Praise for *Relationsick*

"In *Relationsick*, Drs. Lissa Rankin and Jeffrey Rediger name a gnawing truth many of us would prefer to look away from, calling out how many of us are living inside immature oppressive relationships and systems that our bodies experience as unsafe, even when our brains call it love. This is and has made us individually, generationally, and communally sick. When oppressors steal our choice, we become 'monsters in love,' and we carry this betrayal of consent in our nervous systems, in our bodies. The authors don't shame or blame anyone for our relational trauma and the way it might lead to chronic or even life-threatening illness. Instead, they offer us compassionate hope, challenging us to stop abandoning ourselves to maintain connection, to stop spiritually bypassing and calling it kindness, to stop overgiving and enabling and calling it intimacy. The wisdom they share encourages us and gives us tools to build relationships rooted in consent, dignity, and embodied truth. This book is a call to end the quiet violence of self-betrayal and to create real connection that doesn't require it—as medicine for the body, mind, and soul."

—Resmaa Menakem, MSW, LICSW, SEP, *New York Times* bestselling author of *My Grandmother's Hands* and *Monsters in Love*

"This is a must-read book about relationships that can go awry, as many unfortunately do. These red flags are a guide to getting out of—or healing—toxic relationships before they make you sick."

—John Gottman, cofounder of The Gottman Institute and *New York Times* bestselling coauthor of *Fight Right*

"Can your intimate relationship make you physically sick? In this book, two accomplished physicians and writers say it's complicated. It may not be your relationship per se, but the parts of you that overly caretake and don't let you take care of yourself. They back this up with compelling research, theoretical frameworks, and case examples, and offer a variety of practical options for reclaiming yourself and, in the process, your health."

—Richard C. Schwartz, PhD, founder of Internal Family Systems and author of *No Bad Parts*

"*Relationsick* names a hidden epidemic with the precision it deserves: the way chronic overgiving, fawning, and relational inequality do not merely bruise the psyche, but alter physiology. This is what so many women and sensitive, caregiving humans have lived in their bodies for years without language for it. Lissa Rankin and Jeffrey Rediger have written a brave, wise, and urgently needed book about what happens when love asks you to disappear, and what healing requires if you are to return to yourself without hardening your heart."

—Sara Szal, MD, *New York Times* bestselling author of *Women, Food, and Hormones*

"I want to recommend this new book, *Relationsick* by Drs. Lissa Rankin and Jeffrey Rediger. The authors have integrated many valuable elements from a variety of traditions that offer profound understanding and heartfulness, as well as many practical tools for addressing the complexities of relationships with self, others, and the world. They particularly highlight the role of developmental trauma in the development of illness and relational difficulties. This book is very useful for both clinicians and laypeople."

—Laurence Heller, PhD, founder of NeuroAffective Relational Model (NARM), author of *Healing Developmental Trauma* and *Healing Shame and Guilt*

"As a cult recovery specialist, I've witnessed countless cult survivors experience relationsickness, but we didn't know what to call it. Thank goodness two trauma-informed doctors have finally given us language to describe what every survivor of a cult or of narcissistic abuse experiences—that the body bears a significant part of the burden we experience when someone is coercively controlling us. Drawing on both their personal experiences with relational trauma and their knowledge as trauma-informed experts, Drs. Rankin and Rediger have developed an informed and compassionate guide to unpacking toxic relationship patterns, finding your boundaries, and creating new pathways to physical, mental, and emotional wellness. This book is a groundbreaking and much-needed contribution to the recovery space. A must-read—especially for survivors of cults and narcissistic abuse."

—Janja Lalich, PhD, founder of the Lalich Center on Cults and Coercion and author of *Take Back Your Life: Recovering from Cults and Abusive Relationships*

"As a clinician and teacher grounded in Internal Family Systems (IFS) therapy applied to health and illness, I deeply appreciate how Lissa Rankin and Jeffrey Rediger bring attention to the relational environments that shape both our inner worlds and our physical health. This book thoughtfully highlights how protective adaptations to harmful relationships can become embodied over time—and how change in emotional experiences and relational patterns with use of IFS can open the door to meaningful physiological change. It is a compassionate and clinically relevant book."

—Nancy Sowell, LICSW, IFS Institute senior trainer, Harvard Medical School teaching associate, and author of *IFS Health Therapy*

"The authors do a masterful job of weaving together multiple different strands of research and clinical findings about the relationships between trauma and health. The clinical examples that they use to illustrate the science make the book come alive, and will make it accessible to the general public. As we continue to learn about the lifelong effects on our biopsychosocial and spiritual well-being from childhood trauma, particularly the subtle forms of such trauma, a book like this one adds to the resources for clinicians and their clients."

—Laura S. Brown, PnD, ABPP, retired psychologist, Courtesy Clinical professor at the University of Washington, and former president of the American Psychological Association Division of Trauma Psychology

"Just as the science is catching up to what physicians could see with our eyes, *Relationsick* describes the neurophysiological link between developmental trauma, perception of relational safety, and chronic disease. Reading this and learning how to get into a relationship with your hurt parts and repair them when possible is a powerful step toward healthy relationships."

—Christy Gibson, MD, DProf, author of *The Modern Trauma Toolkit*, and cofounder of Safer Spaces Training

"*Relationsick* names something I have witnessed in thirty years of teaching intuitive intelligence: The body keeps an exact energetic accounting of every relationship where you abandoned yourself out of fear or to keep the peace. Give too much, too long, to people who take without reciprocating—and the body eventually sends the bill. Lissa Rankin and Jeffrey Rediger have written a brave, medically grounded book that finally connects the dots between chronic overgiving and chronic illness, showing with precision how the relentless drain of unbalanced relationships disrupts the nervous system, dismisses the spirit, and opens the door to disease. This is not self-help. This is a reckoning. And for anyone who has ever given until there was nothing left—it may save your life."

—Sonia Choquette, *New York Times* bestselling author of *Trust Your Vibes*, *Walking Home*, and *Waking Up in Paris*

"Who in the world ever thought that if you have a dumpkah of a husband, your medical problem might actually be a marital problem? Well, now we know. With such kind clarity and an abundance of trauma-informed compassion for everyone involved, Drs. Rankin and Rediger give us the wake-up call everyone seems to know in our bones but hasn't quite had the courage to say out loud—that our bodies might speak to us about the safety, quality, and reciprocity in our relationships before our minds ever let us admit the truth. But don't despair! These docs don't leave us hanging. They give us a six-step practical model to help us discern which relationships can be transformed to help us heal, and which ones need to get the old heave ho."

—Nancy Slonim Aronie, author of *Memoir as Medicine*

"This book names something many people feel but struggle to articulate: the cost of always putting yourself last. Be forewarned: You might recognize yourself in these pages!"

—Chris Guillebeau, author of *Time Anxiety* and *The Happiness of Pursuit*

"What a practical book! If we're praying for healing while also overgiving in unbalanced or oppressive relationships, we've got one foot on the gas and one on the brakes. With a clear road map that shows how to either rebalance our relationships—or leave—Drs. Rankin and Rediger help us deeply heal relational trauma. Often our bodies follow with much better outcomes as well."

—Tosha Silver, author of *Outrageous Openness* and *It's Not Your Money: How to Live Fully from Divine Abundance*

"For every person in a relationship of too much give and too little take, *Relationsick* offers a compelling reason to change: Toxic relationship patterns aren't good for your health. Filled with a wealth of information on the nervous system's response to trauma and stress, attachment styles, couple dynamics, and Internal Family Systems, *Relationsick* urges readers to stop overgiving for the good of the body, mind, and soul. *Relationsick* isn't simply an invitation for us to change, it's also a guide toward change, giving readers a model for transforming a toxic relationship into a more balanced system of give and take. Drs. Lissa Rankin and Jeffrey Rediger have done it again, creating another beautifully written and impressive resource for all of us wanting to live whole and healthy lives. Bravo!"

—Nicole Wordlaw, PhD, author of *Waking Up Alone: Navigating the Narrow Passage Through Master-Slave Narratives*

"The courageous authors of this book make it clear that relationships can cause or contribute to physical illness. This idea has been immensely unpopular among most physicians so it's very gratifying to see two prominent doctors explain the evidence and mechanisms through which this can happen. Despite the difficulty and challenging nature of the subject, this book is so well written that it's easy to read. A page turner."

—Robert Falconer, IFS lead trainer and author of *Many Minds, One Self*

"In a world full of quick-fix promises, *Relationsick* shows us why trying to hack our way back to health doesn't work. Instead, it offers us a road map to address perhaps the most critical part of our lives and well-being: our relationships. This is for anyone struggling with emotional or physical symptoms who is ready to take back their boundaries and their bodies in order to heal—at last."

—Amy B. Scher, author of *How to Heal Yourself When No One Else Can*

"My life's experience supports all Lissa Rankin and Jeffrey Rediger write about and share. Times have changed due to our experience, and we need to wake up to our power and opportunity and experience the benefits."

—Bernie Siegel, MD, bestselling author of *Love, Medicine and Miracles*

"Lissa Rankin and Jeffrey Rediger understand that real healing starts where polite conversations end. They trace that cost into the body, where it stops being theoretical. The science is real, the stories land, and the way through is more possible than you think. *Relationsick* is honest, uncomfortable, and precise, with a hope that actually feels true. I needed this more than I expected. You might too."

—Chris Grosso, author of *Dead Set On Living* and host of *The Indie Spiritualist Podcast*

"For a very long time, we've been in the dark about how to navigate toxic undiagnosed behaviors in relationships. Finally, there's science-backed evidence to help us understand what happens to our bodies, so we can begin to heal. This book is not just for those who are 'one down' in relationships with unbalanced power dynamics, but also for those who are 'one up,' so they might emerge from denial about the bodily harm, emotional repercussions, and mental health struggles caused by oppressive behaviors. At first, the title made me uncomfortable . . . but we all know what it's like to feel like relationsick."

—Shiloh Sophia, founder of Intentional Creativity and author of *Stardust Bones*

"Research has long shown that healthy relationships are among the most powerful predictors of longevity, well-being, and happiness. But the reverse is also true: Unhealthy relationships can take a profound toll on our bodies. In *Relationsick*, Lissa Rankin and Jeffrey Rediger shine an important light on how relational dynamics influence our health and offer compassionate guidance for recognizing unhealthy patterns and restoring balance. This book is a powerful reminder that caring for our relationships is one of the most important ways we care for our health."

—Shasta Nelson, friendship expert, keynote speaker, and author of *Frientimacy* and *The Business of Friendship*

"I've personally experienced the pain of narcissistic abuse and it literally made me sick. If you can relate, I highly recommend this hopeful book. Lissa provides you with powerful tools to protect yourself and optimize your health, and ways to leave the relationship . . . to save your life."

—Barbara Stanny Huson, author of *Overcoming Underearning*

"Having known Lissa, learned from her, taught alongside her, and witnessed her continued evolution, I can say with full confidence that this book is something special. *Relationsick* is timely, raw, and deeply honest—but more than that, it's profoundly wise. Lissa has a rare ability to translate complex emotional and relational dynamics into something both accessible and transformative. This book challenges our assumptions about what a healthy relationship is supposed to look and feel like, while offering grounded, compassionate guidance for creating something entirely new. Because the truth is life itself is relationship—and most of us were never given the tools to truly master it. *Relationsick* begins to change that. This isn't just a book you read. It's a book that works on you."

—Debbie Rosas, cocreator and founder of Nia Technique

"*Relationsick* is a powerful and much-needed book that bridges the worlds of science and soul in a way few works dare to do. With both compassion and clinical insight, Drs. Rankin and Rediger reveal a truth many of us have felt but couldn't name: that abandoning ourselves in relationships can quietly erode our health. This book is both informative and liberating, and invites us to reclaim our worth, our voice, and our right to receive as much as we give. A deeply healing read for anyone ready to come home to themselves."

—Anita Moorjani, *New York Times* bestselling author of *Dying to Be Me*

"In *Energy Medicine*, we teach that the body's energies follow the heart. *Relationsick* reveals the darker corollary: When the heart is trapped in a relationship that only withdraws, the body eventually sends the bill. Drs. Rankin and Rediger have written the prescription to balance the account."

—Donna Eden and David Feinstein, PhD, coauthors of *Energy Medicine* and *The Energies of Love*

Relationsick

Also by Lissa Rankin, MD

Mind over Medicine

Sacred Medicine

The Anatomy of a Calling

The Daily Flame

The Fear Cure

What's Up Down There

Encaustic Art

Also by Jeffrey Rediger, MD, MDiv

Cured

Relationsick

WHY PUTTING YOURSELF LAST IS DESTROYING YOUR HEALTH—AND HOW TO HEAL

LISSA RANKIN, MD,

AND JEFFREY REDIGER, MD, MDiv

BENBELLA

BenBella Books, Inc.
Dallas, TX

BENBELLA

BenBella Books, Inc.
8080 N. Central Expressway
Suite 1700
Dallas, TX 75206
benbellabooks.com
Send feedback to feedback@benbellabooks.com

Printed in the United States of America
10 9 8 7 6 5 4 3 2 1

Library of Congress Control Number: 2026018736
ISBN 9781637749548 (hardcover)
ISBN 9781637749555 (electronic)

Editing by Leah Wilson
Copyediting by James Fraleigh
Proofreading by Martha Gallant and Marissa Wold Uhrina
Indexing by WordCo Indexing Services
Text design and composition by PerfecType, Nashville, TN
Cover design by Sarah Avinger
Cover Adobe Stock / Irina (apple core) and Nathan Hutchcraft (branch)
Printed by Lake Book Manufacturing

In loving memory of Ralph De La Rosa,
who left us too soon but will be forever in the hearts of many.

We also dedicate this book to every brokenhearted
child who grew up to give too much,
who struggles to break out of relentless people-pleasing
behaviors, who needs help giving voice to the rage that has
no name and the grief that has no place to go, and who seeks
the courage to do what they must to heal their broken heart and
their boundaries, take back their own life, and reclaim the
sovereignty, agency, intimacy, dignity, and equality
that is every human's birthright.

CONTENTS

INTRODUCTION

What do I look like? The Wizard of Oz? You need a brain? You need a heart? Go ahead, take mine. Take everything I have.

—Stephenie Meyer, *Breaking Dawn*

Sophia was in the shower when she discovered a lump in her left breast. After a panicked call to her doctor and a few harried weeks of appointments, mostly with busy doctors emanating an air of aloof authority, she had a diagnosis: metastatic breast cancer.

Sophia was usually the one caring for her husband Bill; although she and Bill both worked full time, she did all the cooking, cleaning, and entertaining. But when she got the news about her cancer, she expected Bill to step up to the plate and care for her for a change. She was shocked when he couldn't be bothered to accompany her to doctor's appointments or help her figure out what to do.

Sophia had always been the devotional type, feeling grateful and mission driven when she had someone to serve and feeling anxious and rudderless when she didn't—an inclination toward service validated by her spirituality and love of God. She knew it might sound antifeminist to admit out loud, but she felt her heart open when she oriented her life around serving her husband with unconditional love and acceptance, even—sometimes especially—when Bill was being demanding. It felt natural and satisfying to express her love through caretaking: anticipating his needs, surprising him with ways to delight him, accommodating his preferences, and making him happy as best she knew how. Except for the times when his needs were just more than she could keep up with, or when he seemed ungrateful or unaware of her sacrifices, she was okay with the way their relationship worked. She told herself she was honored to serve him.

If she were honest with herself, Sophia thought she'd married up—that she didn't deserve someone like him, and the only way she'd have a chance of keeping him was by making his life easy and satisfying his whims. Bill was handsome, smart, and successful, admired by people in the church and community, so she felt like she'd won the husband lottery. But that also made her feel insecure; she always felt like she'd pulled the wool over his eyes in some way. Sophia knew Bill could easily replace her if she let him down or eased off on trying to please him and keep him happy—especially because he worked with many beautiful young women who always seemed to look at her as if they didn't understand why someone like Bill had picked someone like her.

It's not like Bill wasn't good to her. He bought her expensive jewelry and wrote her love songs he played on his guitar. He told everyone he had the greatest wife in the world, and praised her for being so sweet, devoted, and obedient, especially compared to his friends' wives.

So it came as a huge blow when Bill acted like her health needs were an annoying burden. Sophia got the same vibe from her friends and people at her church. She'd always been very generous with others, quick to say yes when anyone was sick or in need. She thus felt devastated when she realized she was on her own for her cancer journey.

Her breast cancer diagnosis settled in her bones like a chill. Her mother had died of it six years earlier after trying all the treatments her doctors offered. The end hadn't been pretty. Her mother had accepted the diagnosis with resignation and perhaps even some unconscious relief, since cancer would be a more socially acceptable way out than suicide. Life hadn't been kind to her, and she died in great pain.

Sophia didn't want to end up like her mother. Although her doctors gave her some hope that aggressive treatment could cure her, after Sophia had seen her mother go that route, and after realizing she wasn't going to have much support on her cancer journey, she decided to accept her fate, decline conventional medical treatment, and try to enjoy whatever quality of life she might have left. It's not that she was actively suicidal, but when it dawned on her that the people to whom she'd been giving so selflessly all those years might have been taking advantage of her rather than loving her, it was hard to muster the motivation to fight for her life. What was the point?

THE GIVING TREE

Like many of us, Sophia grew up hearing messages about how to be a good, noble person like the one in Shel Silverstein's *The Giving Tree.* In this classic children's book, a beautiful female tree laden with apples comes to love a little boy who seems to love her back. He enjoys climbing the tree, gathering her leaves into a crown and playing King of the Forest. He revels in swinging on her branches, eating her apples, playing hide and seek, and taking naps in the tree. This brings the tree great joy.

But as the boy gets older, he loses interest in climbing and playing and begins neglecting the tree. When he does finally come back, the tree begs him to come play, eat her apples, and climb her branches, but he tells her he only wants money. She has no money, she tells him, but offers her apples to sell and make money. So he strips her of her apples and carts them off to the market, selling them for personal profit. And the tree is happy.

Then the boy disappears for a long time, and the tree misses him terribly. When he finally returns again, the tree is excited, but the boy does not want to play. He says he wants a house so he can have a wife and children. The tree says that she has no house to give him, but that he can cut down her branches and build himself a house. So the boy takes every last branch, and the tree, because she loves him, is happy to have helped.

After that, the boy stays away for a very long time, and by the time he returns, he is quite old. But the tree is still delighted to see him, crying, "Come, boy, come and play!" He says he is too old and sad to play, that he just wants a boat that will take him far, far away. He asks the tree if she can give him a boat, but the tree says she has no boat, only a trunk that he can cut down and carve into a boat. So he cuts down her trunk, leaving nothing but a stump, and the tree is happy—for him, if not for herself.

Eventually, the old man finally comes back, and the tree says, "I am sorry, boy. But I have nothing left to give you." She apologizes again and again for no longer having apples to eat or branches to swing from or a trunk to climb. He says he is far too tired for all that anyway, that all he needs is a place to sit and rest. So he sits on the stump, and, we are told, the tree is happy.

Many of us, especially if we were raised in religious households, are trained to think we have to pay a high price to be worthy of relationships. We grow up believing this is the only way to live: to give and give and give, graciously and endlessly, to our own detriment if need be. As children, especially girls, we get the message that we are supposed to admire the sacrificial tree and glorify the nobility of her selfless generosity, to be happy giving.

But the truth is that the tree ultimately dies. Without leaves, branches, and a trunk, she can no longer photosynthesize. By story's end, she is just a stump.

Giving, we are led to believe, should be a one-way street of unconditional love and selfless generosity that requires no gratitude or reciprocation. We are supposed to be like the tree, to feel nourished by the giving itself—even if it sickens or depletes us. Any spark of resentment we might feel when someone entitled is taking, taking, taking and then ignoring us must be completely suppressed; anger, after all, is an unseemly emotion best buried down in our tissues.

Through one lens, *The Giving Tree* is a story of selfless devotion, unconditional love, and sacred sacrifice—of a noble tree and her generous heart. Through another lens, it's a story of abuse and exploitation, in which the boy takes mercilessly while the tree fails to stand up for her own health. While this kind of unqualified giving can indeed sometimes be noble—the kind of giving a mother gives a newborn, or God is said to give us—when there's no reciprocity, when one party in a relationship only gives and the other only takes, the result isn't love. It's martyrdom. And as research increasingly shows, it's also an express ticket to chronic or life-threatening disease.

RECKONING WITH THE PAST

Like the giving tree at the story's end, Sophia had given so fully and so long—to her husband, to the church, to everyone she knew—that she ended up physically spent and psychologically devastated. While she figured it was too late to do anything about her cancer, she decided she could at least do something about her mental health. Sophia's sister Muriel had convinced her to start seeing a psychotherapist who specialized in helping people at the end of their lives make peace with their passing. This meant going back into past traumas and making meaning out of the hard things that had happened to her, facing the rough stuff but also trying to appreciate the good things about her life.

Nobody ever physically abused her, but as Sophia looked back, she realized that she had grown up feeling constantly afraid, walking on eggshells to avoid upsetting her parents, who made it clear they couldn't handle her expressing painful emotions like anxiety, anger, grief, disappointment, or fear. As a result, she stopped expressing her own upset very early in life. She had always been scared of her father. She just figured everyone felt that way growing up. But after reading a lot of books and educating herself at her therapist's suggestion, she realized her father had been very controlling, with narcissistic tendencies that significantly harmed her development. He had a rough childhood, and instead of doing his own healing work, he took out his self-hatred on everyone else.

Things weren't always bad with her father. He could be very charming when he felt bad about blowing up at his wife or kids. It had been Sophia's job to ease his anxiety in those times. He'd tell Sophia how sorry he was for being such a schmuck, and she would reassure him she loved him, that he wasn't a schmuck, and rub his feet while he had a drink. He'd call her Daddy's Little Girl, and she'd feel happy and safe for a blink, like he really needed her.

By the time she left home, she'd been conditioned to read the room, anticipate others' needs, and figure out how to avoid upsetting them, even if it meant ignoring her own needs, which she had buried so far underground that she barely noticed the sacrifice.

The emotional instability in her childhood affected Sophia's adult life in huge ways. She lost the ability to stand up for and protect herself, to say no and set boundaries. She realized that anytime someone asked her to do something, she'd get this panicky feeling in her chest, and the "yes" would come out before she'd even had a chance to think about what she was committing herself to.

Often, others didn't even have to ask; she'd automatically anticipate what they might need and offer to help. All her boss Mike had to do was look anxious and stressed, and Sophia would throw herself into whatever it took to make him feel better. When Mike needed someone to work late or help filling the schedule, she often volunteered, even when she really didn't want to. Her boss was a high-pressure guy, and the more pressure he applied, the more accommodating Sophia became. It was kind of the same with Bill. He was fussy and demanding, always wanting things done in a certain way, right on time. But she prided herself on being able to anticipate what he wanted before he even had to ask.

Sophia would endure and endure, convincing herself she was being a good Christian wife by expanding her heart to grow bigger whenever Bill was being difficult. But then sometimes she'd just blow her lid, and the tears would be uncontrollable. And instead of comforting her, Bill would stomp off and slam doors. Over time, Sophia learned to give him a wide berth.

Everyone said Sophia was the nicest person they knew, and that made her feel good about herself, and special. Being needed felt like her life's purpose, something God had sent her to do: to make life easier for others and have compassion for people who were hard to get along with. But underneath, doubt and resentment nagged at her. And when she saw how others responded to her breast cancer diagnosis, those emotions became overwhelming. For the first time, she saw how imbalanced her relationships were with others—how much she had given of herself, without getting back anything other than the feeling of being useful.

WHEN TOO MUCH GIVING MAKES YOU SICK

Sophia didn't just have metastatic breast cancer. Sophia was what we call *relationsick*. What do we mean by *relationsick*? When we suffer from relational trauma—when consistent safety, trust, or attunement is consistently disrupted by neglect, abuse, or betrayal from our caregivers during childhood—it leads to real physiological changes in the body. Over time, those changes can result in physical and mental health issues.

Most of us are familiar on some level with the relationship between stress and illness. According to the *Journal of the American Medical Association*, 60–80 percent of doctor's visits are for stress-related illnesses. Cardiac issues, gastrointestinal disorders, frequent infections, autoimmune diseases, chronic pain syndromes, dermatologic conditions, and countless others can all be stress related. But chronic stress can be an underlying factor, or at least an exacerbating one, in almost any illness. When it comes to chronic stress, like the kind we experience in unbalanced relationships, our nervous system becomes chronically dysregulated, and the body never adequately relaxes—which directly impacts our ability to heal. Our immune system becomes impaired, raising our risk for infections, cancers, and autoimmune disorders, and we experience chronic inflammation, which increases our risk for almost every disabling and deadly disease out there.

Science links our physical health to our relational well-being, and Sophia's years of doing more than her share, unmet needs, and emotional suppression, accompanied by neglect, devaluation, and exploitation from Bill, suggests relationsickness most likely played a significant role in her developing breast cancer. Fortunately, as part of her psychological healing work, Sophia realized she had been a willing participant in an unequal relationship, enabling Bill to prioritize his needs while they both neglected hers. By understanding and healing her own relational trauma, Sophia began to stand up for her own needs, pull back on taking care of Bill, Mike, and others, and prioritize her own well-being for a change. Healing that relationsickness radically altered her health.

Radical-remission researcher and Harvard psychiatrist Jeffrey Rediger, MD, MDiv, met Sophia decades after her diagnosis, when her breast cancer had been in unexpected remission for many years. Someone had referred Sophia to Jeff because of his research concerning people who had recovered from "incurable" illnesses after they'd either refused conventional medical treatment or somehow wound up healthy when their disease had been deemed incurable. What he learned in that research—and what Lissa Rankin, MD, learned in her own research—was the inspiration for this book.

We're both physicians who have spent a combined thirty-three years observing who gets sick and who doesn't, who gets better and who doesn't. We've researched people who experienced "spontaneous remission" and tried to understand how they differ from those who don't, all in the name of helping people who get sick figure out whether they can do anything proactively to achieve optimal health outcomes. We wanted to know why some with diseases believed incurable get better, while others stay sick or even die, in case what we learned might help us improve the way doctors practice medicine. We wondered if we might find some holy grail that people with incurable diseases could use to improve their health outcomes, not just for diseases considered incurable but for any chronic illness that conventional medicine has failed to cure. Many of these findings have been published in our other books, including Jeff's *Cured* and Lissa's *Mind over Medicine* and *Sacred Medicine.*

While our other books dealt more generally with the many factors that contribute to mind–body health, like stress reduction, meditation, high-quality nutrition, creative expression, and other factors known to optimize health outcomes, this book focuses specifically on the one factor we observed most commonly in those we studied—the relationship between unbalanced "giving tree" relationships and physical disease. We independently came to the conclusion that many people who become sick before their time gave too much to others who gave too little, and their bodies paid the price.

If you're relationsick, it doesn't matter how many medications or supplements you take, how much healthy food you eat, how many yoga classes or workouts you do, how many high-tech procedures or biohacking interventions you undergo, or how positively you think about or meditate on being healthy—as long as your relationships are still unhealthy, your health is likely to suffer. Unless you address the activating factor provoking all this illness-inducing physiology—*your unbalanced or traumatizing relationships,* past and present—your relationsickness is likely to outweigh any other positive health changes you try.

But when you *do* address your relationsickness—when you make the link between unbalanced relationships and your physical and mental health; when you understand how stressful it is to be the one doing most of the giving, without getting your own needs adequately met; when you begin to show up in relationships in a healthier way—the results can be medicine for the body, nervous system, and soul.

GETTING HONEST WITH OURSELVES ABOUT OUR RELATIONSHIPS

When the people we studied got serious about healing, they had to take a long, hard look at the way they showed up in relationships. This wasn't easy, but when they were brave and willing to dive into healing their childhood trauma, when they dared to break out of those deeply indoctrinated patterns—waking up to their true value, worth, and deservingness, and engaging in self-protective rather than just self-sacrificing behaviors—their diseases sometimes got a whole lot better. In rare but notable cases, their "incurable" diseases even disappeared completely.

When Jeff first interviewed Sophia, he asked whether she had any explanation for why her cancer went away. Sophia's eyes lit up and she leaned forward, her voice gathering in intensity.

"I call it my 'Selfish Bitch Project,'" she said.

Sophia had learned in therapy that if she wanted to enjoy as much quality of life as possible before she passed, she had to start saying no and letting other people down, even if she upset them by doing so. She had to think about herself for a change, even though she felt profoundly selfish and guilty when doing so. She had to prioritize her own needs and get fierce and feisty with people who treated her as a doormat—including her husband, her boss, and some of the people at her church. She had to reverse core ideas she had about herself, namely that she wasn't worth being treated better. Realizing she was precious and valuable and deserving of staying alive shifted something deep inside her, which translated into a major change in how she showed up in her relationships.

She couldn't explain how this could have contributed to her unexpected cancer cure, and Jeff couldn't prove her intuition scientifically, but Sophia swore that her Selfish Bitch Project—the change in how she viewed herself and the relational shifts that followed—caused her cancer to go away and stay in remission.

She also believed this shift would have been almost impossible if she hadn't had cancer. In its own way, cancer had been a wake-up call, a gift that changed her life. It gave her a good excuse to start letting others down sometimes, to care about others but also herself, to treat herself as a luminous spark of the divine, worthy of being cared for and deserving of love and belonging.

Jeff asked her why she called it the Selfish Bitch Project. Why did she think it was selfish to take better care of herself when she had a serious cancer diagnosis? Sophia said that she now understands that self-care and self-compassion aren't selfish, but at the time it had been a hard sell. Because she was so used to putting herself last, whenever someone would make entitled requests of her, she'd have to remind herself: *Be a selfish bitch or you might die!* That would calm the panicky feeling in her chest enough to activate a little bit of anger at how much others expected her to do for them, even when she had cancer, and that anger energized her just enough to help her say no.

Almost immediately, something shifted between her and Bill. Maybe it was the thought of losing her or maybe it was a reaction to her getting feistier, but he actually started treating her better. She wondered whether he was starting to see her differently after having lost all respect for her when she let herself be his doormat. Bill agreed to try couple's therapy, despite initially dragging his feet at the request. And while at first he resisted the idea of helping out more at home, grumbling under his breath or giving Sophia the silent treatment at times when she asked him to clean up after dinner, he slowly seemed to come around. In the meantime, Sophia got better at clearly expressing her hurt feelings from years of living on breadcrumbs and feeling like she was more Bill's mother than his cherished wife. She learned to describe in specific terms what kind of real mutual partnership would make her happier and how they could begin looking for ways to better connect and enjoy each other.

Over the next few months, Sophia slowly started to feel better. But those were not easy months. As she reflected back over her life, she cried and cried, not just because she thought she was going to die, but also because she started feeling the pain of all the times when nobody had been there for her, when she'd felt all alone in the world. She felt deep sadness and regret.

Some of her friends didn't like the new Sophia. Her friend Sally, who had often depended on Sophia to watch her bratty children when she and her husband went out for dinner, didn't like it when she started saying no. And Mike practically became apoplectic when she told him she was resigning: "How could you leave me after all I've done to make things easier for you with your cancer?"

Sophia made other changes as well. She purged her pantry after deciding to eliminate processed foods and try a plant-based diet as a way of taking better care of her body. She focused not on what she was giving up, but on the nutrition that she was providing her body, and how she now felt better and had more energy. She took a much less stressful job assisting a writing teacher, which inspired her to start writing herself, something she had always dreamed of doing but didn't believe would be possible.

And the whole time, the lump in her breast was shrinking until it was undetectable. When the doctors went looking for the metastatic tumors or any other evidence of the original breast cancer, they couldn't find a trace. The last time Jeff reached out to her, ten years after she went into remission, she was still alive and doing well.

REVERSING RELATIONSICKNESS

The human body wants to heal. This book is about establishing the physiological and psychological conditions for it to do so, by reversing relationsickness.

In part one, we're going to help you understand and deconstruct the ways of thinking and behaving that make you vulnerable to relationsickness. We'll dig further into the science connecting relationships and health, and how trauma in and around relationships, especially in childhood, can dysregulate the nervous system and impair the body's ability to heal. We'll look closer at the behaviors and relationships that cause relationsickness—the psychological drivers of overgiving and the relational power dynamics that tend to result. We'll also take a moment to explore a major barrier to healing: spiritual bypassing, the use of spiritual beliefs or practices to avoid, suppress, or prematurely transcend uncomfortable emotions, unresolved wounds, or real-life problems, rather than addressing them directly. Last, we'll encourage and inspire you with the many benefits of healing relational trauma and your relationships themselves, while touching on any misgivings you might have as we move into part two.

There, we'll chart a radical road map for relational recovery. We'll offer you the antidote to being the giving tree, with practical self-help and relational tools you can implement to improve both the quality of your relationships and, potentially, your health. We'll accomplish this by using the Internal Family Systems (IFS) model, a therapeutic healing method that views humans as a constellation of both protective and wounded "parts," where transformation happens through the leadership of these parts by the mature, wise Self. We'll also teach you relational skill-building tools, like how to set boundaries, protest mistreatment, and repair relationships when ruptures occur. You'll learn the Six Steps from Fawning to Freedom, a step-by-step algorithm that will help you discern whether you can help your body heal while staying in the same relationships or if you need to distance yourself from those relationships in order to get well.

As we've seen in many patients we have cared for over the years in our medical practices, physical symptoms often develop when psychological trauma hits an intolerable threshold. Every bough has its breaking point. We can only give so much to people who do not reciprocate before our bodies begin to protest. This book is about learning how to stop sacrificing your health and well-being and start fighting for the love, caregiving, protection, and reciprocity you need—so your body doesn't have to do it for you.

Prioritizing your own recovery instead of trying to please or caretake everyone else doesn't mean you aren't good or loving. It means you're loving your own body, your own life—your own delicate heart, your own precious soul—as much as you love everyone else.

If your life force is dwindling, you're struggling with an illness your doctors haven't been able to cure, and you're worried about winding up as a worn-out dead stump, it is our sincere hope that this book's radical road map to recovery from relationsickness will help your branches blossom, so they can once again bear luscious fruit.

PART I
Understanding Relationsickness

CHAPTER 1

Taking Ownership of Your Healing Journey

I have come to believe that caring for myself is not self-indulgent. Caring for myself is an act of survival.

—Audre Lorde

Jill, sixty, and Diana, fifty-four, were both nonsmokers diagnosed with metastatic lung cancer within a month of one another. Both were housewives who were raised geographically close to one another in the same rural Midwest area. Both grew up on farms in conservative fundamentalist religious homes, attending the same church that was influenced by the teachings of the disgraced founder of the Institute of Basic Life Principles (IBLP), an organization widely characterized as cult-like by critics and former members. Both endured abuse and psychological trauma during childhood.

Both had unhappy home lives as adults too. Jill had struggled long and hard with yo-yo dieting and other residual effects of her mother's controlling demands, and suffered from many chronic illnesses. The constant fatigue put a strain on her marriage and left her with less energy to cope with her husband's drinking and his entitled expectations that the house would always be in perfect order.

Like Jill, Diana had long struggled with a host of issues that could be attributed to her family of origin. She kept herself going with religious fervor and church commitments, convinced at some level that with enough dedication and determination, she could drown out the memories of a narcissistic mother whose need to control her children was so over the top that Diana disassociated as a way to endure the relationship without confronting it directly. To give the appearance that she and her mother were still close while also giving herself some space, Diana had moved to Virginia, where she raised her four kids, but she was still the favorite child, the one who remained willing to communicate with her mother frequently despite her mother's continued judgment and extreme religious preoccupations.

Despite all their similarities, psychologically, Jill and Diana approached their cancer diagnoses very differently. Jill accepted her impending death with little resistance. When her doctors suggested chemotherapy but were clear that the best it could do was extend her life somewhat—not cure her—she decided that, at sixty, she had lived a long enough life, and that she would rather forgo the chemo and instead focus on quality of life for her limited time left. She prioritized getting enough sleep, reading, changing her diet, and saying no to commitments and social engagements that would get in the way of her need for rest.

Diana did just the opposite. Although she agreed to undergo the palliative chemotherapy regimen Jill had refused, Diana thought chemo was unnecessary, since she believed God had told her that He would cure her cancer as a reward for her lifetime of piety.

Diana and Jill also viewed their histories very differently. As a protective measure, Diana refused to acknowledge the abuse that her brothers had suffered at their parents' hands, despite having witnessed it herself. From the safe space of Virginia, Diana was adamant that the abuse had never occurred, that her father was beyond reproach, and that her mother could do no wrong.

Jill had been in denial before her cancer diagnosis about the extent of her mother's abuse, but after her diagnosis, she was finally able to face how intrusive and controlling her mother had been. When Jill was a child, her mother controlled her diet and closely monitored her weight. Jill used to hide out in a closet and stuff herself with sweets because her mother would shame her for being chubby, even though her mother was a bit fluffy herself. She pressured Jill to become the straight-A student and perfect ballerina that she herself had wanted to be when young. Since unconditional love was not available, Jill had learned to settle for the approval she could win by complying with her mother's agenda.

Like Diana, Jill also was blind to the depth of the relational trauma in her life. For over thirty years, she had been seeing a Christian counselor whom Jill felt minimized the abuse she was experiencing and encouraged her to stay married and love her husband unconditionally, as a good Christian wife is expected to do. Setting healthy boundaries or even considering divorce was not part of the therapeutic work. But when Jill got cancer, she began to consider that perhaps her counselor was misguiding her, and instead started seeing a therapist trained in trauma recovery. She spent months in therapy, finally allowing herself to feel the intense anger, despair, helplessness, and grief that she had bypassed thanks to a lifetime of spiritual indoctrination. She began standing up for herself, pushing back when her husband's controlling behaviors triggered her. She set boundaries on his perfectionistic expectations of her and quit enabling his alcohol use. She made their continued marriage contingent on him going to couple's therapy, joining AA, and getting help for his recovery.

Unlike Jill, Diana was not going to touch her trauma in this lifetime, much less consider therapy. Whenever an actual emotion would have been appropriate, Diana's family had always praised Jesus and hailed righteous hallelujahs, and Diana had learned to suppress all discomfort.

In looking back on her upbringing, Jill tried to acknowledge the things her mother had done right. But she was also willing to face what was painfully true about her history of trauma. Diana could only glorify the good in her parents, while Jill accepted both the ways in which she had felt genuinely loved by her parents, and also the ways in which she felt she had been abused.

A year after their diagnoses, Jill underwent a thoracic CT scan and was told by her shocked doctors that all evidence of cancer had disappeared, without any conventional medical treatment. As Jill later told Jeff, who had known her long before she got cancer, she had never felt better in her whole life.

Hearing Jill's story was bittersweet for Jeff, because it was so similar, and yet so different, from Diana's. He found out Jill was sick at the same time Diana, Jeff's sister, was going through cancer treatment. (Diana was diagnosed just months after Jeff and Diana's abusive father died from a stroke, and their brother sent the family a photo of the 2 × 2 piece of lumber he would use to beat Jeff and his brother, something that cut through the family denial about their childhoods. It wasn't just Diana who got sick. Everyone in the family—except Jeff's mother—developed a medical problem immediately afterward, as if their bodies couldn't handle facing the truth.)

While Jeff was happy for Jill that her healing journey ended with an unexpectedly good outcome, unfortunately his sister didn't enjoy the same fate. Six months after Jill was pronounced cured, Diana finally broke through her denial about her imminent death when her pain shot through the roof. After an orthopedic surgeon failed to surgically relieve her shooting back pain, she was hospitalized.

Diana died a long, slow, agonizing death, in treatment for both pain and anxiety, finally passing away in an inpatient hospice unit a year and a half after her diagnosis. At the time of writing, Jill is still alive and in remission, three and a half years after her initial diagnosis and two and a half years after her doctors gave her the "all clear."

THE EMERGING SCIENCE OF SELF-HEALING

As doctors who study radical remission, it's our opinion that much more research is needed to determine whether trauma-healing psychotherapies, changing how you show up in relationships, or practicing psychological and spiritual self-help work can improve health outcomes. However, the limited research we do have suggests differences in outcomes between the Dianas and Jills of the world.

While many psychologists stay in their silo of the mind and rarely cross over into the medical treatment of the body, some have ventured out of those confines to examine the mental and emotional factors of healing and disease recovery. One notable example is trailblazing researcher Dr. Alistair Cunningham, who has an unusual ability to stand back and see the big picture, both personally and professionally, and serve as a bridge across disciplines. He has doctorates in both psychology and microbiology, and spent years working as a psychologist in a clinic for cancer patients. He is also a cancer survivor himself, having been cured of stage III colon cancer at forty-seven, when he had been given only a 30 percent chance of surviving.

His main passion has been the intersection between behavioral medicine and health psychology. In 1998, he began a series of research projects that explored the relationship between psychological self-help strategies and physical health. After a few initial studies suggested better outcomes for cancer patients who were more engaged with their healing process than for those who took a more passive approach, Dr. Cunningham's research team focused on following highly motivated cancer patients who had shown a prior interest in psychological work and self-help techniques. The resulting study[1] found a significant correlation between "involvement in self-help" and longevity. In 2002,

Dr. Cunningham designed yet another study to dive even deeper.[2] Although it was moderate in size, it was impressively thorough. Over a hundred hours were spent on each participant, examining a wide range of quantitative and qualitative details associated with their particular illness trajectories and responses.

Dr. Cunningham found that nine patients whom he defined as "highly involved" were spending hours every day engaging in proactive psychological and spiritual self-help activities. Of those nine, eight lived significantly longer than expected, and two of those eight had unexpected radical remissions. At the other extreme, of the eight people who did not engage in psychological or spiritual self-help techniques at all, only one was still alive two years after diagnosis.

Overall, Dr. Cunningham found that people engaged in psychological and spiritual self-help practices* who got very involved in their own healing journey lived three times longer than those who had little to no involvement in their own recovery beyond following their doctor's orders or hoping their faith would cure them. He concluded that the kind of self-help "identity healing" work toward which the nine patients with better outcomes devoted themselves was potentially a major factor in their recovery.

Jeff concluded something similar in his research of radical remission survivors for *Cured*. By looking at the most common overlapping factors to which people attributed their cures, he narrowed the key interventions down to healing what he called the "four pillars of health": one's immune system, nutrition, stress response, and identity. Of all four, healing one's identity rose to the surface like cream time and time again.

---

* Note that Dr. Cunningham's group work includes teachings from Helen Schucman's *A Course in Miracles* and Eckhart Tolle's *A New Earth*, both of which have been widely criticized for promoting oppressive belief systems that are not adequately trauma informed or antiracist. Had he chosen more trauma-informed spiritual teachings, one can only guess how the outcomes might have differed.

What does it mean to heal your identity? It means reclaiming a sense of who you truly are beneath the roles, defenses, masks, and stories you've adopted to survive, so that your choices, relationships, and self-expression arise from authenticity rather than adaptation. It's about integrating the various aspects of our being, rather than splitting, dissociating, being inauthentic, or identifying with the various ways we learn to cope with trauma.

Healing your identity, Jeff found, was especially important for those who carried the burdened belief that they were inherently defective and broken—who believed they didn't deserve to be loved just because they exist and felt they had to somehow earn love by making themselves available for exploitation. In fact, it was arguably the most important factor in their remission. In his research, Jeff found that individuals who spontaneously recovered from severe illnesses often underwent a profound shift in their sense of self, which was key to enabling their recovery. This process involved addressing deep-seated, self-limiting beliefs and unresolved emotional or psychological issues, such as confronting false beliefs like "I'm not worthy" or "I'm not good enough," prioritizing personal needs, releasing unresolved trauma, finding a deeper meaning in life, and moving from passivity to active participation in their lives. This identity healing, he found, was often what provided the motivation to actively pursue the other pillars: nutrition, immune system support, and stress response.

As she described in *Mind over Medicine*, Lissa ultimately came to a similar conclusion. She saw people-pleasing doormat types become what one of Lissa's patients called "unf*ckwithable," going from people who were passively "nice" to healthy boundary setters who took care of themselves while still caring about others. And those same people—the ones who were proactively engaged with their healing process, who took responsibility for their recovery, who took on the hard work of relational healing, and who came out the other side an entirely different person (without losing the core aspects of their being)—often had the best outcomes.

Most notably in Lissa's research, these individuals not only threw themselves into their healing journeys as if their lives depended on it, they also didn't shy away from excavating the deepest recesses of their psyches, facing both the worst things that had happened to them along with their own worst behaviors, toward others they cared about and themselves. They didn't wallow in self-pity or drown in shame, but they took responsibility for the mistakes they'd made. And they did more than simply take personal responsibility. They also extended true unconditional love and self-compassion to those they had harmed—including and especially themselves.

For both Jeff and Lissa, this was especially notable in the people whose identities were like the giving tree, tending toward overgiving, self-sacrificing martyrdom. For them, the healing journey transformed them from compliant, conflict-avoidant people pleasers into more authentic, courageous, honest, compassionately boundaried individuals who knew their own worth. Usually, this shift in identity meant they could no longer engage with other people the way they once had. And that changed everything.

Over and over, we heard stories of people who had changed so much because of their illness and subsequent healing journey that, when they walked down the street, people they had known for years barely recognized them. They stood with their heads high, shoulders back, and a spring in their step. Like Jill, or Sophia from the introduction, they were simply not the same people after their remarkable recoveries.

Sometimes, without ignoring or sugarcoating the genuine suffering they experienced, these people wound up claiming that getting sick was the best thing that ever happened to them. Because their diagnosis propelled them to heal whatever was interfering with their best potential life, they were grateful for the painful nudge, even though it often meant their relationships with both themselves and others had to change significantly.

In short, they recognized their own relationsickness, threw themselves into the work of healing it, and came out the other side healthier—in mind, body, and spirit.

"LEARNED HELPLESSNESS" CAN HARM YOUR HEALTH

Of course, not everyone we worked with and studied during our medical careers prioritized healing relational trauma or altering behaviors in relationships when they got sick. Some, like Diana, just rolled over, resigned to their fate. They might have followed their doctor's orders, but otherwise, they changed nothing, trying their best to maintain the same lives that had made them sick in the first place. Some engaged in magical thinking, believing that they were going to "manifest" their cure or that God was going to miraculously heal them without any efforts on their part. These people often stayed sick or died as predicted by their doctors, even after doing everything those doctors recommended.

A landmark study performed on three groups of rats by Madelon Visintainer and her colleague Martin Seligman, author of *Learned Optimism*, offers a potential explanation.[3] The researchers placed a group of rats in a box where they periodically received mild foot shocks. However, inside the box was a lever. Through trial and error, the rats discovered that if they pressed the lever, the shock would either end immediately or, in some cases, be prevented altogether, depending on the exact protocol. After learning this, the rats consistently pressed the lever whenever the shock began—or just before, in cases where they were given predictive cues, like a warning tone that a shock was coming. Researchers hypothesized that this ability to press the lever gave the rats a sense of control, since they could terminate or avoid the shock once they figured out the association.

By contrast, a second group of rats was placed in a box where shocks were inescapable, with no lever or warning cues. They reacted to the shocks initially by trying to get away from them, running from one side of the cage to the other. But no matter what they did, the shocks kept coming. Over time, because the shocks were inescapable, the rats were rendered listless, helpless, and depressed, demonstrating a behavioral shutdown that Seligman later called "learned helplessness."

But the rats' behavior wasn't what Visintainer and Seligman were really studying. Before setting about shocking these poor rats, Visintainer had implanted a few cancer cells on each rat's flank, carefully controlling the number, such that they could expect that, under normal conditions, about half the rats would reject the tumor and live and the other half would succumb and die.

That's exactly what happened with a third control group of rats who were not shocked at all: After a month, 54 percent had fought off the tumor, while 46 percent had died. Of the rats who couldn't escape the shocks, only 27 percent rejected the tumor. But curiously, the rats given escapable shocks, who had learned how to master the system and felt some control over the trauma that researchers were inflicting, rejected the tumor 64 percent of the time, giving them a survival advantage even over the unshocked rats.

This study demonstrates that it's not so much about avoiding life's shocks; it's more about how you react to them. When stress or disease causes you to roll over, listless and helpless, it harms your chances of getting better. But when you feel like you have agency—if you learn to press the lever, and discover that the shocks stop—your health outcomes can be better than if you'd never experienced that stress at all.

Many of the relationsick people we've worked with have lived a lifetime of learned helplessness, often starting in childhood. Maybe they'd started out fighting to stop the shocks in their lives, but at some point, when fighting failed to stop their suffering, they resigned themselves to those shocks, especially when it came to relationships. In Diana's case, she had learned early on that trying to fight her mother's domination only led to more abuse. When children can't find a way to press the lever and receive the love, comfort, and nurturing they need, they often give up. They learn to live on breadcrumbs and come to think it's normal.

People with learned helplessness thus see illness as just one more bit of bad luck they cannot control. But for our radical remission survivors, the experience of getting sick and watching how others responded was sometimes the wake-up call they needed in order to realize they could metaphorically press the levers in their lives. Faced with a cancer diagnosis or a heart attack, something shifted in them. Some of them had assumed, as Sophia had, that, when they got sick, the people they had been literally killing themselves to take care of would now reciprocate, only to realize these people had no intention, desire, or capacity to offer caregiving in return. Finding themselves without adequate caregiving support after a lifetime of caregiving others, they often felt stunned, betrayed, and heartbroken. And that betrayal and heartbreak led to a justified anger, one often suppressed for decades, shocking them out of their passivity and putting them back in touch with their biological will to live. Instead of rolling over passively, with learned helplessness, they broke out of their dissociated numbness and finally started fighting for their lives.

SPONTANEOUS REMISSION, DIVINE INTERVENTION, STATISTICAL OUTLIER, OR PERSONAL AGENCY?

The medical literature is riddled with case studies of the rare health outliers who have been cured from severe or deadly diseases, including nearly every type of cancer. They've recovered from life-threatening maladies like HIV, end-stage heart failure, aneurysms, heart defects, abscesses, hydrocephalus, and liver and kidney failure. They have also been cured from common chronic diseases like asthma, hypothyroidism, rheumatoid arthritis, ulcers, gallstones, diabetes, high blood pressure, ischemic heart disease, cataracts, herniated discs, and epilepsy.

The medical establishment labels these unexpected cures "spontaneous remissions," and doctors write them up in medical journals as curious flukes. Religions call them "miracles" or "divine intervention." And skeptics argue that those lucky enough to experience spontaneous remission are mere statistical outliers, falling into the margins based on pure mathematical probability. All three interpretations encourage some people to write these outliers off, suggesting that they are not worth studying because the phenomenon is so rare that it is unlikely to yield helpful new information. We beg to differ.

It's true that most tennis players don't become Serena or Venus Williams; most entrepreneurs aren't Steve Jobs; most scientists don't discover what Einstein, Marie Curie, or Stephen Hawking did; and most artists never become Frida Kahlo or Claude Monet. Yet we study these people to find out what makes them remarkable in their respective disciplines—because while not everyone can be an outlier, what we learn from those outliers can help us improve.

You are not a statistic. And you deserve the best possible chance to heal. Our research suggests that means getting proactive about doing what is within your power to improve your odds, especially if you're relationsick. Are you ready to learn how to press the lever, so you can grow beyond learned helplessness and stop the relational shocks in your life?

ASSESSMENT

DO YOU SHARE QUALITIES WITH "OLYMPIANS OF HEALING"?

In *Cured*, Jeff calls people who had better-than-usual outcomes from medical conditions believed to be incurable "the Olympians of Healing." Do you have the qualities researchers have associated with these sorts of health outcomes?[4] Try this list of self-assessment questions.

1. Am I flexible enough to consider new ways of thinking about what might and might not help the body heal? Am I prepared to let go of my certainty about my world view?
2. Am I prepared to adapt to new ways of being in the world, to do what it takes to change how I think, what I believe, and how I behave in my relationships?

3. Can I keep my critical thinking and skepticism engaged enough to make a clear choice about what I believe will or won't help me heal, without being so rigid in my skepticism that I shut down potentially helpful new ideas that are backed by science, psychology, and my gut instincts and wisdom?
4. Am I practicing reality-based optimism while resisting the temptation to engage in denial, magical thinking, or believing that God or positive thinking alone will cure me?
5. Am I allowing my psychological or spiritual self-help practices to comfort and illuminate me without using them to avoid my past trauma and any other hard issues I might need to face in order to heal?
6. Am I prepared to put my healing journey at the top of my priority list, even if it means deprioritizing other things that are important to me or letting down others whom I care about? Am I willing to turn my focus inward, centering my own healing, instead of focusing on what everyone else wants, needs, or expects from me?
7. Can I imagine a future that my body would love and allow that vision to motivate me to face difficult obstacles that might need to be overcome in order to achieve the best possible health outcome?
8. Am I able to consider the possibility that I have been taught by my culture, religion, spirituality, or family to live in a way that makes it difficult for me to center my own authentic needs and deeper desires?
9. Am I willing to engage with conflict or confront people assertively in order to solve problems in my life that might improve my health?
10. Do I accept that all of us will die at some point, and that, no matter how much I try to get better, at some point my

time will come? And that healing emotionally, even if I'm dying, can help me embrace my inevitable mortality and die gracefully?

Take some time in silence to ponder these questions and notice what arises in you. Do you already have the qualities associated with the best possible health outcomes? Or would it be helpful to work on shifting the way you engage with your healing journey, in order to improve your odds?

CHAPTER 2

The Physiology of Relationsickness

Crawl inside this body—find me where I am most ruined.
Love me there.

—Rune Lazuli

Lifelong people pleaser Jamar attended a workshop led by Gabor Maté that Lissa had been asked to guest-teach. Based on Maté's book *When the Body Says No*, the workshop attracted many people who were sick with life-threatening diseases, and Jamar was one of those people. He told a heartbreaking story of why he believed his body said no—because his voice wasn't capable of doing so. For most of his life, he prided himself on being the "yes-man" to the women in his life, and especially his romantic partners. Even if a woman asked for something outrageous, he would stay up all night, if need be, trying to find a way to please her. As long as she was happy, he was happy. Or so he thought at the time.

Sure, this created a lot of stress for him, given that the women in his life were very entitled, used to Jamar working his ass off for them. But until the workshop, he never thought that his people-pleasing tendencies might be related to why he got sick. He'd also never realized where those tendencies might have started: As a young boy, he'd been expected to be the yes-man to his demanding mother.

During one of the workshop exercises, Jamar got in touch with the part of him that was terrified of letting a woman down, for fear of activating her rage. Even the idea of saying "no" sent him into a cold sweat. When he tried saying it out loud with a practice partner, he stuttered and could feel his heart pounding in his ears. He'd always identified as being a nice, accommodating guy. It wasn't until the workshop that he realized that his lack of boundaries and inability to say "no" might have attracted women who would reenact his relationship with his mother, while putting him at risk of the illness he was now fighting. He also hadn't considered why, when the women in his life had no problem saying no to him and what he needed, he hadn't felt angry now that he was sick and in need of their help. He'd just assumed they wouldn't. If he was honest, he hadn't even wanted them to, since he thought he'd look weak to them if they saw him so vulnerable.

It's not surprising that Jamar didn't initially link relational trauma and disease. Most of us think illness is caused by bad luck, bad genes, or unhealthy behaviors, like a poor diet, bad habits like smoking, or failing to stay in shape at the gym. But make no mistake about it. Overgiving to the point of depletion in any of your core relationships—"pretzeling" yourself to try to please someone else while your own needs go unmet—is a severe stressor that can reduce both your quality of life and your life expectancy.

The way we're defining it, you're *relationsick* when cumulative relational trauma leads to real physiological changes in the body, resulting in physical and mental health issues. So let's take a closer look at how that happens, starting with the impact of stress and trauma on the nervous system.

MEET YOUR AUTONOMIC NERVOUS SYSTEM

The nervous system is as ubiquitous in the body as the circulatory or lymphatic systems. Your nerves go to every organ, traveling through every part of you, so whatever affects the nervous system impacts your entire body. When we talk about "mind–body medicine," that's really kind of a misnomer—because the mind/brain is part of the nervous system, and the nervous system *is* the body.

When we experience stress—whether it's the stress you feel when a car cuts you off and you have to slam on the brakes not to hit it, or when your child acts out, or your partner denies wrongdoing after hurting you—the body may experience a "fight-or-flight" response in the sympathetic nervous system—part of the autonomic nervous system.

The fight-or-flight stress response was first identified by Walter Cannon, PhD, at Harvard, and it can be a life-saving physiological reflex if a tiger is chasing you or you're about to get in a car accident. The resulting hormonal cascade diverts most of the body's resources away from processes not essential to immediate survival (like digestion, reproduction, and physiological self-repair) and instead mobilizes them to the heart, muscles, lungs, and other systems that can help you survive the tiger or the car crash.

Once the threat is gone, depending on how severe the stress was, the fight-or-flight response is intended to turn itself off within a few minutes to an hour. This is what happens for most other animals. But for modern humans who encounter a *traumatic* stressor—such as almost being hit by a car when we were previously hospitalized after a car wreck—our thoughts, beliefs, and feelings about the stressor may continue long after the initial threat. We may ruminate, have visual or emotional flashbacks, and experience persistent emotional distress, even after our bodies are safe again. And because the nervous system is still registering a threat, it continues to release stress hormones—and to divert resources *away* from things like self-repair. The result is increased wear and tear on the body—premature aging, early-onset disease and disability, decreased quality of life, and a shorter life span.

The nervous system is not a single, sole-purpose system. It can roughly be broken down into two branches: voluntary (somatic) and involuntary (autonomic). The somatic nervous system controls movements and sensations that we consciously regulate, such as moving an arm. The autonomic nervous system regulates automatic body functions outside conscious control, such as heart rate, digestion, and breathing rhythms. This system can be further subdivided into two main parts: the sympathetic nervous system, which is responsible for the fight-or-flight response just described, and the *para*sympathetic nervous system, which is responsible for rest and repair.

The research of Harvard cardiologist Herbert Benson, MD, author (with Miriam Z. Klipper) of the widely read bestselling book *The Relaxation Response*, made huge inroads in helping us understand how the parasympathetic nervous system impacts physical disease and how to heal stress in the body.* In his research, he found that when people engage in certain practices—such as meditation, prayer, yoga, saying mantras, or deep breathing—they activate the vagus nerve, part of the parasympathetic nervous system, which leads to a slew of positive physiological changes, including decreased heart rate, breathing rate, and blood pressure; reduced muscle tension; lower levels of stress hormones; positive alterations in gene expression; increased activity in the prefrontal cortex; decreased limbic brain activity; and greater telomere health, which helps slow aging. These physiological changes translated into improved disease outcomes for almost every disease he studied, including cardiovascular

---

* While Benson and Klipper's book popularized the notion of using mindfulness meditation to activate the parasympathetic nervous system for the purposes of improving disease outcomes, Benson was promoting as his "medicine" a version of Transcendental Meditation that was later outed as an abusive cult. Nonetheless, Dr. Benson did great work to move the needle on our understanding of the link between nervous system regulation, meditation, and disease recovery.

disease, chronic pain, gastrointestinal disorders, autoimmune conditions, side effects of cancer treatment, and type 2 diabetes.

Why? Benson found that when we feel safe, relaxed, connected, and calm, not only do stress hormones not get released, but our cells get bathed with healing hormones: the bonding hormone oxytocin, the natural-opioid endorphins, our pleasure-reward hormone dopamine, and our inborn antidepressant serotonin. Only in this relaxed parasympathetic state can the body's natural self-healing mechanisms do their job of repairing the wear and tear of everyday life.

Benson's research dovetailed nicely with the research of Candace Pert, PhD, the founder of "psychoneuroimmunology," who published her research in over 250 scientific articles and her bestselling book *The Molecules of Emotion.* Psychoneuroimmunology is the study of the relationship among the psychological, neurological, endocrine, and immunological systems in our bodies, unpacking how our emotional lives—our thoughts, beliefs, and feelings—impact our physiology. Dr. Pert's research demonstrated that when the body launches a stress response, the resulting hormonal cascade affects our cellular biology and downregulates the immune system's natural healing process.

This process is important not just for fighting off bacteria and viruses we're exposed to in daily life, but also for repairing what normally breaks down in the body. For example, we all make cancer cells every day, but we don't usually wind up with tumors because our immune system wipes those cells out before they can take hold. Remember those rats that got injected with cancer and then were exposed to the stress of either escapable or inescapable shocks? About a quarter of them still survived, even when they got inescapable shocks. Our immune systems can sometimes fight off cancer, when our self-repair mechanisms are working right.

The same is true for many other diseases. We make atherosclerotic plaques that can block our coronary arteries, but as Dr. Dean Ornish demonstrated in the Lifestyle Heart Trial,[5] by optimizing the body's self-repair mechanisms through intensive lifestyle changes, patients can unclog blocked arteries. Even diseases believed to be incurable by medical science, can, in rare but notable instances, be cured—without medical treatment. The Spontaneous Remission Project database,[6] a collection of medical case studies published in reputable medical journals and compiled over fifteen years by Caryle Hirshberg and Brendan O'Regan with the Institute of Noetic Sciences, lists 3,500 medically documented cases of diseases like metastatic cancer, heart disease, seizure disorders, HIV, and numerous others that were cured without conventional treatment. Some of the cancer cures seemed to happen after an infection, suggesting that ramping up the immune system to fight off the infection might also have killed the cancer cells.

We're not suggesting you should avoid medical treatment or deliberately infect yourself to try to kill your cancer, but it is worth highlighting these examples to show exactly how remarkable the body's self-repair mechanisms can be when things are working the way they should. When the nervous system is calm and relaxed, our bodies are self-organizing systems designed to heal from many diseases and injuries. But stress disables our self-healing mechanisms. And when the body lives in a stressed state chronically, as can happen in response to ongoing stressors or after trauma, our self-healing mechanisms stay disabled, allowing disease to overwhelm the body's capacity for repair.

UNDERSTANDING POLYVAGAL THEORY

In other words, the body can sometimes heal itself, even from very severe medical illnesses, if the nervous system conditions are right. But what's necessary for the body to self-repair turns out to be more nuanced than what Benson and Pert originally thought. With the emergence of psychologist and researcher Steven Porges's "polyvagal theory," the role of the parasympathetic nervous system in trauma and trauma recovery was significantly reimagined.

The primary driver of the parasympathetic nervous system is the vagus nerve, the tenth cranial nerve, which runs from the brainstem down into the body, connecting with the heart, lungs, gut, and other organs. It's a key player in regulating heart rate and breathing, social engagement (through facial expression, voice tone, and eye contact), digestion, and inflammation, and returning the body to calm after stress.

But the vagus nerve is more complex than we once believed. It's not simply the nerve of involuntary organ functions and nervous system relaxation. It's also the nerve of safety, bonding, and connection, mediating whether we can relax and engage, or disconnect and collapse. It communicates between the body and brain, carrying the story of whether we feel safe or threatened. If we feel safe, the body is free to self-repair. If not, self-healing is not a priority and may be disabled.

Activating the parasympathetic nervous system is also not just about turning on the relaxation response, as when we're sleeping or meditating. As amply illustrated in Barbara Fredrickson's brilliant work at UNC Chapel Hill, which she wrote about in her book *Love 2.0*, the parasympathetic nervous system is also activated when we make authentic positive connections with each other, whether with the barista during a brief encounter at the local coffee shop, with our neighbors as we walk the dog down the street, or with those we love the most. That momentary upwelling of positive emotion and mutual well-being, along with biochemical and behavioral synchrony with the other person, lights up our parasympathetic nervous systems and releases those healing hormones.

Whenever we share a moment of eye contact with a baby in a stroller, a joke with the grocery store clerk, or a cuddle with a golden retriever; when we activate our facial muscles into a genuine, authentic smile, born of happiness—that's the vagus nerve activating our social engagement system in what Fredrickson calls "micro-moments of positivity resonance."[7] The more of them we experience, the stronger and more toned our vagus nerve becomes, leading to what she calls an "upward spiral" of mutual reciprocity between positive emotions, social connection, and improved physiological health.

However, the vagus nerve isn't just involved in relaxation or bonding with others. Just as the sympathetic nervous system is responsible for causing us to fight or flee, the vagal system is associated with the two other common, more severe responses to stress: the "freeze" response, and sometimes the "fawn" response. According to Porges, the vagus nerve has evolved over time to include two distinct pathways, each associated with different behavioral responses to stress and social engagement: the dorsal vagus and the evolutionarily more recent ventral vagus.

Scientists are still debating the accuracy of polyvagal theory because some of its key claims about distinct vagal pathways and their evolutionary hierarchy aren't fully supported by current neuroanatomical evidence, and many of its ideas are difficult to test empirically. While clinicians often find it useful as a metaphorical or therapeutic framework, critics argue that it oversimplifies complex autonomic processes and isn't yet grounded in robust, reproducible data. But for the purposes of our discussion, we find the assertions of polyvagal theory clinically useful, as do many other clinicians in the trauma field.

The dorsal vagus pathway is active during normal sleep or meditation, when you're calm and safe but not necessarily engaging with others. But it can also become active in response to severe relational stress, leading to a "freeze" state that may cause us to collapse when we're terrified, like a prey animal dropping and playing dead to try to avoid getting eaten, or a human freezing when someone is threatening them with a gun. When fighting and fleeing don't work to stop trauma, or when those options feel too dangerous, the dorsal vagal system kicks in.

For example, people who experience trauma in childhood usually respond to that trauma at first with hyperaroused fighting or fleeing. They resist being oppressed and typically try to rebel. Just like the rats in the learned helplessness study, who initially ran back and forth in an attempt to avoid the shocks, these people run or fight back to try to stop the shocks inflicted by abusive parents. But if fighting and fleeing only get them beaten down more, at some point they will run out of energy. The adrenal glands collapse, and so do they—mentally, emotionally, physically, and spiritually. We call this kind of learned helplessness in humans "dissociation."

As with fight and flight, this stress response evolved to be protective. If a gazelle freezes and drops to the ground when a lion is gaining on it, the lion may lose interest, hesitate, or believe their prey is already dead or spoiled. If the lion does eat the gazelle, the dissociation and endorphins released in the dorsal vagal state mean the gazelle will feel less pain. This survival strategy is why child abuse or sexual assault victims often report either having little or no memory of the abuse or having watched the scene from above—and possibly why such victims sometimes don't fight back.

However, humans can have a more complex reaction than rats do to repetitive shocks that they're helpless to stop. While rats can't flatter the researchers in order to try to stop the shocks, humans can—and sometimes do. Enter fawning: the attempt to placate those we deem threatening as a way to survive. We might see fawning as a kind of human-specific lever we can learn to push along with freezing and dissociating. Fawning behaviors are designed to deescalate conflict, access positive attention, and potentially prevent further abuse. "Fawn types seek safety by merging with the wishes, needs and demands of others," writes therapist Pete Walker, who is widely credited as the first person to describe fawning as a fourth kind of stress response in his book *Complex PTSD*. When fighting or fleeing might make the situation worse, fawning might actually save your life, even if it's also putting you at risk of long-term health issues down the line.

WHAT FAWNING ISN'T

The ventral vagal system is typically associated with feelings of safety, connection, attachment, and social engagement. It's the part of the nervous system that is active when we feel calm, relaxed, and connected, like when we're holding hands on the beach with a partner, picnicking with friends, or nursing a baby we're happy to be holding. When the ventral vagus is firing, it's like our body is in "safe mode." We can engage with the world around us in peaceful and harmonious ways, which in turn foster healing and self-repair when the body breaks down and gets sick. This is the medicine of "coregulation," where we humans calm our nervous systems *together*.

On the surface, fawning can look very similar to ventral vagal connection. When we're fawning, we often appear friendly and socially engaged. We might smile, nod our heads, talk in a singsong voice, and utter sweet words. On the outside, we can look just fine. But if you were to monitor our vital signs and other physiological markers of stress, you'd see that, deep inside, our body is revved up and signaling "Threat!" We might look as if we really like or even love the person we are fawning. We might even think we do. We might eroticize the unconscious feeling of danger (something we'll talk about more when we discuss limbic resonance in chapter four). When we feel genuinely safe and connected, our nervous systems tend to show more flexible, regulated patterns, including higher heart rate variability and more synchronized communication between the heart and brain. When we're fawning, our heart rate variability drops, and our cortisol and stress hormone output increases. It's a more disorganized state for your heart and mind, combining high-arousal sympathetic stress with immobilization-based numbing, like pressing the gas pedal while the emergency brake is on.

As trauma therapist Ingrid Clayton, PhD, explains in her book *Fawning*, while the word *fawning* is relatively new in trauma language, it points to something many of us have known in our bones for a long time. Earlier psychological frameworks, like codependency, people pleasing, and submissive accommodation, tried to name the same dynamic. They helped us see ourselves and gave us language for a relational pattern that had long gone unnamed. But these frameworks described the symptoms rather than the root cause. They told us what we were doing, but not why we were doing it. And when we focus on these behaviors without understanding the nervous system that drives them, we end up pathologizing what are, in truth, brilliant survival adaptations. Fawning isn't evidence of brokenness; it's evidence of innate survival intelligence. It's the body's way of trying to keep us safe in unsafe environments. When we can see it through that lens, the shame begins to loosen, and compassion for ourselves can take shame's place.

If the language of codependency has been helpful for you, we don't want to take that away. But we do want to overlay a trauma-informed lens. Born out of the addiction recovery movement, the term *codependency* was meant to describe those who enabled or took on too much responsibility to compensate for the irresponsibility of an addict. Melody Beattie, who popularized the term in her classic *Codependent No More*, defined a codependent as "a person who has let another's behavior affect them and is obsessed with controlling that person." Ouch! This implies that our motivation for fawning is to exert control, when usually we fawn out of fear—not because we want to manipulate, but because we're terrified of losing connection. In our nervous systems, disconnection equals danger.

Viewed this way, what looks like "control" is often hypervigilance. What gets labeled "dependency" is often hyperattunement on overdrive. We are wired to coregulate—to live together, to impact one another, to be interdependent. Healthy dependency is part of being human. But our lone-wolf culture, steeped in rugged individualism, often shames caregivers, mothers, healers, and helpers for anticipating others' needs, as if attunement and caring were a sin. For many of us, these patterns were not learned dysfunctions but assigned roles, often along gender lines. We were socialized to anticipate, serve, and soothe as our ticket to belonging—only to be insulted later in life for doing the very things that once made us lovable and safe.

People pleasing is subject to a similar misunderstanding. It's become the buzzword of our times, especially on social media, where "recovering people pleaser" has become shorthand for anyone who struggles with boundaries. But for many trauma survivors, the term is insufficient and misleading. Fawning may look "pleasing" from the outside: We smile, we say yes, we avoid conflict. But deep inside, our bodies are flooded with fear. The goal isn't to please anyone; it's to survive. The label "people pleaser" evokes an image of a sweet, compliant, weak, naïve goody two-shoes—someone who is "too nice." But it's not niceness driving those smiles; it's survival.

The truth is, these patterns don't develop out of nowhere. The language of codependency and people pleasing often frames these issues as personal problems we need to work on in therapy, without acknowledging that these are often issues born of environments that require us to fawn to avoid harm. Fawning tendencies grow in families where love and safety are conditional, in societies that punish self-assertion or shame it as selfish (especially in women or people of color), and in hierarchical systems that reward fawning behaviors. Fawning isn't a character flaw; it's a creative adaptation to powerlessness. It's the body's way of saying, "If I can keep everyone calm and happy, maybe I'll finally be safe."

Many fawners bristle at language that implies weakness, words like *doormat* or *enabler*, because, deep down, we know our fawning took strength, skill, and courage. Fawning worked. It kept us alive, housed, and fed. It allowed us to maintain some semblance of control in uncontrollable situations. We became experts at reading the emotional weather, taming monsters, holding families together. We were acrobats of empathy, holding everyone else upright so nothing would collapse. Under untenable circumstances, fawning is how we made it through.

WHAT HAPPENS IN THE NERVOUS SYSTEM WHEN WE FAWN

Physiologically, the fawn response is a paradox, an elegant yet excruciating strategy for survival. When we fawn, our nervous system is doing something extraordinary: activating both the sympathetic (fight or flight) and parasympathetic (freeze or collapse) branches at once. On one hand, the hyperaroused part of us is hypervigilant, busy scanning for danger, managing moods, smoothing tension, and tending to the emotions of those in charge. Yet beneath that hypervigilance lies the quiet numbness of hypoarousal, a disconnection from our own sensations, needs, and knowing. It's as if we're pressing the gas and the brakes at the same time, frantically active on the outside, frozen on the inside. Fawning isn't passivity; it's an exquisite balancing act that keeps us safe by keeping us small. It's not "playing dead," but "playing life"—performing aliveness to survive proximity to danger, while losing touch with the pulse of our own authenticity.

In survivors of severe trauma, freeze and fawn often go hand in hand, as you dissociate from the body while, on the surface, appearing to be calm, friendly, and collected. Even though you're in a severe state of autonomic nervous system shutdown and activation, you may present to others as accommodating and sweet, in hopes that they won't hurt or abandon you. In essence, fawning behavior is an attempt to elicit empathy from someone we're actually afraid of, whether they're a real threat or not.

People who fawn suppress their own desires and needs, mirroring or merging with someone else's desires or expectations as a way to avoid conflict so that they stay safe. As such, this fawning tendency can also cause them to overgive, since fawners often neglect their own needs and preferences, focusing on what others want and need. Like with Jamar, your "yes" is an automatic reflex—a sign that your body is experiencing a severe stress response—rather than an expression of authentic connection or a reflection of true consent.

Physiological self-repair requires ample time spent in the calm version of the dorsal vagal state, as when we're peacefully sleeping or meditating. But researchers now understand much more than they used to that good health also requires logging many hours each day in a ventral vagal state of coregulation and connection. When we instead get stuck in the unhealthy version of the dorsal vagal (freeze and fawn) state, just like when we get stuck in a sympathetic (fight or flight) state, it causes the body to prioritize survival over repair, and compromises our ability to heal from illness and injury.

Polyvagal theory is still a theory, not a fact, and research is ongoing. But understanding the dynamics of the autonomic nervous system can offer valuable insights into how we respond to stress and trauma, as well as how we form connections with others and navigate social interactions. Individuals who have experienced relational trauma may have dysregulated vagal responses, leading to difficulties in feeling safe, connecting with others, and managing emotional reactions. And since the body's copious self-repair mechanisms only function optimally in the ventral vagal parasympathetic state—which individuals still suffering from trauma rarely enter—this makes disease worse and impairs recovery.

WHAT'S NEEDED TO DEVELOP A HEALTHY VAGUS NERVE

While trauma can lead to unhealthy activation of the dorsal vagus nerve at any age, relational trauma in the first three years of life has an especially strong impact, because it can directly interfere with the development of the vagus nerve.

Infants rely on consistent, attuned caregivers to coregulate, borrowing the adult's steadiness until their own nervous system learns the art of settling. Just as two or more metronomes placed near one another can gradually fall into the same rhythm,[8] human nervous systems can influence one another toward greater calm through connection and safety. When a child is overwhelmed by terror, rage, loneliness, or disappointment, and a caregiver responds with presence, mirroring, and validation, the child's body learns that emotion is survivable, connection is possible, and regulation can return, laying the groundwork for resilient vagal tone and lifelong nervous system flexibility.

But when a caregiver is chronically frightening, unavailable, or dysregulated, the infant experiences relentless stress, with their bodies in either a sympathetic (fight or flight) or dorsal vagal (freeze) state, and this inhibits the development of the ventral vagal pathway. If the ventral vagus doesn't develop normally, a child grows up either chronically hyperaroused (stuck in fight or flight), hypoaroused (stuck in freeze and fawn), or a combination of both.

Part of the reason for this is that stress hormones interfere with the production of myelin, a fatty substance that coats nerve fibers, acting like insulation on a wire and allowing signals to travel quickly and efficiently. Healthy myelination of the vagus nerve is essential for benefiting from the self-healing properties of the ventral vagal states. Low myelination, in contrast, creates a brain and nervous system more biased toward threat detection and less equipped for self-regulation, relational coregulation, and physiological repair.

Fortunately, research in neuroplasticity is revealing that deep changes in nervous system structure and function, including remyelination, can occur even late in life.[9] People who have never experienced ventral vagal states of connection can strengthen vagal tone through a variety of trauma-healing modalities, which we'll teach you about in part two, as well as refer you to additional resources for nervous system healing on page 353.

STRESS INFLAMES OUR BODIES

Stress has another impact on disease and healing that's important to discuss: its role in chronic inflammation, which a large body of research in immunology, psychiatry, and behavioral medicine identifies as a central contributing factor in many chronic illnesses, as well as mood and anxiety disorders. Acute inflammation is a normal part of the body protecting itself from disease. When the body spots a pathogen or a foreign body that doesn't belong, like the virus that causes COVID-19 or cancer cells, it mounts an immune response designed to fight off the invader. Just as with the body's stress responses, immune responses can be life-saving in the short term but dangerous in the long term. Chronic inflammation leads to autoimmune activation, in which immune cells become confused and begin attacking your body's own cells. The result is metabolic diseases such as type 2 diabetes, cardiovascular disease, stroke, Alzheimer's, nerve degeneration, and cancer.

As we age, we all develop some degree of chronic inflammation, which is associated with the natural degeneration of the body. But the most powerful driver of chronic inflammation, along with an inflammation-inducing diet, is chronic stress caused by trauma. This has profound consequences for disease onset, progression, and recovery.

Remember, when we're under stress, the body enters a state of biological threat that kicks off a cascade of physiological changes. One of these is the release of stress hormones like cortisol, epinephrine, and norepinephrine. Normal cortisol release suppresses inflammation, but in long-term stress, cells can become resistant to cortisol, leading to unchecked inflammation. The vagus nerve normally works like a brake pedal to keep inflammation in the body under control. But when you're under chronic stress, this braking system gets weaker, so the body has a harder time shutting down inflammation. Chronic stress can impair the regulatory mechanisms that maintain gut barrier integrity. When that barrier becomes too porous, bacteria and toxins that normally stay inside the gut can slip into the bloodstream, which triggers more inflammation, thereby weakening the immune system.

Chronic inflammation is now known to be a common driver or amplifier of many diseases. It inhibits tissue repair and creates a cellular environment that promotes cell mutation, making it a well-established risk factor for several types of cancer. It also shortens telomeres and increases oxidative stress, which speeds up aging and increases your vulnerability to all kinds of diseases. As Jonathan Saw writes in *Harvard Magazine*, "Can seemingly unconnected illnesses of the brain, the vasculature, lungs, liver, and joints really share a deep biological link? Evidence has been mounting that these common chronic conditions—including Alzheimer's, cancer, arthritis, asthma, gout, psoriasis, anemia, Parkinson's disease, multiple sclerosis, diabetes, and depression among them—are indeed triggered by low-grade, long-term inflammation."[10]

Importantly for our discussion about relationsickness, relational trauma keeps the body in a pro-inflammatory state, impairing the immune system. When you marry a chronically stressed nervous system to an impaired immune system, you have a recipe for difficult-to-treat disease.

CHILDHOOD RELATIONAL TRAUMA AND CHRONIC INFLAMMATION

Studies show that childhood trauma is surprisingly widespread and carries serious long-term health consequences. In a landmark study that assessed people's score on a scale tallying adverse childhood experiences (ACEs), measuring ten common childhood traumas (e.g., physical or sexual abuse; neglect; or the divorce, domestic violence, mental illness, substance abuse, or incarceration of parents), about two-thirds of adults reported at least one ACE, while around 12 percent experienced four or more. Those with four or more ACEs faced dramatically higher odds of adult illness, having roughly two to three times greater odds of developing conditions like cancer, heart disease, and respiratory disease, and those with six or more ACEs risk dying twenty years younger versus those who do not experience severe trauma in childhood.[11]

Since the 1990s, when research into ACEs and physical disease began, researchers have sought a physiological mechanism that would explain how traumatic experiences that happen in childhood could lead to adult-onset disease. While psychoneuroimmunology and polyvagal theory partly explain this, new data is giving us a better understanding of how childhood trauma may impair the adult body later on. In a meta-analysis of multiple research-study results published in *Molecular Psychiatry*,[12] researchers found a significant association between childhood trauma and inflammatory markers, like C-reactive protein and interleukin-6, which are hallmarks of chronic inflammation, providing strong evidence that childhood trauma significantly alters the inflammatory system and leads to chronic inflammation long term. Chronic inflammation, in turn, can damage blood vessels, disrupt metabolism, and impair immune function—explaining how early relational trauma "gets under the skin," and why its effects can persist decades into adulthood, shaping both physical health and longevity.

HEALTHY BODIES NEED RECIPROCAL RELATIONSHIPS

True healing—cellular regeneration, immune repair, hormonal balance—depends on the body feeling safe enough to stop defending and start repairing. But people who give too much—people who, like the giving tree, are doing more for others than their bodies can afford, without enough reciprocation—rarely feel comfortable enough to do this, because they tend to have nervous systems that are stuck in chronic stress responses. Their plates are too full. Their mental loads are too high. But this chronic stress often occurs even when there's no obvious stressor. This is because, for people who have experienced past relational trauma, especially as children, relating *itself* is stressful.

When we find it hard to relax around other humans, when we struggle to feel worthy of being in a relationship unless we're overgiving, when relationships are transactions and we're getting the raw end of the deal, the day-to-day wear and tear adds up. Not only does the chronic stress from our relationships lead to immune system dysfunction, chronic inflammation, and other physiological harm; it also makes it harder to enter the ventral vagal parasympathetic state that allows for repair.

Most adults who find themselves in unbalanced relationships were set up to choose unequal, unfair relationships because of how they were exploited and mistreated in childhood, for reasons we'll look at more closely in chapter four. This puts their nervous system on high alert and can lead to overgiving as a type of fawning, in an effort to avoid upsetting others and win love, something we'll talk about more in the next chapter.

For now, understand that this is how relationsickness works: Relational trauma causes nervous system dysregulation, which leads to hormonal imbalances, chronic inflammation, and immune system malfunction, increasing the risk of incurring almost every chronic disease process. When your nervous system is in fight-or-flight sympathetic nervous system hyperdrive 24/7, or in freeze-or-fawn parasympathetic hypodrive beyond when you're resting and sleeping, your body is practically guaranteed to pay the price.

You can get the best medical care on the planet; eat the healthiest, most nutrient-dense and anti-inflammatory foods; take dozens of supplements; work out with your personal trainer; and practice yoga and meditate—but if you do not have healthy, reciprocal relationships, your body cannot heal, repair, and thrive.

CAN WE IMPROVE HEALTH OUTCOMES BY HEALING TRAUMA?

All this leads us to the million-dollar question: If trauma causes nervous system dysfunction that leads to chronic inflammation and immune dysfunction, does treating trauma—thus returning the nervous system to the self-healing ventral vagal parasympathetic state, reducing chronic inflammation, and rebalancing the immune system—reverse disease?

Well, sometimes, for some diseases. Even when inflammation is the main driver of a disease, other factors are involved, like genetics, environmental toxins, and random bad luck. Illness and human suffering are complex, multifactorial, and layered. It's tempting to blame trauma for every form of human suffering, but reducing all diseases to trauma would be flattening and insulting to anyone who actually struggles with chronic illness. Trauma is a significant risk factor for disease, but it's not the only one.

It's also not the only cause of chronic inflammation; an inflammatory diet, immobility, and other factors can provoke it. A sedentary lifestyle and a diet full of food that the body doesn't recognize as nutrition can certainly contribute to early-onset disease. Overeating or eating processed foods with low-quality nutrition stimulates an inflammatory response that kicks off a whole cascade of autoimmune activity. Exercise can reverse some of this, but if your diet is poor and you're not exercising much, the effect is amplified.

The good news is that some diseases caused or exacerbated by chronic inflammation can be reversed by reducing inflammation. Diet-related inflammation can be reduced by limiting overconsumption and prioritizing anti-inflammatory, nutritionally dense foods. Immobility-related inflammation can be treated with exercise. And chronic inflammation due to trauma can be reversed by healing that trauma and its effects on the nervous system. This is as true for relational trauma as any other kind.

We hate to break it to you, dear reader, but trauma treatment is sometimes a long, slow, emotionally painful process. This does not make it a popular intervention for medical conditions in a quick-fix culture that likes the relative emotional ease of popping a pill or doing a green-juice cleanse. The reality is, if you want to heal your nervous system and its related illnesses, you need to transform the thoughts, behaviors, and emotions that contributed to that illness. We believe that to really optimize your health outcomes, treating your trauma is one health intervention you can't afford to skip.

The root of the word *healing* means "to be whole." Trauma fragments us, and we need to reintegrate those fragmented parts before we can truly heal, or be whole, again—before we can access and live from our deeper, more authentic, uninjured selves. As long as such trauma goes untreated, it can be nearly impossible to cure disease.

While all of this is true, let us be crystal clear that, in sharing these stories and this science, we are not blaming anyone for their illness. It's easy to feel at fault when you hear the science linking trauma and disease, or stories about patients who took ownership of their healing journeys differently from how you did and had radically different outcomes. True, healing is your responsibility; nobody else can do it for you. But your trauma—and any disease that contributed to or resulted from it—is not your fault.

We also know it's hard, and it hurts, to face the past and reckon with what has sometimes been decades of pain. Not everyone will be interested in doing this kind of deep work, especially as even highly trained medical professionals don't realize how important, effective, and liberating it can be. We understand that. You have every right to control your own choices, especially when your body is breaking down. Every one of us is entitled to our own journey when we get sick, and you are not beholden to anyone else to work on yourself or listen to unsolicited advice.

However, if you're curious, open, and willing to consider getting more involved in your own recovery, if you're open to facing past relational trauma and taking steps to change the way you show up in your current relationships, you just might get better. While you can be healed without being cured of disease, sometimes, when people heal their trauma, cures follow.

The first step is learning more about *why* we overgive to the point of depletion. And this means understanding more about fawning.

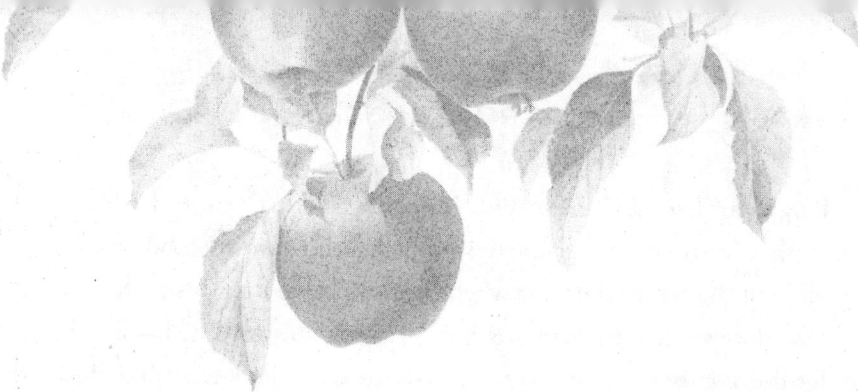

CHAPTER 3

Are You Nice, or Are You Fawning?

Stop setting yourself on fire to keep others warm.

—Anonymous

When Celie met Jude, it was love at first sight. The instant their eyes locked, her whole body melted, and she felt a rush of desire she had rarely experienced. She didn't usually think of herself as sexy or sensual, but Jude awakened something in her she didn't even know was there. She couldn't believe someone like him had chosen her.

She adored all his little quirks, even the ones that might have annoyed another woman. She loved how he always sat with his back to the wall at restaurants, eyes fixed on the door like a Secret Service agent. She thought it was gallant that he'd maneuver her to the inside of the sidewalk, shielding her from passing cars. Because she'd felt unprotected in the past, like nobody had her back, every protective gesture made her feel cherished, feminine, looked after, and cared for in a way she'd longed for her whole life. With Jude, she couldn't wait to lay out clean clothes in the morning, make sure he had his favorite foods for lunch, and put dinner on the table when he came home from his high-powered job. She even started changing how she dressed, swapping her fitted suits for flowing dresses and soft sandals so she could look more like the kind of woman she imagined he wanted. When he barked out orders in the bedroom, she thrilled at the sound of his voice, grateful that he desired her at all.

At first, Jude showered her with flowers and chocolates, handwritten notes and romantic songs. But when those gestures faded, Celie didn't complain—she redoubled her efforts to please him instead. She convinced herself it was natural for him to get busy with his important work; he was running a whole city! And she prided herself on being able to attune to his needs, anticipating them and accommodating even his most mercurial expectations. On the rare occasions when her intuition was off, she profusely apologized, kicking herself for failing to nail it the first time. When he criticized her for not doing something he needed perfectly enough, she twisted herself in knots to try to appease him, acquiescing to his sometimes-challenging demands and counting her blessings that she had the opportunity to be the wind beneath his mighty wings.

To ease his burdens, she cooked every meal, folded every load of laundry, and spent long hours helping him research a major city improvement project. She even volunteered to handle the messy legal details of his still-pending divorce, telling herself it was an honor to smooth the way for a man with such a vital mission. Whenever doubt crept in, she reassured herself that once his work settled down, he would return to his old romantic self.

Her devotion came at a cost: her first negative HR review at work. She accepted it as proof she needed to reprioritize, and when she timidly told Jude about it, he suggested she just quit her job so she could keep supporting his needs full time. He offered to take care of the bills, and to her own surprise, she felt almost relieved, grateful to be freed from the stress of work so she could pour her energy fully into loving him.

Over time, Celie's health began to falter, but she brushed the headaches, rashes, and digestive troubles aside, telling herself it was probably just perimenopause. Even when she developed long COVID and then a heart condition related to it, she hated to complain too much. When she asked Jude if he might help around the house or consider hiring some outside support, he lashed out, accusing her of being lazy. Instead of standing up for herself, she panicked at the thought of losing his approval and redoubled her efforts to prove her devotion.

One time, Jude dangled the idea of helping take care of her, offering to come with her to a doctor's appointment and take her out afterward, and she clung to that suggestion as if it were a lifeline. When he withdrew his offer at the last minute, claiming he was too busy at work, she collapsed in tears, not so much angry at him as ashamed of herself for wanting too much.

Even though it was a stretch for her, she reached out to her friend Lucy to accompany her to the appointment, and she took the risk of telling her friend about how much it hurt that Jude canceled after getting her hopes up. Lucy confessed to Celie that she'd been worried about her since she'd gotten involved with Jude, that it had been hard to witness her friend morphing into someone she didn't recognize. She invited Celie to join her for a Zoom workshop Lucy had enrolled in with Lissa about fawning, how chronic fawning behaviors can cause medical issues, and how to heal.

Celie had never heard of fawning, but she'd heard of codependence, and she figured she probably fit the description for that. It had never occurred to her, though, that codependent behavior might be linked to getting sick. She signed up to join Lucy for the workshop, and the psychoeducation she received was a glaring wake-up call. Celie had to face the parts of herself that confused love with sacrifice, that equated devotion with self-erasure, and that kept giving, even when it was her turn to receive.

UNDERSTANDING THE FAWN RESPONSE AND ITS IMPACT ON THE BODY

People in situations like Celie's can get so accustomed to fawning that it becomes a reflex. We think we're just being nice, that this is how we're supposed to be. We may not even realize that we're stressed or feeling threatened. Survivors of relational trauma can end up fawning out of sheer habituation, as automatic as breathing, not even realizing we're doing it. And the threat we're responding to may be as simple as the fear that others will abandon us if we stop fawning. Habitual fawners, Pete Walker explains, "act as if they unconsciously believe that the price of admission to any relationship is the forfeiture of all their needs, rights, preferences and boundaries."[13] Those who fawn are very sensitively attuned to those they seek to placate, anticipating others' needs before they even express them and seeking to appease them, even when it leads to unwise choices.

Habitual fawning is often the result of socialization. It can be a foundational part of one's upbringing, training, religion, or education, or an intrinsic part of the way certain families and communities function. Think of the parent who demands their children's obedience, or how women in certain cultures are taught to be subservient to men. Or it may be such an important part of survival that an individual truly has no choice, if they want to stay alive. If you were born into a marginalized group where you might be in danger outside your own home, like individuals in the United States who are Black, Indigenous, or people of color (BIPOC), or those born into the lowest levels of India's caste system, habitual fawning may become a life-sparing mechanism that keeps you safer. But it's still a trauma response, from living in a world where some people matter less. And regardless of the reason for it, habitual fawning is dangerous for your long-term health.

In chapter two, we detailed what happens to our health when our nervous systems are stressed most the time: The body bears the burden.

And while chronic stress responses of any kind can be destructive in the long run, the burden can be worse for those who freeze and fawn than for those who fight or flee.

Fighting and fleeing are further up what therapist Deb Dana, LCSW, calls the "polyvagal ladder"—a simple model developed by Dr. Stephen Porges to help us understand how we move through states of regulation and dysregulation. Imagine a ladder with three rungs. The top rung is the ventral vagal state, the relaxed, socially connected nervous system state associated with love and belonging. The middle rung is the sympathetic state, the state associated with mobilization, like playing sports, and also fighting or fleeing if you're in danger. The bottom of the ladder is the dorsal vagal state, which is associated with the most severe kinds of stress responses, like freezing. The fawn response is a combination of the bottom two rungs: sympathetic activation and dorsal vagal shutdown and immobilization.

The more time you spend higher up the ladder, and the more easily you can recognize the signs of stress in your body, the sooner you can take measures to reduce your stress. For example, maybe you can tell physiologically when your mother, spouse, or boss makes you want to run or scream. You can either fight, to try to make them stop doing whatever is stressful for you, or you can get yourself away by fleeing. This ability to fight or flee is actually protective for your health—because it spurs action.

But if you're frozen or fawning, you may not even realize something is wrong, so your reaction to the stress is likely to be more passive. Maybe you just feel sluggish when you get up in the morning, and you tell yourself you're just not a morning person. Or you feel the need to take frequent naps, or you struggle to force yourself to exercise, or you feel depressed. One of Lissa's clients, a frontline ER doctor and chronic fawner who got burned out during the COVID pandemic, described his slow start in the morning as "morning cancer," not realizing until he read in a book Lissa recommended that morning cancer was how his body responded to the fawning and dissociation.

While a sympathetic stress response is less damaging to the body than dorsal vagal dissociation, the ventral vagal state is where Olympians of Healing win their gold medals. This is why a flexible, healthy nervous system is so important. It allows us to move up and down the ladder all day, often without conscious awareness, letting us return to a ventral vagal state after we've been triggered through coregulation in safe relationships or body-based tools like breathing, movement, and sound.

Just to be clear, all chronic repetitive stress responses, whether fight, flight, freeze, or fawn, can make us relationsick. Staying in a chronic state of fight or flight because of our relationships will take a toll on our bodies. The problem is that chronic fawners often do not look or feel stressed, so the health complications can sneak up on us. Fawning often rides shotgun with dissociation, so someone who is fawning may look so calm, cool, and collected that nobody, including the fawner, has any clue how stressed they are.

At least in a hyperaroused fight-or-flight state, we might recognize the signs of stress in ourselves: blood pounding in our ears, tightness in our neck or jaw, diarrhea, or our heart skipping a beat. Doctors will often pick up on early warning signs of too much time spent in a hyperaroused state, like high blood pressure, tachycardia, physical pain, and other physical exam or laboratory evidence of physiological wear and tear. After we recognize the problem, we can take action to relieve our stress.

But fawning comes with a combination of both hyperarousal and hypoarousal. We're hypervigilant, but we're also frozen, with the freeze response dominating. We don't always experience the typical stress-related warning signs, and doctors may more easily miss the signs of toxic stress in the body during screening exams. Because the vagus nerve is firing, someone frozen and fawning might even have normal to low blood pressure and a normal to slow pulse. We can *look* like the calm picture of health, even to medical doctors—until we wind up with a cancer diagnosis or test positive for an autoimmune condition.

Even Jeff, a medical doctor and chronic fawner, missed the signs of stress in himself. Since he always passed his physicals with flying colors—normal blood pressure, heart rate in the low 50s—he had no idea how much his fawning was stressing his nervous system (though he'd always wondered why he scored so poorly on heart rate variability monitors, which monitor how much stress you're under). Then he met Lissa and realized that his ability to tolerate even the most outrageously stressful situations with equanimity was not a mark of his advanced spiritual development, as he'd previously thought; it was a survival strategy. It was him fawning and dissociating whenever things got intense in his relationships. And once he realized that healing the tendency to fawn could prevent illness as much as his rigorously healthy diet and exercise regimen, he got into therapy and began to heal—as preventive medicine.

Since fawning is such a common factor leading to relationsickness; since it's a risk you can mitigate, change, and heal; and since most people who are fawning don't realize they're stressed when engaging in fawning behaviors, it's crucial that we be able to identify when and if we're fawning. Let's dive deeper into what fawning looks like and its impact on relationships, so you can learn about this largely unconscious behavior and start identifying it as a marker of stress that can lead to relationsickness.

THE 8 A's OF FAWNING

Fawning tends to show up as what Lissa calls "the 8 A's": Attuning, Appreciating, Anticipating, Accommodating, Appeasing, Acquiescing, Apologizing, and, in extreme cases, Assimilating.

Attuning: Hyperfocusing on the other person's words, behavior, and body language to determine what would make them happy. As the giving tree might say, *"Hey, boy, you look like you're having a hard day. Why don't you come climb my trunk and swing from my branches so you can cheer up?"*

Appreciating: Expressing excessive gratitude for and approval of the other person's behavior, even when that behavior is abusive. This can include justifying one's treatment with spiritual beliefs. *"I'm grateful to* *the boy who is giving me the chance to sacrifice all my apples, branches, and trunk. He's helping my soul grow and teaching me unconditional love."*

Anticipating: Anticipating the other person's needs before they even ask and practicing anticipatory compliance, even when it's not necessary. *"As long as I mind-read what the boy might need and offer it to him without hesitation, I will earn his loyalty and love."*

Accommodating: When the other person does make a request, reflexively accommodating that request, whether we want to or not. *"Yes, of course you can have my apples, branches, and trunk."*

Appeasing: Placating the other person, even if they're making entitled demands, including going back on our no or relaxing our boundaries to make them happy. *"I'm sorry if I didn't seem excited about cutting down my trunk so you could build a boat. Of course I want you to row off into the sunset!"*

Acquiescing: Accepting intolerable behaviors without protest. *"Well, I won't be able to photosynthesize if I cut down all my branches and have no leaves anymore. But of course you can take my branches to build yourself a house."*

Apologizing: Preemptively or reactively apologizing for not answering the other person's demands, even if we've done nothing wrong. *"I'm sorry I have nothing left to give you, boy. I'm devastated that I've let you down."*

Assimilating: Being absorbed into another's identity such that you lose your own sense of self. At the most extreme end of the fawning spectrum, we wind up socially isolated, cut off from others, and financially severed from funds and freedom—yet we still fawn our abusers as a survival strategy and even convince ourselves we're in love with them. *"I'm nothing but an old stump with all the life taken out of me, but I love you, boy."*

Most people who act out the 8 A's have little to no awareness that these behaviors are typically driven by fear and an unconscious need to stay safe. When we're fawning, we may have driven our fear so far underground that we don't even feel afraid. But the minute you ask a fawner to consider modifying these behaviors, panic often sets in. Even imagining doing something different can feel terrifying because of deeply ingrained subconscious programming.

FAWNING ISN'T KINDNESS—IT'S CONFLICT AVOIDANCE

How is fawning different from just being nice, kind, or altruistic?

People who are genuinely being kind discriminate based on their values. They know the difference between saying yes when they're really a no or giving to the point of overriding their own needs and boundaries, because they're kind to themselves, as well as to other people. When these kind folks think about doing something for someone else, they filter it through their own needs, preferences, and other responsibilities. And they're willing to let down people in the outermost reaches of their social network if that's what it takes to show up in loving ways for those they most love and cherish.

When we fawn, we are nice or deferential to others, not because we have made a conscious choice to do so, but because of a perceived threat. We may extend that niceness only to people we fear, or people we deem higher up on a power hierarchy—those we believe we need to please in order to stay safe. Fawning is a way to avoid conflict, which doesn't feel safe—usually because, in some way, it wasn't safe when we were small.

Many of us worry that if we put some limits on our fawning, people might stop liking us. Sometimes that does happen. But not always. Most reasonably healthy people are willing to respect our "no" and cooperate with our boundaries, without labeling us unkind. But fawning can become so reflexive that we find ourselves walking on eggshells, trying not to upset anyone—even when we're around safe, healthy people who wouldn't blow up if we did something they didn't like.

Fawning can look like compulsively trying to anticipate other people's needs, even if it means stuffing down our own. It can mean saying yes when we really mean no, or becoming a chameleon, trying to be who we think people want us to be, rather than who we are, because our relational trauma has left us scared of not being liked. It can look like people pleasing, being nice when an expression of displeasure would be more authentic, and flattering people we aren't actually very impressed by.

That's not being kind, even if other people perceive it as such. That's pretzeling ourselves to please others, because we're terrified of what will happen if we don't.

FAWNING CAN MAKE OUR RELATIONAL LIVES RISKIER, NOT SAFER

When we fawn, we center the person we're fawning, making them the object of our undivided attention. The object of fawning can come into hyperfocus, as the rest of the world fades away. The person being fawned absorbs all our attention, so much so that we might neglect everyone else in the room and anything else happening around us.

This kind of attention can feel very seductive to others, especially if they've never had it aimed their way before. Even healthy people can begin to take up a lot of space in response to someone fawning them. Those with strong fawning behaviors will continuously recenter the person they're fawning, even when the other person tries to put the attention back on the fawner. And because of the way trauma rewires the nervous system, this can happen with anyone the fawner is attached to, even if they're not scary or intimidating and haven't required fawning for people to stay in their favor.

Those with strong fawning behaviors rarely take up much space themselves, which can partly be a strategy for avoiding intimacy, resulting from the kind of attachment trauma we'll discuss in chapter 4. We are protecting ourselves from being truly known, for fear of being discovered as essentially unlovable for who we really are. Because we were conditioned to believe our worth comes from pleasing other people—to believe others cannot possibly love us unless we earn our keep by meeting their needs, while making our own invisible—we are sacrificing true intimacy and the opportunity to be loved for ourselves.

In short, fawning results in the opposite of what we intend to create—*safety in relationships.* Even if we are lucky enough to have people around us who *are* safe, we miss out on the opportunity for true closeness because we're not being authentic about what we want and need and where our boundaries lie. And if we aren't so lucky, fawning behaviors can enable others with tendencies toward selfishness, narcissism, or exploitation to behave poorly toward us. What might start out as a mildly unequal dynamic is ramped up until it becomes full-blown narcissistic abuse (something we'll talk about more in chapter five).

TRADING LOVE FOR POWER

The kind of fawning we're talking about in this chapter is not the same as the Merriam-Webster dictionary definition of the word: "exhibiting affection or attempting to please; obsequiously flattering, to court favor by a cringing or flattering manner." That's not the unconscious survival strategy version of fawning; that's an intentional choice, a conscious manipulation designed to get something you want.

Some relational trauma survivors learn to obsequiously flatter people in positions of authority not just to stay safe, but as a way to get what often turns out to be a poor substitute for the love they didn't get enough of growing up: power. Some part of them, whether conscious or unconscious, decides that, since unconditional love isn't on the menu, they might as well settle for power—whether that's the power of intellect and education; the power of celebrity influence; the power of beauty; the power of talent; or political, financial, or spiritual power.

> Manipulating others for the sake of getting what you want depends on a spoken or an unspoken power hierarchy, in which one person is "one up" and the other is "one down." When we're the one in a position of authority, we may feel safer than when we're one down. In response, some people who flatter others try to acquire power as a way to stop being one down, and instead start being one up—the person who should be fawned. They seek out leadership positions or pair up with partners they think of as "less than," so that they are more frequently in the one-up position.
>
> But being on this side of the power equation also comes at the price of intimacy. It may feel better to be one up than one down, but you can't love from either.

OVERGIVING AS FAWNING

The important thing to understand is that fawning is not—despite how it sometimes looks from the outside—just the behavior of a good, generous, caring person. It's a *stress response,* arguably the most severe kind. And it can make you relationsick.

Fawning in the context of our romantic relationships in particular leads to overfunctioning, in which we take excessive responsibility for others—managing, fixing, or doing more than our share—while neglecting our own needs or boundaries. It prevents us from asking for what we need and getting the help we deserve. And it depletes us psychologically, emotionally, and physically, because it puts too much pressure on us to survive on our own, without enough help from others. Our nervous systems are firing severe stress responses because we're simultaneously afraid *and* not getting our own needs met. We're not receiving the comfort, nurture, support, and coregulation humans rely on to live healthy lives.

The fawner who gets relationsick is the wife who, while working outside the home as many hours as her husband does, also does much more than 50 percent of the parenting, domestic work, social and travel planning, and emotional labor of the relationship, because she's not asking for help, delegating what's beyond her capacity, or saying no when she needs to. It's Celie, attending to Jude's responsibilities, the ones that don't even have anything to do with her, like his work project and his divorce issues. It's the tree who sacrifices apples, branches, and trunk to an ungrateful little boy, because why else would he love her? It might, dear reader, be you.

If you recognize yourself in this discussion about fawning, please don't blame yourself. It's not your fault. It's how you survived. It's an understandable adaptation that got you through childhood or some other traumatic experience.

What's needed to begin to heal from fawning tendencies is a nonjudgmental open heart. See if you can contact that tender-heartedness as we take a compassionate look in the next chapter at what causes some people to fawn while others don't: childhood relational trauma.

ASSESSMENT

SELF-INQUIRY FOR FAWNERS: WHY DO I GIVE MY POWER AWAY?

If the descriptions in this chapter resonated with you, it's worth taking a moment before we move to the next one to see if you can explore some of the impulses that underlie fawning behaviors. The following questions are not a quiz; they're an invitation to reflect deeply and honestly. There are no right answers—just insights. Take your time. You can write your responses in a journal or talk them through with someone you trust.

- Why do I gravitate toward relationships where I feel smaller, less powerful, or unable to speak up?

- How do I make decisions? If I ever willingly hand over decision-making to others, when do I do so? In what circumstances?
- What stops me from setting limits or saying no?
- Have I ignored warning signs, gut feelings, or hard truths in order to avoid conflict or stay connected? If so, why?
- Do I believe I deserve to be protected—or that I'm allowed to protect myself?
- Am I looking for someone to save me, take care of me, or give me a sense of purpose through caretaking others?
- Do I prioritize other people's needs over my own? If so, why?
- If I sometimes hold on to unhealthy relationships too long, what is the story I tell myself about why I do this?
- How do I usually respond to hurt or disappointment? Do I address it, suppress it, or do something else?
- What am I most afraid might happen if I stop people pleasing?

This inquiry is meant to stir curiosity, not criticism. If your answers reveal patterns that don't feel aligned with your well-being, know that you're not alone; many of us were conditioned to fawn in order to survive emotionally or physically unsafe environments.

The good news is that these patterns can be unlearned, without sacrificing your kind heart or your loving spirit. In part two of this book, you'll learn how to rebuild your relational confidence, reconnect with your inner knowing, and practice setting healthy boundaries—without guilt, shame, or fear.

You deserve to take up space. You deserve to be safe, seen, and sovereign.

CHAPTER 4

Understanding Relational Trauma

The child you once were needed someone to love you, to protect you, to put you first. When that didn't happen, your nervous system encoded the absence as danger.

—Janina Fisher

To say that Elizabeth's childhood was challenging would be, by any measure, an understatement. Her father had untreated bipolar disorder and a rap sheet a mile long, and while he worked nights, her mother's revolving door of drunk boyfriends touched Elizabeth in places therapists and social workers would later have her point to on a naked doll. While her mother was hitting the bottle and then hitting Elizabeth, the girl was the sole caregiver of her younger brother and had to mother them both, far too young for that kind of responsibility.

Then, when Elizabeth was twelve and her brother was nine, her mother disappeared. Elizabeth still doesn't know what really happened—whether Mom just walked out on her family, as her father claimed, or whether her father drove Mom out into the middle of a corn field on a deserted highway and told her he'd kill her if she ever came back, as her mother later said. All she knew is that, one night, the bottles, the boyfriends, and her mother were gone.

Nobody ever explained to Elizabeth or her brother why their mother was gone. It was left unspoken, and she and her brother never asked. In their mother's absence, the father they barely knew was in charge. Elizabeth remembers looking at him, thinking, *We don't even know this loser, and now he's responsible for us.* Elizabeth's mother may not have known how to take care of them, but at least she was familiar. Their father was just this amorphous figure who skirted the edges of their lives, and now he was all they had.

Elizabeth's father turned out to be clueless about how to raise kids. He frequently forgot to feed them when he went to work and left them at home alone, leaving Elizabeth to beg the cashier at the local convenience store for canned ravioli. When the cashier who took pity on her wasn't working, Elizabeth would sometimes have to steal dinner. And when that didn't work, she and her brother ate cat food.

Although they lived right across the street from a gas station, her father would take the kids on an outing with the gas tank on empty, just to terrorize them. "We're riding with the devil," he'd say. Then he'd pretend to run out of gas and wander off, allegedly to go find more. But just before he left the kids alone in the car, he'd warn them, "Don't let the Hatchet Man in."

The kids would shake in their boots and startle at every peep, terrified that the Hatchet Man would come and get them while Dad was off pretending to get gas. After a while, the kids realized that they never actually ran out of gas, but still to this day, they get the shivers if it's dark and someone mentions the Hatchet Man.

Around this time, social workers appeared in Elizabeth's life. Word must have gotten out about her mother's booze and boyfriends, or it could have been because of her father's trouble with the law. When she asked him later, as part of her application for a security job, whether he had ever been arrested, her father laughed, asking how many pages of his rap sheet she wanted him to include.

Today, Elizabeth is finally healing from the relational trauma caused by her crappy parents. After years of hopping from culty church to culty church, trying to find a spiritual explanation for the injustices of her early life, she finally gave up trying to make sense of how unfair her life was. She realized in therapy that her attempt to explain the "why" of all her childhood suffering was really just an attempt to bypass the brokenheartedness of her little-girl self, who would never get the parents other kids did.

Elizabeth still struggles with loneliness and chronic pain, but to lighten the heaviness, she jokes that, somewhere, there's a parent factory where they pop out parents. Because the factory only operates Monday through Friday, the factory workers are at their best Monday morning, and this is when they produce the best parents, the ones who make their kiddo feel safe, who love them unconditionally, who treat them fairly, with dignity and respect, and who don't exploit them. On Tuesday afternoon, they're still rolling out decent parents, but the factory workers are getting a little tired and sloppy; these parents might be kind, attuned, and loving some of the time, but they slip up more often than Monday morning parents. By Wednesday, the factory workers are starting to fantasize about happy hour on Friday night, so they're a little distracted, and Wednesday parents have more flaws. But by Friday afternoon, the parents they're churning out are of clearly inferior quality. Not only do they not behave the way Monday morning parents might, they're flat-out awful. They're mean, abusive, violent, neglectful, exploitative, and terrifying.

The kids who get Friday afternoon parents did nothing to deserve such bad parents. We don't believe they're being punished by karma because of misdeeds in past lives, or that their souls chose their parents so they could learn lessons through abuse—two spiritual beliefs that are often used to justify oppressing people or let people feel in control of things they can't control. They just lost the parent lottery. The problem is, that's not how these kids grow up feeling.

Those of us who don't get our early needs met grow up with broken hearts. We see other kids with loving caregivers, and we can't understand why we're not good enough to get the same affectionate closeness, comfort and nurturing, and permission to feel our emotions and become our own well-boundaried little beings. We're too little to understand that the way these Friday parents treat us has *nothing to do with us*, and everything to do with how our parents were parented themselves. We can't comprehend how our parents' own traumas are interfering with their capacity for empathy, healthy bonding, and loving care. As a result, we grow up feeling less lovable, less worthy, and unable to relax and bond with other people in healthy ways. Instead, we fight, flee, freeze, or fawn.

The worse our childhood trauma, the more likely we are to learn to fawn as a way to survive childhood. While this adaptive strategy gets us out alive, it can create havoc in our adult relationships and, as we've seen, put us at risk of relationsickness—unless we realize we're doing it and make sense of why.

Whenever we talk about trauma, we are talking about what happens in your body, in your nervous system and your endocrine system, because of something distressing that happens to you. Trauma refers to a single or repetitive experience that impairs your stress response system, making it overly reactive and sensitive in some cases and inadequately reactive—numb, dissociated, and insensitive—in others. Trauma is related to but not quite the same as stress.

Trauma is not about a tough day at work or how you feel when you don't get something you want. It's more serious than that. Some people endure very stressful, tragic experiences that do not register as traumatic, because they were supported by loving people who helped them get through it. Most deeply traumatic experiences stem from feeling alone, invalidated, or unloved in the aftermath of a difficult event.

We most often hear about trauma in relationship to natural disasters, war, medical issues, or accidents. But trauma can also be relational. When we are used, exploited, controlled, neglected, or betrayed by the people who are supposed to care for us, that's trauma too—sometimes the most devastating kind. And especially in childhood, even things that might not seem like that big a deal can be traumatizing in ways that harm your nervous system, and your relationships, later in life. So it's worth taking some time to dig into childhood relational trauma, to explore how and why it leads to fawning behaviors.

BREAKING THE CONTRACT OF CARE

In her book *Not the Price of Admission*, trauma therapist Laura Brown, PhD, describes the required relationship between parents and their children as the human "contract for care." Humans cannot just give birth and then expect their kids to grow up as functioning members of tribal society. There are certain rules of being human that all kids need to learn from their parents: basic social skills and how to get along as an adult without undue dependency; when it's safe to trust and when to be suspicious of someone; how to tolerate difficult emotions, like anger, disappointment, terror, and shame; and how to be autonomous, without either being controlled or controlling someone else. But not every parent fulfills this contract, and the result is that kids grow up thinking they have to pay an unfair price in order to be worthy of love.

As Dr. Brown writes:

> If you are a survivor [of relational trauma], you were raised by people who were impaired in some way in their ability to engage in the most important human task. They broke the "contract for care." They did not make you central. Perhaps they exploited your normal childhood vulnerability to believing what adults say. Maybe they took advantage of you needing comfort and connection even though the one to whom you had to go for that comfort was scaring or hurting you. Or they simply were unable to show up for the task of giving you the attachment experiences that you needed because they were themselves too affected by emotional distress, physical illness, and/or inadequate resources.

> At the same time . . . they were simultaneously teaching you that it was your job to keep your relational agreements with them, as well as others. They expected loyalty from you, even when they hadn't any to you. They taught you that you had to pay a price to be in relationships by exacting prices from you that children can't pay without suffering damage to their developing senses of self and capacities to be in relationships of any kind.[14]

As a result, Dr. Brown says, relational trauma survivors grow up confused about how to show up in relationships, knowing they don't want to be like their parents—disloyal, disengaged, and untrustworthy—but not knowing how else to be. They grow up not knowing that it's okay to say "enough already" or "no," and not realizing that they don't have to be the only one investing in the relationship.

As Dr. Brown puts it, "You don't quite grasp why it's perfectly moral to drop your end when other people drop theirs. You've overridden your inner warning signals too many times and trusted people who were dangerous to you. Or you're on the other end of the spectrum, thinking that you hear a tsunami warning when it was just the siren of a distant ambulance going by, and you've kept people at a distance in order to feel even a little bit safe."[15]

Kiddos don't need perfect parents. They just need what Donald Winnicott calls "good enough" parents: caregivers who are generally attuned, present, attentive, and playful, and who know how to repair any relational ruptures that inevitably happen. When we have good enough caregivers, we feel safe, nurtured, loved, and supported. Our nervous system can relax and our brain and peripheral nervous system can develop neural pathways in optimal ways. We learn to feel safe and connected with people we can trust.

When our caregivers aren't safe or trustworthy—when closeness is intrusive but lacking in warmth or intimacy, or when our caregivers neglect us, reject us, or exploit us—we grow up with relational confusion, not knowing who to fear and who to trust. Since leaving an unsafe situation at home is not an option for us as vulnerable children, we almost always grow up assuming that *we* are the problem—that we are defective, broken, unlovable, and unworthy of being treated better. To help ourselves feel as safe as possible in an unsafe situation, we learn to ignore our Spidey-Sense that something is wrong, suppress our hurt and anger (especially if fighting gets us beaten, humiliated, or abandoned), and develop conflict-avoidant and fawning tendencies in order to survive.

The developing nervous system is not the only casualty of having caregivers who break the contract of care. The developing psyche suffers as well. Relational trauma in childhood distorts a child's developing personality structure. It interferes with the healthy development of identity, the cohesive sense of *who a person is*—their stable self-concept that integrates personality, values, beliefs, preferences, and the felt continuity of being the same person over time. When relational trauma is extreme, children can experience splits in identity that are severe enough to cause dissociative identity disorder. But even survivors of relational trauma without this disorder can end up with a divided and disorganized sense of identity.

To survive severe childhood relational trauma, a child must find a way to feel safe when safety is nowhere to be found, to trust when our caregivers are not trustworthy, to develop a sense of control when life is out of control, and to feel some sense of power when we are powerless. This is a double-edged sword: It allows us to survive intolerable conditions, but the psychological defenses and adaptive strategies we develop to help us survive show up in adulthood as a false self that chameleons itself to become whoever we believe others want, rather than an authentic identity rooted in an inherent sense of our own value.

In short, when our caregivers break the contract for care, our little psyches are deeply affected, which influences how we relate to others for the rest of our lives. In this chapter, we'll examine how the adaptive strategies we're forced to learn to protect our fragile young psyches from the intolerable pain of rejection, neglect, and abuse impact our development. These ways of coping, while necessary for survival, outlive their usefulness when we grow up and try to have relationships with other, healthier people whom we may struggle to trust.

THE STILL FACE EXPERIMENTS AND ATTACHMENT

A heartbreaking YouTube video[16] titled "Still Face Experiment Dr Edward Tronick" demonstrates how distressing even a brief moment of relational rupture between an infant and its "good enough" mother can be for an infant's developing nervous system. If you watch the video, which we encourage you to do, you'll witness a smiling, attuned, and responsive mother cooing with her adorably happy and securely attached infant. The cheerful baby smiles back at her mother, laughs, points to get her attention, and giggles. Her mother plays along, receiving and reacting to her bids for connection. But at a certain point in the Still Face Experiment, the mother is instructed to adopt a "still face"—to remain expressionless and unresponsive for a brief period, no matter what her baby does. She's still there. She's not abandoning her child. But she stops responding to her baby's cues.

This sudden change in the responsiveness of her mother's face creates a stark change in the child's behavior. The infant initially tries every trick she can think of to get her mother to smile and play again. Rapid fire, she cycles through every bid for connection that had gotten her mother's attention only a moment earlier. She smiles. She points, because she's used to the mother looking where she points. She uses both hands to reach for her mother. But these strategies don't work this time. The baby begins to look distressed. She claps her hands and makes a screeching sound. She turns away and presents her back to the mother, so she is no longer looking at her mother's painfully still face. And finally, she starts sobbing and pretzels her body in a full-on meltdown.

At this point the researcher instructs the mother to reconnect. The baby is able to be soothed quickly; the repair to the rupture of connection is swift, and the mother is forgiven.

The reason this baby is so easily soothed is because of the baby's bond with her mother. The bond is stable, based on months of experience that, when she coos or cries, her mother responds, playing with her and meeting her needs as best she can. This baby recognized the Still Face Experiment as an anomaly—a breach in an otherwise-fulfilled contract for care, something *not normal*. While it created extreme stress in her little nervous system, the experiment didn't last long, and her well-established maternal bond allowed her to be easily comforted once the short experiment was over.

The deep emotional bond between an infant and their primary caregivers is called *attachment*. According to John Bowlby, the originator of *attachment theory*—the study of how humans relate to one another, based on how their parents related to them—this bond is biologically driven and essential for survival. When, as a baby, we experience stress, we have an innate drive to seek emotional and physical proximity, safety, and soothing from our primary caregivers. And in both theory and experiment, it's clear that a child's development depends not only on physical caregiving but on emotionally attuned, consistent responses from their caregivers.

Securely attached babies can rebound from the pain and fear of the Still Face Experiment, assuming it only lasts a couple of minutes before the mother reengages and comforts the child. But imagine if you were a baby who grew up with caregivers who always had a still face, or even worse, a mad, scary, or threatening face, or no face at all because you were abandoned and left to cry alone. Your tiny baby nervous system would be so jacked up in a sympathetic hyperaroused state that you'd be arching and screaming and begging for connection. And if that didn't work, you'd likely become listless and hypoaroused, feeling helpless and hopeless and winding up disembodied, dissociated, and disconnected in a dorsal vagal state.

When babies pull out all the stops to try to engage bonding behavior in their caregivers, and repetitively fail to get their attachment needs met, it hurts so much that they quit trying. They roll over like the rats who couldn't avoid being shocked in Martin Seligman's learned helplessness studies, and give up making bids for connection. Unable to tolerate the pain of rejection, they reject their caregivers: crying, leaning away, and not making eye contact, even when their caregivers do try to engage.

The reactions of the babies in the Still Face Experiments have been validated across a wide span of cultures around the world, including in the United States, Japan, Germany, China, South Africa, Israel, Cameroon, Peru, and India, and they appear to reflect one of our most basic, universal human patterns. We are driven to connect and attach, and when this doesn't occur, our attachment systems go haywire, causing the attachment bonds we do form to be insecure.

ATTACHMENT TRAUMA INCREASES DISEASE RISK

Researchers have been able to draw a direct line between adult-onset disease and unhappy relationships in childhood. In the Harvard Mastery of Stress Study,[17] which followed Harvard college students from the mid-1950s and 1960s until the 1990s, 87 percent of subjects who lacked closely attuned parenting as children had at least one disease thirty-five years later. This was compared with only 25 percent of those who felt very cared for by their parents. In other words, the absence of closely attuned parenting had a massive impact on how likely these college students were to develop at least one disease over the next thirty-five years. Because attachment trauma sets kids up to experience chronic nervous system dysregulation, the resulting immune system dysfunction and development of chronic inflammation, as well as impairment in the natural repair that occurs in the ventral vagal state, most likely contributes to this higher disease rate later in life.

FAILURE TO ATTACH

Sometimes the reason children do not get their initial bonding needs met is because they've ended up with Friday parents, but there are plenty of other reasons bonding needs may not get met that are nobody's fault and have nothing to do with how much their caregivers love them or care for them. Sometimes children are separated from their caregivers for unavoidable reasons, such as neonatal ICU stays or caregiver death or hospitalization.* Traumatized primary caregivers who themselves have attachment trauma are not always wired to give their babies the kind of love, attention, and bonding needed to develop healthy attachment. Babies can fail to bond with primary caregivers and develop attachment trauma if the primary caregiver has postpartum depression, is overwhelmed by the demands of parenting, is "checked out" because of their own mental illness or substance abuse, or has been given parenting advice around dealing with a crying baby that lacks an understanding of attachment needs. War, significant poverty, or separation of children from parents (for example, at immigration detention centers) can also interrupt this key developmental need for attachment, and intergenerational or collective trauma can make it harder for caregivers to be attentive to a baby's needs.†

---

* Scientists and therapists are still learning at the cutting edge of attachment theory what happens when babies are separated from the birth mother, even when connection with the birth mother is replaced very quickly by a birth father, an adoptive parent, a gay parent of a surrogate's baby, or a nanny, for example. There is controversy around this issue, as these concerns bump up against issues of women's rights, LGBTQIA+ rights, social class issues, and patriarchal notions that mothers belong at home with the children. While most data suggests that alternative caregivers who are not the birth mother can still raise securely attached kids, activists who were adopted or became adoptive parents, like Nancy Verrier, the author of *The Primal Wound*, controversially claim otherwise.

† This is not to suggest that there aren't plenty of wonderful parents who are Holocaust or Gaza genocide survivors, BIPOC, or refugees—just that systemic

Regardless of the reason, when kids don't get the secure attachment experiences necessary for normal child development and healthy brain and nervous system development, they experience a kind of relational trauma that trauma researchers also call *developmental trauma* or *attachment trauma*. Buddhist psychiatrist Mark Epstein, MD, calls this kind of trauma "the trauma of everyday life." It's also known as "little t" trauma, to distinguish it from the "Big T" traumas we usually think about when discussing childhood trauma.

But the suggestion that developmental trauma is less traumatic is erroneous, since developmental trauma may happen every day for years, while some traumas that we think of as more severe, like physical violence or sexual abuse, might only happen once. Because of that consistency, developmental trauma affects the way a child's personality develops and may lead to personality disorders, like narcissistic, borderline, or antisocial personality disorder.

We are all literally wired for connection and attachment, and when that doesn't occur, our nervous systems become dysregulated.

ATTACHMENT THEORY

Attachment is now a well-studied field of research in the traumatology sphere. Our understanding of attachment helps us make sense of why we act the way we do in our most intimate relationships in adulthood. Remember the Still Face Experiment? The same kind of bid for connection occurs in all of our interactions with others, even as adults. Though we might learn to suppress the desire for it, we all want and need to feel seen, valued, and loved. And when we don't get that, we are, like the baby whose mother would not respond in the Still Face

---

or collective oppression or trauma may make parenting in a responsive way more difficult. It's not the parents' fault, but the children can still bear the scars and carry on generational wounds.

Experiment, forced to take on different patterns of protective behavior, or *attachment styles.*

Pioneered by British psychologist John Bowlby and picked up later by Mary Ainsworth, attachment theory is the study of how we relate to one another, based on how our parents related to us as infants and how we learned to get our needs met—or didn't. Bowlby posited that the bonds formed between children and their primary caregivers, typically the birth mother, are crucial for healthy psychological development.[18] He began his groundbreaking work in the 1950s by observing children who had been separated from their families during and after World War II. Noting that these children exhibited distress and behavioral issues, he theorized that a secure attachment to a caregiver is essential for emotional stability. Bowlby proposed that attachment behaviors—such as crying, clinging, protesting when a caregiver is unresponsive or leaving, and following a parent around—are innate. They function to keep the caregiver close, thus ensuring the child's safety and care.

In the 1970s, Mary Ainsworth, one of Bowlby's colleagues, performed her research on what she called the Strange Situation, in which infants were observed in a series of episodes involving separation from and reunion with their mothers in a controlled environment. From these experiments, she distinguished several different patterns of response, which she called attachment styles. Importantly, Ainsworth theorized that these patterns were neither random nor solely a matter of temperament, but were shaped by the infant's prior experience with the caregiver's responsiveness. When caregivers had been consistently available and attuned, infants developed a *secure* style: They explored freely when the caregiver was present, showed distress when the caregiver left, and were quickly soothed upon reunion. When caregivers had been rejecting or emotionally unavailable, infants tended toward an *insecure avoidant* style, showing little overt distress when the caregiver departed and avoiding or ignoring them upon return. And when caregivers had been inconsistent—sometimes responsive, sometimes not—infants developed an *insecure anxious* style, becoming highly distressed upon separation, and showing both a strong desire for contact and difficulty being soothed during reunion.

Mary Main, a psychologist and one of Ainsworth's doctoral students, later expanded this framework by identifying a fourth pattern, disorganized attachment, or the *fearful avoidant* style, which Ainsworth endorsed. In this attachment style, the infant showed contradictory or confused behaviors during reunion, such as approaching the caregiver while averting their gaze, freezing, or collapsing. Main theorized that this style emerged when the caregiver was simultaneously a source of comfort and a source of fear, leaving the infant with no coherent strategy for seeking safety.

In other words, kids who couldn't get their attachment needs met wound up with a series of predictable behavioral patterns resulting from that primary attachment trauma, making it harder to feel secure relationally, even when those kids later engaged in relationships with people who were more trustworthy than their early caregivers. Later behavioral psychologists have expanded this attachment theory research to include adults in relationships. Even though the attachment strategy we learned in childhood may no longer be necessary for our survival as adults, the patterns we learned back then can return to haunt us, causing us to unwittingly sabotage even the healthiest adult relationships because of the distrust and lack of safety we learned early on.

Understanding your attachment style—how you respond in relationships based on how well your attachment needs were met as a child—and the attachment styles of those you love helps you make sense of otherwise confusing behaviors in yourself and others, and develop compassion for those exhibiting such behaviors. For our purposes, understanding attachment styles can help us understand why some of us give too much without expecting adequate reciprocity: as a way of trying to secure otherwise insecure attachment bonds.

A DEEPER DIVE INTO INSECURE ATTACHMENT STYLES

In the best of circumstances, babies cry when they have needs, and their caregivers respond, figuring out through trial and error what they need and doing their best to provide it. These babies learn to recognize and express their needs, and trust that those needs will mostly get met. They feel comfortable relying on their caregivers, and safe reaching out to them for help. If their caregivers get it wrong and their needs remain unmet, they know it's safe to protest until their caregivers get it right. These babies grow up securely attached. And as adults, they bond readily, exercise discernment in who they trust, and flexibly navigate both closeness and distance.

As described by Laurence Heller, PhD, founder of the NeuroAffective Relational Model, in his book *Healing Developmental Trauma*, children who grow up to be relationally healthy learn to stay emotionally attached to others without collapsing their sense of separateness, allowing them to bond emotionally with others while protecting their sovereignty. They maintain the right to set limits while respecting the limits of others. They have learned they can say no without fearing that they will lose the love of their attachment figures. And they are capable of respecting "no" from others without withdrawing emotionally.

People who grow up with one of the three *insecure* attachment styles, in contrast, struggle to trust other people and lack a secure base, the foundation upon which healthy relationships are built. This makes it difficult to have reciprocal, functional, mutual relationships in adulthood and causes them to feel perpetually unsafe, which can drive chronic stress in the body.

Any insecurely attached person is at risk of fawning, but the styles that include anxious attachment (both anxious and disorganized) are most likely to fawn, because they fear abandonment if they don't do exactly what the other person wants. In a classic match made in hell, people with avoidant attachment often pair up with people who have anxious attachment. The anxiously attached person pursues, and the avoidantly attached person distances, creating a classic cat-and-mouse chase: The more the former pursues, the more the latter gets scared and runs, and then the more anxious the former gets. So it's worth taking a closer look at all three of these insecure attachment styles, to better understand what makes some people wind up like the giving tree, and others feel entitled to take, as the boy did, without appropriate reciprocity.

Anxious Attachment Style

Some babies receive intermittent care and bonding, mixed with neglect. Sometimes their parents respond when they need something and cry. Other times they don't. But since *sometimes* their efforts were rewarded, these babies grow up learning that trying harder—crying harder, complaining more, acting clingy and needy—is the only way to get what they need. These babies grow up with the anxious attachment style and are at greater risk of overgiving and fawning in adulthood. Since they learned that trying harder sometimes got them what they needed, they might try too hard to win over unpleasable people as adults, resulting in unbalanced relationships.

Babies who grow up anxiously attached hate to be alone, and may experience "departure stress," getting anxious if they're preparing to separate from an attachment figure. They do want closeness, but because of inconsistent caregiving, they also fear it won't last, which can make them ambivalent: sometimes pushing away after seeking comfort, struggling to actually take in any emotional nourishment they do receive, and seeming hard to satisfy, even to someone who's trying hard to please them. It's almost like love doesn't *land* for them, even when someone genuinely caring is showering them with affection.

Adults with this attachment style often crave intimacy but feel insecure about whether others will reciprocate, which can lead to passive-aggressive protest behaviors: sulking, guilt-tripping, picking fights, or withdrawing affection to test loyalty. As adults, those of us with anxious attachment frequently yearn for people who are only sometimes or partially available. The unavailable person creates a familiar emotional pattern, echoing early inconsistent caregiving. We may even eroticize this attachment wounding, feeling the most attracted to people who are not fully available to give us the love, care, and reciprocity we need and deserve. We may develop crushes on people who are married, who "just aren't that into us," or who have a sexual preference we don't fit. We may chase incarcerated prisoners, workaholics, people who live far away from us, or anyone just out of reach who recreates the "sometimes there, sometimes not" availability of our early caregivers.

If we do find an available partner, we often merge and lose ourselves in the other person, anxious to keep them but always waiting for the other shoe to drop. We may struggle to say no and hold our boundaries. We also may have a hard time respecting other people's boundaries, showing up as too intrusive or demanding. We may overfocus on the other person in an obsessive sort of way, to our own detriment. We badly crave connection, yet we struggle to self-soothe and rely too much on others to calm us down when we become distressed. This can create the classic behaviors we associate with codependency.

In some ways, those of us with an anxious attachment style are less traumatized than those with other types of insecure attachment styles, because we *did* get our attachment needs met some of the time. As a result, we're neurologically more wired for connection than other insecure types. We just don't quite know how to take in emotional nourishment and feel secure in the connections we do make, so we tend to seek out people who can't or won't give us what we need—like avoidantly attached people.

Avoidant Attachment Style

When babies are neglected but not violently abused, when they don't get enough attention and are ignored too much, they might wind up with avoidant attachment. Initially, when babies who grow up to have an avoidant attachment style need their caregivers, they'll cry and cry, ramping up their protests the way the babies in the Still Face video do, in an attempt to get their needs met. But if enough time goes by, and their caregivers do not come to meet their needs or comfort them when they're hungry, poopy, gassy, or experiencing overwhelming feelings like terror, anxiety, or loneliness, they stop protesting and start rejecting their parents as a defense against the heartbreak of that broken connection.

Over time, these babies shut down, no longer bothering to cry when they are lonely or scared, sitting in a poopy diaper, or feeling hungry, because crying doesn't get their needs met, and it simply hurts too much to keep crying out for help and getting ignored. They give up, resigned to their fate, and often dissociate from their bodies as a way to adapt to the emotional neglect.

Sometimes these kids are thought of as "good children," because they are quiet and compliant, but in truth, they have just learned helplessness, like Visintainer and Seligman's poor shocked mice. As they grow, they become little rugged individualists and stop reaching out for comfort, help, or support, even when they're with people who want to meet their needs and would help out if they could. These babies tend to grow up with an avoidant attachment style.

As adults, those of us with this attachment style tend to put the brakes on attachment, keeping intimacy at arm's length and finding creative ways to avoid getting too close to people. We become John Wayne–like lone wolves, convinced that it's safer to be independent, isolated, and alone than to risk the vulnerability of reaching out and being rejected. Even though we get lonely and, at our core, want connection, we find it easier to be alone than to be in a committed, long-term relationship. When we do seek relationships, we tend to jump from one superficial connection to another without diving into the depths of real intimacy, making it difficult to get close and relate in healthy ways. Or we pair up with others who are independent lone wolves, don't expect real intimacy, and are satisfied with distance and disconnection.

Those of us who are avoidantly attached may exhibit fawning behaviors like people pleasing and accommodating, but it's usually a strategy to maintain distance or keep conflict low, not a way of clinging for closeness. The difference between anxious fawning and avoidant fawning is the motivation. In anxious fawning, it's "If I please you, you'll stay close." In avoidant fawning, it's "If I please you, you won't expect too much from me (and I can stay safe)." We might act agreeable or compliant to avoid exposing our real needs or emotions, as a way of protecting our inner vulnerability and avoiding too much intimacy. In professional, family, or romantic settings, we might overfunction, overgive, or stay "the capable one" as a way to avoid being seen as needy. This can come across as similar to fawning, but it's driven more by a need to be powerful and in control than by the terror of abandonment fears.

Because avoidant people often give off the vibe of being emotionally unavailable, they frequently attract anxiously attached partners. The anxious partner tends to fawn them in hopes of securing closeness, while the avoidant partner withdraws, and both feel stuck.

Disorganized Attachment Style

The most severe kind of attachment wound happens when babies have caregivers who override healthy or safe boundaries and neglect their core attachment needs. When the people who are supposed to be our safest source of attachment are instead frightening, exploitative, or sexually or emotionally abusive, babies grow up with disorganized attachment, sometimes called *fearful avoidant* attachment. This style exhibits a mix of avoidant and anxious attachment behaviors.

Those of us with disorganized attachment styles both crave connection and also fear intimacy. The anxious aspect of the attachment style may cause us to people-please, fawning and overgiving, while the avoidant aspect may cause us to erode connection by sowing distrust, acting out in hurtful ways, withdrawing, or rejecting others before they have a chance to reject us. This can be very confusing for others who want to partner or even have close friendships with us. One moment, we're trying to please them. The next, we're breaking our promises and sabotaging the relationship. Because it wasn't safe to say no, push back, and rebel when we were children, we learned blind obedience—fawning—in order to survive. But because we had caregivers who crashed through and destroyed any sense of healthy boundaries, we perceive even healthy closeness and well-boundaried intimacy as terrifying and invasive.

We crave connection, because closeness is what's familiar. But we also fear it, because the type of connection we experienced as children was invasive and terrifying. So we push people away, sabotaging even healthy connection, which we confuse with intrusiveness. Alternately, we may choose partners who do not threaten our fear of intrusiveness and are emotionally unavailable for real intimacy, allowing us to have superficial companionship while avoiding genuine intimacy. People with disorganized attachment often seek out long-term relationships, marry, and have children; we just ensure that the people we partner with are essentially distant, even when we live in the same house. That way, the anxiously attached part of us can avoid being too lonely, while the avoidantly attached part can sidestep too much intrusiveness. But to other people, the push/pull pattern can feel disorienting.

Those of us with this attachment style tend to be dissociated from our bodies and disconnected from what we really need. We tend to stuff down any feeling or impulse toward self-care or self-protection, rationalizing it away or considering it less important than what someone else might need. Because we may have been abused when asking to have our needs met, we learned to put ourselves forth as needless and wantless. But underneath, we may feel desperately needy, scared, and lonely.

We may stay quiet and pretend to be unbothered when others are treating us badly. But deep down, we're brokenhearted. Still, we may sincerely believe that dissociating from our needs and fawning others is the only way we can have a relationship, so we settle for "white-knuckling" it through our human connections in a way that is at best unfair to everyone involved and at worst abusive.

ASSESSMENT

WHAT'S YOUR ACE SCORE?

We like to think we have free will and are making conscious choices about which people we let close and which ones we keep at a distance. But attachment research suggests that we are far more unconsciously controlled by our relationship role models from childhood than we might expect. Unless you undergo relational recovery work, how your childhood caregivers treated you establishes how you will choose relationships and behave relationally for the rest of your life.

Sometimes it's obvious that we got the wrong childhood programming about relationships. If we experienced one or more Big T traumas, like physical or sexual abuse, or a parent that intentionally abandoned us, it's easier to understand why we might experience challenges in intimate relationships when we grow up.

While many developmental traumas go unrecognized by any standard trauma scaling, the scale psychologists use to measure the more obviously traumatic childhood dynamics is called the adverse childhood experience (ACE) scale. Marking your baseline ACE score is important for exploring the depth of your trauma burden, since we know from good science that the higher your ACE score is, the more likely you are to develop physical diseases prematurely. A low ACE score does not mean you haven't experienced significant trauma that can lead to relationsickness, but a high score almost always means you've also struggled with interruptions to healthy childhood development.

In a 2014 TEDMED talk, California surgeon general and pediatrician Nadine Burke Harris, MD, summarized the findings of a landmark study conducted by Vince Felitti at Kaiser Permanente and Robert Anda from the CDC: "Thirty years ago, the CDC and Kaiser Permanente discovered an exposure that dramatically increased the risk for seven out of ten of the leading causes of death in the United States . . . This exposure is not cigarettes, alcohol, junk food, pesticides, or a sedentary lifestyle; it's childhood trauma."[19] At the time this pivotal study was published, we didn't fully understand the mechanism for why this was so. Some of the "why" is still a medical mystery, but we now have much more scientific data linking ACE traumas to chronic nervous system dysregulation and its associated health impacts.

Because we learned in chapter two that a high ACE score can decrease life expectancy by twenty years and increase the risk of almost every disease out there, it's important for you and your doctor to know your ACE score. That way, you can get help implementing adequate prevention and treatment for trauma-related medical conditions. You can determine your ACE score by answering the following questions:[20]

1. Did you feel that you didn't have enough to eat, had to wear dirty clothes, or had no one to protect or take care of you?
2. Did you lose a parent through divorce, abandonment, death, or other reason?
3. Did you live with anyone who was depressed, mentally ill, or attempted suicide?
4. Did you live with anyone who had a problem with drinking or using drugs, including prescription drugs?
5. Did your parents or adults in your home ever hit, punch, beat, or threaten to harm each other?

6. Did you live with anyone who went to jail or prison?
7. Did a parent or adult in your home ever swear at you, insult you, or put you down?
8. Did a parent or adult in your home ever hit, beat, kick, or physically hurt you in any way?
9. Did you feel that no one in your family loved you or thought you were special?
10. Did you experience unwanted sexual contact (such as fondling or oral/anal/vaginal intercourse/penetration)?

You get one point for each "yes"; your ACE score is the total number of yeses.

It's important to note, however, that both ACEs and childhood relational trauma can be counteracted by positive childhood experiences. If you had neglectful, intrusive, or otherwise abusive parents, but you also had a very kind grandmother who lived nearby and looked out for you, or a best friend who had your back in school, these positive experiences can help minimize trauma's impact. Even if you only had one person who showed empathy for what you were going through, helped coregulate you, and reminded you that you're a good, lovable, valuable human being, traumatic events might have had less residual impact on your mental and physical health—and your relationships—later on.

HOW FAMILY POWER DYNAMICS IMPACT OUR HEALTH

What attachment theory makes clear is that kids, to grow up healthy, have to feel safe, supported, loved without controlling conditions, and permitted to become their own individuated selves. Even if your family looked harmonious on the surface, and even if your ACE score is zero, if you were worried about losing your caregivers' approval when you weren't perfect, or if your acceptance in the family was contingent on being what your parents wanted you to be, rather than who you really were, your nervous system will feel under assault. As children, we have to know we are loved unconditionally—not because our parents will approve of us if we fawn well enough (that's a stress response). Rather, we have to know we can be our imperfect, authentic selves and our caregivers will still love us, even if they're not always thrilled with our choices.

Many of the relational distortions that develop in a trauma survivor's personality revolve around power. If, in childhood, we do not experience healthy attachment—feeling helpless, hopeless, worthless, controlled, and overpowered instead of loved for our authentic selves, or figuring out how to win approval by being little "parentified" adults who comply with what our caregivers want us to be—we may grow up to be either disempowered or power hungry. These two adaptations look very different on the surface, but they are both trauma symptoms resulting from inadequate caregiving in childhood.

As elegantly delineated in Pia Mellody's *The Intimacy Factor* and taught at The Meadows in her relational recovery programs, many childhood trauma survivors develop one of two core wounds that can lead to fawning behavior. The first is the "not enough" wound of *disempowering abuse*, in which we were unable to win the affection of our caregivers, causing us to believe we are inherently damaged and broken. Because we were either neglected or actively abused no matter what we did, this daily drip-drip-drip of disempowering abuse can harm us as much as any Big T trauma.

The second is the "too much" wound of *falsely empowering abuse*, in which we were only able to win our caregivers' oh-so-conditional approval by being who and what they wanted us to be, rather than ourselves. This kind of wound is equally destructive to a young psyche, even though it can look less so on the surface, since it falsely inflates you, rather than cutting you down. But underneath the inflation is the same message: *You're not good enough just as you are. You have to pretend to be perfect instead.* Kids like this know, deep down, despite the praise they earn, that it's a setup, a sham, and not real love. What the targets of both kinds of abuse share is the brokenheartedness of not being unconditionally loved.

When a Child Is Disempowered

Disempowering abuse occurs when a child is repeatedly made to feel powerless, inadequate, defective, or broken, or is not allowed to develop independence, autonomy, agency, and a healthy sense of their personal power. This form of abuse includes actions or messages that undermine a child's self-worth and sense of competence and efficacy, communicating to the child that they lack intrinsic value and reinforcing a sense of helplessness and dependency on others. Under the burden of disempowering abuse, children are shamed, belittled, neglected, controlled, and/or infantilized. They wind up feeling worthless, as if they are fundamentally deficient, rather than realizing their caregivers are the deficient ones.

As a result, the disempowered child may hide, going invisible and playing the role of the "lost child" or the wallflower, withdrawing and becoming invisible and self-sufficient to avoid adding to family conflict. They might escape into books or fantasies, becoming a rebel, nerd, or hermit, terrified that others will discover how damaged and worthless they believe they really are. Or they might wind up the scapegoat, burdened with the family's secrets—the psychiatric patient, troubled teen, addict, bad seed, or "good for nothing" loser.

The disempowered child thus may fail to step into their power in a healthy way, or never optimize their potential as a fully actualized individual. When we are continually disempowered or treated as a problem, we often grow up feeling incapable of handling life independently. This creates a deep need for reassurance from others, which often manifests as clinginess, indecision, or dependency in relationships. As adults, we may constantly seek approval or fear abandonment.

Because disempowering abuse has chipped away at our self-worth, often leaving us with chronic self-doubt, low self-esteem, and insecurity, we frequently fear rejection, obsess about being abandoned, or are hyper-aware of perceived threats to the relationship. Those of us with disempowering abuse histories are often highly attuned to emotional shifts or signs of withdrawal from others. Because we learned to depend on external validation for our sense of safety and worth, we may become overly vigilant or preoccupied with keeping relationships intact, the way anxiously attached people do.

Underneath our feelings of defectiveness often lies a kind of scrupulous perfectionism that is designed to keep us under the radar, and we may overcompensate for our low self-worth by being hyper-responsible. Or we may avoid taking on adult responsibilities because we don't trust ourselves to be competent enough and fear reprimand. Because we lack self-trust, we tend to put our trust in others who seem more capable, giving our power away in the process.

Disempowering abuse can lead to reflexive fawning with almost everyone around us, since we perceive others as more valuable than we are, and don't believe we deserve the same basic care, protection, and boundaries that others do. Most people who grow up with a severe case of the giving-tree pattern were victims of disempowering abuse—but not all. Some also end up fawning as a result of falsely empowering abuse.

When a Child Is Falsely Empowered

Sometimes caregivers, due to their own unresolved issues, impart an inflated sense of worth, superiority, power, and control to a child, which can lead to significant distortions in self-perception and relationships. Pia Mellody points out that while this attention might appear positive, especially if it involves lots of parental praise, approval, and pride, it also comes with unrealistic or inappropriate expectations. For example, a parentified child is one who is expected to take on family responsibilities that rightfully belong to adults, like parenting younger children, supporting the family financially, or becoming a caregiver's emotional support person or, in the case of molestation, sexual partner.

These responsibilities can make a child feel as if they are "better than" others—more morally righteous, more important, more helpful and competent—with no guarantee they are developmentally ready for that kind of adult responsibility.

Those of us who are parentified as children are the hero, the helper, Daddy's little girl, or Mommy's little man. And because we are often rewarded for these prematurely responsible roles, we grow up believing the only way we can get love is by being exploited. We confuse exploitation with love, because we learn to get attention, praise, and approval by accommodating others' needs.

Whether we feel special and better than others because (as with child stars or prodigies) we develop a talent that brings in fame and money, or because we have been parentified, the sense of value imparted by falsely empowering abuse is precarious. Because the falsely empowered children's source of value comes from the outside, they fail to develop a true, inherent sense of worth, substituting the esteem of others for actual self-esteem. They learn to seek others' approval by being cuter, smarter, more helpful or accommodating—so nobody can discover that, deep down, they don't feel good enough. They wind up feeling superficially special, but at the price of sacrificing their authenticity and their boundaries.

Growing up with a false sense of empowerment can make us very successful professionally but leave us floundering in relationships. We tend to be perfectionistic, obsessive, and fixated on being perceived as "good," because our nervous system is fragile. Our falsely inflated self-image can't handle criticism and so hides behind a wall of defensiveness and invulnerability that forecloses on intimacy.

We can struggle in adult relationships because we have been taught to over-rely on ourselves. We may grow up believing that depending on others is a weakness, whereas self-sufficiency is the mark of strength, so we avoid vulnerability and dependency at all costs. As adults, we might feel uneasy with or resistant to intimate connections, fearing that we might lose our independence or sense of superiority if someone gets close enough to discover that, secretly, we feel small, powerless, and worthless. In addition, our built-in fragility prevents us from being able to accept accountability or change our behavior when we cause injury to others. As a result, although we may still be highly respected by people who barely know us, we may wind up estranged from our kids and rejected by our spouses.

False empowerment inflates a child's self-image, but at the cost of their perceptions of others. They feel "better than" other people, especially those they help, because, to a child's mind, the helper is superior to the one in need of help. Those of us who were falsely empowered often seek out relationships with people we can rescue, whether they want the help or not, in order to both earn their love and continue to protect our feeling of specialness.

How much power we successfully acquire determines whether we fawn. If we make it to the top of the privilege hierarchy, whether because of unearned privileges (like being white, tall, male, able-bodied, stereotypically attractive, or heterosexual) or privileges we've worked for (like education, professional success, wealth, or skill), we are more likely to be fawned by others. If we lack these privileges, we're more likely to wind up fawning. But that doesn't mean people with a lot of power and many privileges won't also fawn.

Those of us who have survived falsely empowering abuse tend to fawn those we judge as more powerful or better than us, pleasing and accommodating them the way we learned to do our parents. As children, we learned that love has a price we can't afford not to pay: becoming who we believe everyone else needs and wants us to be, rather than who we are. But we often expect those we judge as "less than" or in need of our help to fawn us, and sometimes seek out relationships with people like this because it feels safer.

Especially if we took on way too much adult responsibility as children, we may continue to overfunction and overgive in our adult relationships. However, we also tend to become resentful when our own vulnerable needs go unmet because of the partners we've unconsciously chosen—often people who struggle to carry their weight in relationships due to their own disempowering abuse.

ASSESSMENT

WERE YOU DISEMPOWERED OR FALSELY EMPOWERED?

If you're unsure whether you experienced falsely empowering abuse, disempowering abuse, or both, try taking this quiz. It isn't meant to label or diagnose; it's here to help you reflect with curiosity and compassion.

Read each statement and note how strongly it applies to your childhood experience using the following scale:

0 = Not true at all
1 = Somewhat true
2 = Very true
3 = This was a constant pattern

Section A: Signs of Disempowering Abuse

1. I was often told I was "too much," "not enough," or a burden imposed upon my parents.
2. I was ignored, dismissed, or treated as if my needs didn't matter.
3. I was frequently criticized, shamed, or made to feel stupid or wrong.
4. I was physically hurt, threatened, or controlled through fear.
5. I made myself small, stayed under the radar, or tried to be invisible to feel safe.
6. I was discouraged from expressing anger, jealousy, frustration, or sadness, and I couldn't trust my parents to help me manage my emotions.
7. My parents found my joy or exuberance threatening.
8. I felt like I couldn't succeed or do anything right.

9. I was compared unfavorably to siblings or peers.
10. I feared making mistakes because the consequences were harsh.
11. I had a parent who infantilized me, thwarted my attempts to grow up, and kept me from becoming my own person "for my own good," or who expressed hurt or anger when I tried to pull away or become independent.
12. I was frightened by people and preferred being alone, often isolating in my room.
13. I lived with a sense of nameless dread or terror without knowing why.
14. I was not taught healthy boundaries and didn't learn how to say no, set limits, or protect myself.
15. I struggled to know what I needed or was too shy or scared to ask for help.

Total for Disempowering Abuse: _____

Section B: Signs of Falsely Empowering Abuse

1. I was praised only when I was achieving, performing, or "being good."
2. I was told or expected to be "better" than other kids, or to uphold a family image.
3. I was encouraged to be strong, independent, or perfect, even when I needed support.
4. I was the "parentified child" and felt like the only adult in the house. I was given inappropriate responsibility for siblings or finances; was the confidant or lover of an adult; or was the peacemaker of the family.
5. I felt I couldn't show weakness or vulnerability without being shamed or ignored, so I learned to live in my head, rationalizing everything instead of feeling my emotions.

6. I was used and idealized, treated like a "golden child," or exploited to meet a parent's needs for pride, validation, and their own self-worth.
7. I was rewarded for being useful, smart, talented, financially valuable, or entertaining, but not loved for just being me.
8. I felt pressure to hide pain, pretend I was okay, or protect the family's reputation.
9. I had a parent who made me their best friend, confidant, spouse substitute, or emotional partner.
10. I felt pressure to be a perfect, high-achieving child or risk shame, punishment, or abandonment.
11. I was treated as special for being gifted—intellectually, artistically, athletically, or because of my looks.
12. I had mystical or spiritual experiences that made me feel "chosen," "different," or otherworldly.
13. I was rewarded for being sick or fragile, gaining extra love or attention when unwell.
14. I was the "golden child" or the "proud rebel"/scapegoat, known for being the best or the worst.
15. I learned to get what I wanted and needed from adults by flattering, pleasing, or performing to win special treatment.

Total for Falsely Empowering Abuse: _____

Interpreting Your Responses

If your score is higher in Section A, you may have experienced more disempowering abuse, where your basic worth, needs, and voice were minimized, denied, or punished. This can result in a dysregulated nervous system that leads to fawning, chronic self-doubt, people pleasing, or underfunctioning in adulthood.

If your score is higher in Section B, you may have experienced more falsely empowering abuse, where you were given adult-like roles or pressure, often at the cost of your own development. This can lead to overfunctioning, perfectionism, or difficulty receiving help or feeling safe being vulnerable.

If you scored high in both, your parents might have alternated between shaming you one moment and idealizing you the next. Or one parent may have disempowered you while another falsely empowered you. This often creates confusion about identity and worth, and is common for those with complex post-traumatic stress disorder (CPTSD) and/or disorganized attachment. This can lead to a confusing mixture of fawning some people and expecting to be fawned by others—or flipping between fawning the people we're close to one moment and rebelling against them the next.

WHY WE CHOOSE THE RELATIONSHIPS WE PICK

We hope it's now clear that how your attachment style developed in childhood, what ACE traumas you lived through, and how disempowering or falsely empowering abuse you may have experienced in childhood sets the stage for the kinds of relationships you'll seek out in adulthood. Any negative patterns we experience in childhood tend to repeat as we replay the brokenheartedness at the core of our childhood dynamics again and again.

In *Getting the Love You Want,* couples therapist Harville Hendrix calls the internal blueprint of love shaped by our earliest caregivers our "imago"—a full-spectrum emotional imprint of what love is and isn't, based on how our caregivers both nurtured us and also neglected, hurt, or failed to see us.

As adults, we're magnetically drawn to partners who reflect that imprint—not because we're broken, but because some deep part of us is longing to rework the original wound. By reenacting old family dynamics, we're trying to rewrite our origin story with a happier ending. The problem is, the people we choose may not cooperate with this agenda of healing our core wounds. More commonly, these imago relationships become traumatic reenactments, retraumatizing us by pressing on our oldest, most tender places. But if we find the right partners and get the right therapy, it's possible to leverage those imago attractions to help us heal.

This dance of attraction also has roots in neuroscience. The limbic brain, the seat of emotion and attachment, learns not through logic but through experience. This is the realm of *limbic resonance*, the unconscious coregulation of nervous systems that occurs in close relationships. In ideal early environments, a child's brain learns that emotional connection is safe, and that others help soothe distress. Through limbic resonance, we literally "sync up" with the brains of our caregivers, mirroring them and being mirrored, reciprocally responding to each other's verbal and nonverbal cues in an exquisite kinetic dance. This is what helps to wire our attachment system. We become attuned to our caregivers, whether they're good caregivers or not, and certain patterns of emotional and physical arousal come to feel familiar to us. We recognize this as "love."

When caregivers are frightening, absent, or unpredictable, our limbic systems still attach, but our learned definition of "love" involves rejection, volatility, and abuse, creating a kind of "love reversal" wherein we mix up love and abuse. To return to our discussion of how stress affects the nervous system: A chronically stressed nervous system becomes normal and familiar, rather than abnormal and uncomfortable. This feeling of familiarity then turns our safety compass upside down. Our developing nervous system adapts to an unsafe environment by wiring itself to register danger as "home." As a result, we perceive danger signals when we're around someone safe and only feel comfortable or aroused when we're around someone abusive or unsafe.

This backward compass can lead to tremendous relational confusion, causing survivors of relational trauma to choose and attract unsafe people time and time again, failing to register unsafe behaviors as worrisome while rejecting safe people as threatening or simply finding them unattractive. As Thomas Lewis and colleagues describe in *A General Theory of Love*, negative early experiences program the nervous system to resonate with what is familiar—even if what's familiar is painful or dangerous. Limbic resonance wires us to find intensity erotic, to mistake chaos for chemistry, and to feel most "seen" when someone seems likely to activate our core wounds.

This is why survivors of trauma often feel most drawn to people who might retraumatize us. We eroticize what feels familiar, even if we might know cognitively that it's not good for us. We attach with our emotions more than our thoughts, so even if you've done a lot of great cognitive therapy and psychoeducation, but haven't healed the emotional heartbreak underlying attachment wounding, you're likely going to choose what feels familiar. Then you'll wind up wondering, "How did I end up here *again*?"

Without awareness, we keep cycling through these patterns. But with the right kind of attuned connection, whether in therapy, safe relationships, or conscious partnership, those well-worn neural grooves can begin to soften. Thanks to limbic resonance, the romantic partners to whom we are the most attracted can be our biggest nightmare—but they can be our greatest healers if they're on board to do the work with us. Such a person is our imago. When both people are willing to do the inner work, a painful reenactment can become a sacred crucible for healing and transformation. What once felt like love because it mirrored our pain can be redefined by safety, presence, and true intimacy. Love becomes not a repetition of the past but a chance to rewire it.

This process is crucial when it comes to healing relationsickness. Because of limbic resonance and the way imagos work, those of us with relational trauma are more likely to choose relationships with unsafe people. In relationships like this, the nervous system rarely gets to relax—and the body isn't able to heal. But if we have relationships with others who are motivated to heal with us, we can interrupt these patterns, change our nervous system, and direct the freed-up energy to physiological self-repair.

ALL TRAUMA HAS THE POTENTIAL TO BE HEALED

By adulthood, children who have experienced significant relational trauma carry heavy burdens that have distorted their sense of their own value and pushed them into roles they'd rather not play. They take on adaptative strategies as children that aid survival into adulthood, but at the price of a solid and stable identity, their ability to live authentically, and eventually their health.

This is heavy stuff. You might feel resistance to even reading about it, and that's normal. Many of us, especially those of us with low ACE scores who score high on disempowering or falsely empowering abuse scales, may have minimized the pain of what we went through and are reluctant to open up Pandora's Box, convinced the past is best left in the past. But if you want to optimize your chances of full recovery, you might need to dive more deeply into healing your relational traumas and committing to a path of relational recovery.

Giving-tree behaviors don't typically disappear overnight just because we now know better. Because fawning is a reflexive stress response, something we can't consciously control, it takes time to interrupt automatic patterns and lay down new, healthier neural pathways.

The good news is that nervous systems are neuroplastic, relational trauma can be treated, and deep healing allows these distortions to untwist and unveil the existing wholeness underneath. Learning to trust this inborn wholeness and recognize your true wants and needs is a necessary step in also learning the relationship skills necessary to have authentic, balanced relationships. These are skills you may not have learned in childhood: how to set boundaries, how to negotiate and uphold agreements, and how to repair relational ruptures so you're in integrity in your relationships—not giving too much in order to prove your worth and not taking more than your fair share.

CHAPTER 5

Is Being "One Down" in Relationships Making You Sick?

The Narcissist's Prayer
That didn't happen.
And if it did, it wasn't that bad.
And if it was, that's not a big deal.
And if it is, that's not my fault.
And if it was, I didn't mean it.
And if I did, you deserved it.

—Dayna Craig

When Aaron and Ginger met on Match.com, back before many other people were dating online, Ginger didn't realize that their first date was really a kind of first-round job interview. Aaron was a celebrity who traveled the world speaking and writing books about leadership—and he was in the market for a wife who would be his unpaid beck-and-call girl, even though he hadn't been quite that direct in his dating profile.

For their third date, Aaron asked Ginger to go on the road with him, to enjoy a "free" romantic trip to Paris while also helping out with logistics, managing the travel details, assisting with his speaking engagements, and otherwise supporting him. Ginger must have passed the job interview, because within three months, they were married in a small civil ceremony at a local courthouse, and she was working twelve-hour days to attend to Aaron's many needs.

It seemed like a strange arrangement, but before meeting Aaron, Ginger had been struggling to make ends meet as a life coach. So the idea of going on the road and helping out a famous motivational speaker sounded meaningful and exciting. The fact that she quickly ended up Aaron's unpaid personal assistant didn't bother her much, at least in the beginning.

While Aaron didn't exactly insist on only green M&Ms in his green room, he did like to have things just so. There had to be a fresh green juice waiting in the refrigerator for him before his lectures, and Ginger would frequently end up scouting small towns in the Midwest for the only juice bar within miles when local staff forgot. He liked to have his back massaged right before he went out on stage, and sometimes preferred to have a postcoital glow when greeting his cooing fans. His suits had to be pressed a certain way, and he only ate paleo, which sometimes made finding the right foods for him difficult. He also insisted on taking his pit bull everywhere they went, which others didn't always welcome.

To please his increasingly particular tastes, Ginger wound up becoming his travel agent, portable green-juice maker, on-the-fly chef, housekeeper, dogsitter, massage therapist, and agent. She lost touch with most of her former friends because she was on the road so much and found it hard to make new ones when Aaron never stayed put for long.

Ginger put up with all this because she believed in Aaron's mission and saw being the wind beneath Aaron's mighty wings as her life's purpose. But as the years went on, Aaron expressed less and less appreciation for the tasks Ginger performed for him each day. He found fault with every little thing she did and criticized her endlessly. Then he began accusing Ginger of taking advantage of him financially, expecting him to pay all of the bills, without acknowledging that Ginger had quit trying to build her own life-coaching practice in order to support him.

Aaron wound up removing Ginger's access to the bank accounts and insisted she get a job to take some of the pressure off him to provide for them both. After having been out of the job market for over a decade, Ginger found it hard to find gainful employment, but finally found a gig leveraging some of the talents she'd acquired from serving Aaron for all those years, working for another author and speaker who needed an assistant. But the new job made her less available to Aaron, who started accusing her of "sucking up" to her new boss, and after only a few weeks, Ginger quit just to stop Aaron's constant complaints. She was in a double bind: If she worked only for Aaron, she got accused of exploiting him financially, and if she found other work, she got blamed for neglecting Aaron and being a shitty wife.

It wasn't until she felt pain in her chest and radiating down her left arm that Ginger asked the event coordinator they were working with to get her to a hospital—STAT. And even then, Aaron berated her for making it all about herself when he was about to go on stage in front of five hundred people and needed his green juice. The coordinator had one of the event's volunteers drive Ginger to the hospital while Aaron went ahead with his talk, leaving Ginger scared and unsupported at the hospital.

The doctor diagnosed a mild heart attack and saved her with cutting-edge cardiology treatments, but insisted she'd have to take it easy during her recovery. Following doctor's orders, Ginger stayed at home while Aaron went to his next gig without her, hiring someone to pinch-hit and leaving her feeling discarded, abandoned, and replaced. Without Aaron around, when she slowed down just enough to feel her feelings, she was overwhelmed with sadness and regret. What had happened to her life?

Had she just been taken advantage of for an entire decade, only to be tossed as soon as she could no longer be used? Had what she'd thought of as love and devotion only been exploitation?

From the previous chapters, we know that overgiving and always putting others' needs first, at our own expense, can lead to illness. We know that this kind of reflexive fawning is a trauma response, born usually from childhood relational trauma. And we know that, because of childhood relational trauma, we often choose to pair up with people who are likely to light up our core wounds, ending up in relationships that feel familiar from a nervous system perspective, even if they also feel awful.

If you examine Aaron and Ginger's relationship through a trauma-informed lens, you recognize that they both acted as if Aaron's life mattered more than Ginger's. Their relationship was *unbalanced*: Her life had become all about him and his needs. He expected she would sacrifice her own needs willingly, and she hadn't done anything to make him believe otherwise. As a result, Ginger enabled Aaron to dominate her, tolerating the inequality without protesting—until her body protested for her. Aaron's actions weren't Ginger's fault, but Ginger also wasn't exercising the power she did have: the power to speak up and express what was unfair in the relationship. By abdicating that power, even unwittingly, she allowed someone who didn't care enough about her needs to take over her life, putting her body, heart, and soul at risk. And without the wake-up call of her heart attack, it could have killed her.

OUR RELATIONSHIPS INEVITABLY AFFECT OUR HEALTH

Science, including medicine, has historically underplayed the role that relationships play in health and illness, but this is slowly changing for all kinds of reasons—and what we've learned is eye opening. "Social relationships, or the relative lack thereof, constitute a major risk factor for health—rivaling the effect of well-established health risk factors such as cigarette smoking, blood pressure, blood lipids, obesity, and physical activity,"[21] according to James House and fellow researchers at the universities of Michigan and Texas. Chronic loneliness is considered a risk factor for disease comparable to or greater than obesity, alcohol abuse, air pollution, or smoking fifteen cigarettes per day.[22] Those without strong social support have a 29 percent increased risk of heart disease and a 32 percent higher risk of stroke.[23]

The opposite has also proven true. Good science indicates that people with positive social connections and healthy attachments are more likely to recover from a variety of diseases. A landmark study by Lisa Berkman and Leonard Syme in Alameda County, California, found that individuals with strong social ties were three times less likely to die over a nine-year period than those with fewer connections.[24] A meta-analysis conducted by Julianne Holt-Lunstad and colleagues of 148 studies concluded that social connections with friends, family, neighbors, or colleagues increases the odds of surviving serious disease by 50 percent.[25] And studies on heart disease and social support have shown that individuals with strong social networks have a reduced risk of developing cardiovascular disease, experiencing complications from heart conditions, and having another heart attack.[26]

It appears that romantic relationships can play a particularly crucial role in improving the possibilities of recovery from illness. In a large study analyzing data from over 1.2 million patients who had been diagnosed with one of the ten cancers most associated with death, Ayal Aizer, Ming-Hui Chen, and their team reported that for five of the cancers studied (prostate, breast, colorectal, esophageal, and head/neck cancers), the survival benefit associated with marriage was actually larger than the published survival benefit of chemotherapy![27]

But as we know, not all marriages are created equal. And research has shown that some people's medical problems are actually exacerbated by unhealthy, unbalanced, or toxic marriages. Researchers have also looked specifically at the relationship between the quality of romantic partnerships and the trajectory of serious illness. Chiara Acquati and

Ellen Miller-Sonet and team found that it wasn't just the presence of a spouse or other supportive relationships improving the odds of surviving cancer; the *quality* of one's relationships has an impact on if and how long people live.[28] Similarly, Hae-Chung Yang and Tammy Schuler found that women in distressed partnerships experienced slower recovery from breast cancer and poorer outcomes compared to women in stable, nondistressed marriages or partnerships.[29] They were less active, slower to recover, and had more symptoms and signs of both illness and treatment side effects throughout all three years of the study. The researchers concluded that marital distress is associated with not only worse psychological outcomes for breast cancer survivors but also poorer health and less physical activity overall.

If you're in an unbalanced, giving-tree-like relationship like Aaron and Ginger's, in which you find yourself overgiving to the point of illness, this is likely to play a role in your recovery—or rather, the lack thereof. So let's take a closer look at unbalanced power dynamics and the way we divide up responsibilities, get needs met, respect each other's boundaries, and prioritize equality and reciprocity in relationships. We'll pay particular attention to how unbalanced relationships can lead to or exacerbate the stress-based fawning behaviors that can predispose us to getting sick.

A PRIMER ON UNBALANCED RELATIONSHIPS

Healthy, healing, reciprocal relationships—the kind that help the body repair damage and stay well—are those where power and responsibilities are shared; where decisions are made together, consensually; where boundaries and agreements are negotiated and respected. Unhealthy, unbalanced relationships are those where they aren't.

Some couples have an arrangement where one person is the wage earner while the other supports the home, the children, or the wage earner's career. Although this often creates power imbalances, it's still possible to have a healthy relationship with shared power, as long as both people understand that both parties' contributions are equally valued, and nobody gets more than 50 percent of the vote in decision-making.

In unhealthy, unbalanced relationships, one person often acts as if they are "one up" from a power perspective (as Aaron did), while another person acts as if they are "one down" (as Ginger did). Maybe one person goes one up in relationships because they were raised to think they're special by overindulgent parents who saw their kids as narcissistic extensions of themselves, or because they were victims of falsely empowering abuse. Or they may go one up because they were bullied and overpowered in childhood and feel safer in that position.

Likewise, someone might go one down because they're victims of disempowering abuse and were shamed and degraded into believing they don't deserve equal, reciprocal relationships. Or they might feel safer as the damsel or dude in distress, being "rescued" by someone they see as more competent, responsible, or powerful than they are.

While there are many different kinds of developmental trauma that can cause people to choose and tolerate unbalanced relationships, it notably takes two to do this particular one-up/one-down tango. Aaron's behavior is selfish, narcissistic, exploitative, and abusive, and the onus of apologies, relational repair, and amends should absolutely be on him, not Ginger. But Aaron could not have taken advantage of Ginger unless her trauma caused her to let him get away with doing so. If Ginger had had the ability to recognize when she was in consent and fawning, if she had had the nervous system regulation and courage to speak up and say no when things weren't fair, Aaron couldn't have used Ginger so readily. Sure, he might have kicked her to the curb and replaced her if she hadn't cooperated with his exploitative agenda, and that might have had stressful financial consequences for her. But considering the relationship's impact on both her health and her dignity, she still would have been better off.

Power imbalances can be both personal and systemic. Although we don't always act this way, all humans are inherently equal. Nobody is more or less valuable than anybody else, no matter what we were raised to believe about ourselves or others. So while we might go one up or one down solely because of childhood relational trauma, systemic issues—like patriarchy, which casts women as inferior to men; white supremacy, which dictates that light-skinned people are superior to dark-skinned people; homophobia, which judges straight people as better than queer folks; or social class hierarchies, which consider the rich superior to the poor—also play a role. The marginalizations and/or unearned privileges someone was born with can add to or exacerbate power issues in relationships.

Some relationships have a power imbalance built in—between employee and boss, for example, or child and parent. Still, the transaction between employee and boss should be equitable: The employee is expected to do certain jobs, and the boss is expected to pay a fair salary and offer benefits. And while the parent typically has more power in the relationship than the child when both are younger—a power dynamic that can swap if the child becomes a caregiver to an elder parent—nobody who becomes one up is entitled to abuse that power.

Intimate relationships are different; when it comes to friendship and love, power should be shared. As Relational Life Therapy (RLT) founder and couples therapist Terry Real says regarding intimate relationships between equals, you cannot love from the one-up superior position, and you cannot love from the one-down inferior position. Love and intimacy demand democracy.

Of course, this isn't always how it works. Think mean girls and their minions. Or the bossy bestie who tells her BFF how she should live her life. People who prefer to be one up in their relationships often choose friends they consider one down—people they can control or rescue, people who look up to them, people they deem inferior or less important than they are. And when it comes to romantic relationships, one-up/one-down dynamics are unfortunately more common than not.

This is true whether we're talking about straight or queer couples, and about men, women, or nonbinary folks. But it's particularly ubiquitous in heterosexual couples, thanks to lingering patriarchal expectations about men and women's expected roles (where the man works outside the home to provide financially and the woman works inside the home caring for the children), and the value and importance of each. Too often, women are still carrying more than their fair share of work inside the home while also working outside of it. The domestic work they do also is devalued, in a way that leaves the relationship unbalanced.

Imbalances in relational power aren't always totalistic; a division of labor that is not 50/50 on everything does not necessarily mean the relationship is unbalanced. Many couples share power by delegating responsibilities and taking leadership roles in various areas: one person ruling the roost when it comes to the housecleaning, child-rearing, and socializing, while the other handles breadwinning, managing the finances, car maintenance, and repairs around the house. The key is that responsibilities are divided equally, fairly, and with the consent of both partners, who are respected and valued for their contributions. Problems arise when breadwinning is considered more valuable than child-rearing or housekeeping, such that one person's needs and wants get prioritized over the other's.

Whenever this imbalance in priorities happens, relationsickness becomes a risk—particularly in relationships like Aaron and Ginger's, where one person is controlling, entitled, and overbearing, and the other is not only fawning but also unhealthily dependent on the other, lacking agency, financial independence, or the ability to leave if a relationship becomes abusive.

Many people never even think about whether their relationships are balanced. Especially if you were raised in a family where power dynamics were unequal between your caregivers, or where you were manipulated and overpowered, being controlled or controlling others might feel completely normal to you. But to figure out whether you might be relationsick because of an unbalanced relationship, you're going to need to examine the close relationships in your life to determine whether they are equitable or compromising your health and well-being.

ONE UP VERSUS ONE DOWN IN RELATIONSHIPS

A useful way of conceptualizing power dynamics in relationships is through Terry Real's Relationship Grid. This grid is an elaboration of work done by one of Real's mentors, Pia Mellody, and helps people conceptualize and make sense of the power dynamics and boundary issues in their relationships, while supporting them in finding their way to greater relational health. Although Real developed this grid in his work with couples as part of the couples therapy model he developed, these same principles can be applied to any close relationship, like siblings or intimate friends.

THE RELATIONSHIP GRID

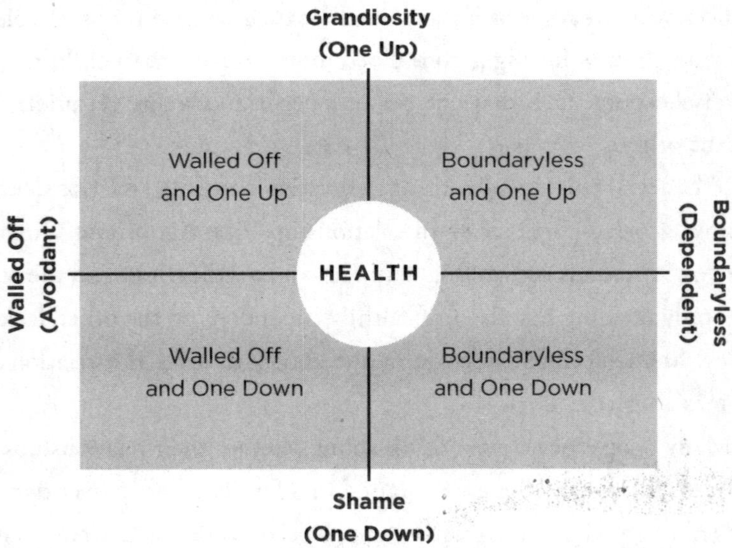

On the vertical axis lies power: one up (grandiosity) and one down (shame). If you were using older psychological frameworks, you might call the top half of the grid "narcissism" and the bottom half "codependency," though we don't prefer that language (see "Narcissism, Codependence, and the Problem with Labels" on page 115). The horizontal axis shows the state of one's boundaries, with lack of boundaries, or boundarylessness, at one extreme, and rigid avoidance or boundaries that are too strict—being "walled off"—at the other. Understanding where we land can help us return to our relational center.

Real originally developed the RLT model to upend patriarchal conditioning in heterosexual relationships because the traditional patriarch is usually the one-up partner, while the one-down partner fawns and accommodates. Any gender can engage in one-up or one-down behaviors, however. Who's one up and who's one down can vary from situation to situation, but most people have a go-to pattern. Real says that, in his experience with heterosexual couples, about two-thirds of the time, the one-up partner is male, and one-third of the time, they're female. And both men or women can be either boundaryless or so walled off that they're unavailable for connection or repair when inevitable relational ruptures occur.

One Up, Walled Off (Upper Left Quadrant)

One-up, walled-off individuals can be dismissive, withholding, and emotionally armored, believing that feelings are dangerous and connection equals weakness. They tend to withhold love, praise, or attention as an act of control. They minimize the experience of others and stay emotionally distant, even in intimate relationships. They believe feelings are messy or irrational, and use silence, logic, or stonewalling as defense mechanisms. They may avoid conflict at all costs—by freezing or by walking out.

They might say:

"I'm fine. I don't want to talk about it."
"You're making a big deal out of nothing."
"I'm so out of here." [Shuts door, disappears.]
"At least one of us needs to stay rational here."

One Up, Boundaryless (Upper Right Quadrant)

One-up, boundaryless individuals can be dominating, intrusive, and entitled, leading with control to avoid vulnerability. They tend to interrupt, monologue, and talk over others, making unilateral decisions in the relationship. They often use sarcasm or biting humor, impose solutions without collaboration, make decisions that impact the other without their consent, intrude into others' inner worlds without permission, and may frequently express righteous indignation and moral superiority.

They might say:

"I know what's best for you."
"You're just being too sensitive."
"My intuition tells me that you're just acting out of your mother wound."
"This is how we're doing it—end of story."

One Down, Boundaryless (Lower Right Quadrant)

One-down, boundaryless individuals can fawn, overdisclose, and self-abandon in a bid for love or approval, oversharing as a way to earn closeness. They tend to overapologize or take on too much self-blame, excessively attune to others, anticipate others' needs, desperately seek reassurance when under stress, and collapse their boundaries in order to stay connected.

They might say:

"I don't care what you do—just please don't be mad."
"I'll change, I promise—just tell me what you want."
"I know I'm probably crazy for feeling this way."
"I'm sorry I didn't have your coffee ready when you got up."

One Down, Walled Off (Lower Left Quadrant)

One-down, walled-off individuals can be shut down, avoidant, and depressed, burdened by feelings of deep shame and unworthiness and avoiding the vulnerability of intimacy to avoid being seen as "too much" or "not enough." They tend to retreat into silence, invisibility, or depression, and feel hopeless, powerless, or broken in their relationships, thinking they'll never be good enough for love.

They might say:

"Why bother? It's not going to change anyway."
"I know I'm the problem. Just leave me alone."
"I don't know why anyone would love me."
[Disengages, is barely present in the room.]

When you think about the close relationships in your life, notice which quadrant your behaviors tend to land in. Then think of the people you're closest with. Which quadrant best describes them?

We're going to spell out some common one-down and one-up behaviors next, to give you a feel for how these behaviors show up in action. It's possible to act out from all four quadrants. But most of us have one go-to quadrant that's dominant in our most intimate relationships. We suspect many of you reading this book will resonate with the one-down behaviors, but remember, you can be one down in some relationships and one up in others. For example, you might be one down with your spouse and one up to your kids, your clients, or your closest friend. It's helpful to be honest about where we go one up and where we go one down, not as a way to beat ourselves up, but as a way to heal.

NARCISSISM, CODEPENDENCE, AND THE PROBLEM WITH LABELS

In the world of pop psychology, we might describe someone one up in an unbalanced relationship as a "narcissist" and someone one down as "codependent." The problem with labels is that they can be stigmatizing, polarizing, and totalizing, as if you or your loved one are *only* that label. Truly understanding one-up and one-down behaviors, and why we end up in unbalanced relationships, requires a more nuanced understanding of the relational traumas that lead to such behaviors, so we can understand why these behaviors occur and how we respond to them.

It's useful to know, first of all, that unequal power dynamics in relationships are often two sides of the same coin. Unless you have healthy, clear boundaries, you may be the overpowering one in relationships where you have more power. Where you have less power, you're likely to get overpowered. This means you might behave more one up in a relationship where you judge yourself as superior or more powerful than someone else, and you might fawn and behave one down in another relationship where you feel inferior or less powerful.

Keep in mind that both tendencies are trauma symptoms caused by childhood relational trauma and/or the result of systemic forces like patriarchy and white supremacy. What we commonly think of as narcissism is often the result of falsely empowering abuse in childhood, as well as collective traumas that position some people as better than others. Both tendencies—one up and one down—are not our fault, but they are our responsibility to heal.

Second, not all narcissism is created equal. As Craig Malkin explains in *Rethinking Narcissism*, the personality traits and behaviors we associate with narcissism exist on a spectrum. On a scale of 1 to 10, someone who meets the criteria for narcissistic personality disorder (NPD) might be an 8–10 on the spectrum, while someone who is a 0–3 on the spectrum might have low self-esteem and not have enough healthy narcissism. Someone with a healthy amount of narcissism—someone who is assertive without being aggressive, knows that they are entitled to healthy boundaries, and expresses their needs without entitled expectation—would fall in the 4–7 range.

Because narcissism is so prevalent in Western cultures, you're bound to encounter some people who are high on the narcissism spectrum, whether in your personal life or at work, school, or your place of worship. Having narcissists in your outer circle can work out fine, since they're often fun, interesting, talented, attractive, and sociable at a superficial level. As long as you have good boundaries, you can safely have distant relationships with narcissistic individuals you enjoy. But if you're closely engaged with someone who is a 10 on the narcissism spectrum, or if you don't know how to identify and deal with people like this, you're at high risk of ending up relationsick—or worse.

Third, it's essential to separate the narcissistic psyche from narcissistic behaviors. As asserted by Dr. Mark Ettensohn, founder of the *Heal NPD* podcast, narcissism isn't just defined by how someone behaves toward others; it's about what's happening inside. Clinically, it reflects a disorder of self-esteem regulation and a disturbed sense of identity, often rooted in early developmental trauma. Pop psychology often equates narcissism with bad or abusive behavior, but this oversimplified version mistakes the symptoms for the underlying psychic structure. While narcissism can lead to harmful actions, abusive behavior alone does not define narcissism. You can be abusive and narcissistic, or you can be abusive and not narcissistic.

From Ettensohn's perspective, narcissism develops when early emotional needs for unconditional love, attunement, and validation go unmet. To survive, the child constructs a "false self" to gain approval and avoid shame, while the real self becomes hidden, fragmented, and psychologically fragile. Ettensohn argues that the relational volatility, defensive rage, and collapse of empathy associated with narcissism are better understood as survival mechanisms, rather than intrinsic moral failure or simply "bad behavior." What later looks like arrogance, entitlement, defensiveness, or lack of empathy is actually a protective structure built to regulate unbearable feelings of inadequacy and disconnection. Ettensohn emphasizes that beneath the defensive grandiosity lies profound insecurity and loneliness, and that healing requires compassion, not condemnation. He believes that with the right treatment, even those with full-blown NPD can gradually integrate their fragmented self-states; develop authentic relational empathy; form a more stable, coherent sense of identity; and behave differently.[30]

Just as we don't want to shame or blame those who fawn as a result of childhood relational trauma, we also don't wish to pathologize or stigmatize the identity and self-esteem struggles that underlie narcissism, which develop because of relational trauma. But we do want you to get honest with yourself about the power dynamics in your relationships. If you're sick and in a relationship with someone who regularly one-ups you the way Aaron did Ginger, accurately diagnosing the root cause of what might be making you sick helps you get the right treatment—not only the appropriate medical treatment, but also the trauma and relational treatment that will help you heal.

ONE-DOWN BEHAVIORS

One-down behaviors stem primarily from shame, insecurity, and feelings of unworthiness related to disempowering abuse in childhood. Most of the fawning behaviors we talked about in chapter three, including the 8 A's, fall under the one-down category.

So do the behaviors therapist Pete Walker lists as part of the fawn response in his book *Complex PTSD*. If you fawn, he says, you might stifle your own needs, find authentic self-expression challenging, and do your best to fly under the radar. You might have trouble saying no, overapologize, and hold back opinions or preferences that might seem controversial, as a way to avoid conflict. You might struggle with boundaries and change your preferences to align with others. If you get relationsick and experience chronic pain or illness, you might deny your own discomfort, complaints, pain, needs, and wants, minimizing your own suffering and failing to pursue the help you need and deserve.

Those of us who are one-down fawners tend to feel easily rejected and overwhelmed. We feel like a failure when we make the smallest mistake and walk on eggshells to avoid conflict, apologizing for our feelings or our very existence. We feel selfish or guilty when asserting ourselves. As a result, we tolerate behaviors that violate our boundaries, often without complaint, giving up our own truth and authenticity to keep the peace.

One-down folks often take on an exaggerated sense of responsibility for the actions of others, overfunctioning and doing more than our fair share, usually without protesting the injustice. Then we are hurt when people don't recognize our often-extraordinary efforts, and as a result can feel chronically resentful and may act out passive-aggressively.

We tend to second-guess ourselves, lacking trust in our own judgment, and struggle to make decisions without an inordinate amount of advice and reassurance from others. Figuring out what we want or need—and saying it out loud—can be challenging. We also tend to have difficulty adjusting to change because we lack confidence in our own resilience, competence, and ability to cope.

In relationships, our boundaries may be porous (boundaryless) or too rigid (walled off), but either way, we tend to center the person we're with, to our own detriment. We may demonstrate an unhealthy dependence on the other person, with a deep fear of being abandoned if we mess something up. We see them as one up in the relationship, and may tolerate bullying one-up behaviors without adequate accountability. As a result, we may wind up saying yes when we mean no, looking the other way when we feel hurt, convincing ourselves we're okay when we're not, and getting relationsick.

YOU'RE NOT FORGIVING, YOU'RE ENABLING

Those of us who are survivors of childhood relational trauma often learn early in life to enable abusive behavior, rather than push back against it, as a way to survive. Enabling is the intentional or unintentional denial, justification, overlooking, neurotically tolerating, or minimizing of behavior that misuses or abuses power, rather than responding with a clear and firm expression of displeasure.

We don't mean to shame anyone for enabling. Forgiving our caregivers or telling ourselves everything's okay when it's really not is an understandable and effective adaptation to intolerable conditions in childhood. But we do want to name this pattern and unpack it, so you realize—now that you're an adult—you have a choice,.

When we forgive instead of holding someone accountable, when we avoid conflict rather than calling out behaviors that aren't fair or kind, the locus of our empathy may reside primarily with the person we are enabling, while we withhold or minimize empathy regarding those they hurt, including ourselves or our own children. We may sacrifice our own needs or the needs of our children to please someone one up and to avoid rocking the boat, while turning on others who fail to enable and appease the person we're fawning and enabling. We may even spiritualize or feel proud of ourselves for how good we are at forgiving/enabling, thinking of ourselves as selfless martyrs who have an infinite capacity for unconditional love, when we're really just conflict averse in ways that prevent us from protecting ourselves and others.

Enabling can manifest in different ways. On her *Navigating Narcissism* podcast episode "Are You An Enabler?,"[31] clinical psychologist and narcissism expert Dr. Ramani Durvasula describes six types of enablers:

Pollyanna enabler: This well-meaning enabler thinks everyone is doing the best they can, there's good in everyone, and we shouldn't talk badly about anyone.

Toxically positive enabler: This enabler takes Pollyanna enabling to a new level, shaming anyone who isn't "positive," "spiritual," or giving everyone the benefit of the doubt. These "high vibes only" people see themselves as superior to those who try to hold abusers accountable, judging those who feel angry when they're being abused as "less than" or "unspiritual."

Transactional enablers: These enablers excuse others' behavior because they are benefiting from staying in the one-up person's good graces. Whether they're getting a one-up spouse's financial support, seeking to secure a parent's money through inheritance, gunning for a promotion at work, or just hoping for an elevation in status, transactional enablers don't want to rock the boat because they don't want to give up the perks of the relationship.

Trauma-bonded enablers: These enablers are enmeshed with the one-up person they're enabling, and will not only fail to protest abuse, but also make excuses for, justify, and/or minimize their abuser's behavior, gaslighting anyone who tries to point out what they're doing. The goal of the trauma-bonded enabler is to maintain and stabilize their tie to the abuser at all costs, a motivation that is often unconscious and deeply rooted in trauma.

Cultural enablers: These enablers protect abusers not because they believe abuse is acceptable but because of loyalty to the family, group, or institutional system and a desire to protect its reputation or ensure its survival. Some families put secrecy first, at all costs—think of the elders in a region's dominant religion or families that cover up members' criminal behavior, like sexual abuse or child abuse. Revealing an abuser's actions is viewed as betraying the family, group, or institution and so the abuser is not held accountable.

Flying-monkey enablers: This is the most severe type of enabling. The flying-monkey enabler, like the flying-monkey army that protected the Wicked Witch of the West in *The Wizard of Oz,* is a one-up person's "Abuser in Chief," carrying out abuse on behalf of the person they enable. Their primary goal is to please the one-up person—no matter who they hurt in the process. And because the flying monkey is the one doing the dirty work, the one-up person may even escape accountability, retaining plausible deniability even though they are the one masterminding the abuse.

Why is discussing enabling behaviors so important, especially in the context of healing from relationsickness? Because chronically fawning a one-up person isn't only bad for the fawner. It also isn't good for the people we think we're helping, rescuing, or extending empathy to by forgiving and enabling them. When we allow a person to get away with one-up behaviors, we are rewarding and reinforcing those behaviors, effectively making the person relationally worse. Every time we fawn and appease someone's entitled demands, we give them permission to become more entitled and abusive, rather than helping them learn to handle their disappointment or frustration in a healthy way, so they can learn to treat you—and others—more fairly.

ONE-UP BEHAVIORS

While it's beyond the scope of this book to get into a detailed, trauma-informed, nuanced discussion of the psychological underpinnings of narcissism and NPD, we still want to talk briefly about the behaviors commonly associated with people who tend to go one up in relationships.

People with certain types of relational trauma may toggle between two poles: one down (shame, collapse, inferiority) and one up (control, inflation, superiority). But keep in mind: One up is not genuine self-esteem. It's a defensive strategy meant to ward off the terror of falling into the one-down pit of shame. Both strategies come from the same root wound of not feeling safe, loved, or enough as they are. People in a one-up stance manage their insecurity by putting themselves above others—sometimes obviously, sometimes subtly. They may act arrogant and controlling, or they may be more sullen, resentful, and victim identified, while still feeling and acting entitled. Both versions are fueled by the same underlying fear: *If I don't put myself above, I'll be crushed below.*

Some therapists who specialize in narcissism divide the condition into two styles: the aggressive grandiose style and the more easily overlooked covert style. But as Dr. Mark Ettersohn asserts, most one-up types exhibit elements of both styles, depending on whether they're flying high or collapsed. When things are going their way, when they feel strong, confident, and successful, they can be more grandiose. When they fail, lose, make mistakes, or get called out or humiliated in public, they tend to react more passive-aggressively, feeling like a victim while still acting entitled. The underlying psychology—a fragile self-esteem based on performance and being liked—is the same, whether the presentation is grandiose or covert.

Either way, it can be helpful to pick apart these styles, so you can recognize these behaviors in your various relationships, understanding that the behaviors might change depending on circumstance.

Grandiose One-Up Behaviors

Let's start with the kind of one-up behaviors that tend to ride shotgun with grandiosity. These are the people at the top of Terry Real's Relationship Grid, who seek out power and tend to use it to subjugate those they view as one down. Those who are one up and grandiose can be masters of flattering people and working the room until everyone around them is swooning. They're often charming, confident, attractive, talented, intelligent, successful, and may seem spiritually evolved. They can be extremely impressive, influential individuals who may inspire envy in others.

These one-up folks can be slick politicians, Wall Street hedge fund managers, Grammy-winning rock stars, gorgeous movie stars, record-breaking sports stars, celebrated CEOs, or high-powered attorneys at competitive law firms. They can be authors, speakers, influencers, teachers, activists, or healers. They might be overtly materialistic, like the pastor of a megachurch who drives a Ferrari, or they may dress up their grandiosity in holy drag and practice extreme asceticism as a priest, monk, or spiritual guru. Anywhere you find power—be it worldly, financial, secular, spiritual, political, physical, or psychological—you're likely to find people who tend to go one up in relationships.

One-up folks may come from an impressive family lineage that they brag about, or they may have come from a meager background and worked their way up in the world. Either way, because they did not get enough unconditional love growing up, they are approval seeking and addicted to praise, and have figured out how to win a lot of it through their intelligence, beauty, strengths, and talents.

In the beginning, when you first meet these folks, you may come away feeling as if you've fallen under a spell. One-up individuals can be the life of the party, loving to put on a show, and may bowl you over with over-the-top gestures that leave you feeling like you're in a romantic comedy. Like the Richard Gere character in *Pretty Woman*, they can be the sugar daddy or fairy godmother you always dreamed would whisk you away from it all and solve all your problems.

Grandiose one-up individuals are masters of "love bombing"*: going above and beyond in an effort to manipulate someone into a relationship with them. This looks different for every person, but it usually involves some form of excessive flattery and praise, overcommunication of positive feelings, showering the object of attraction with over-the-top gifts, and premature and intense talks about a fabulous future together.

But things are not always what they seem if you happen to get close to these people. Underneath all the pizzazz run rivers of grandiosity and entitlement, covering up extremely fragile self-esteem. One-up people tend to be transactional and exploitative in relationships, stratifying human beings into those they judge as one up and those they deem one down. They may objectify others, seeing them as things they can use rather than humans to be loved, perceiving even their own children as extensions of themselves, rather than individuals with rights to their own agency and individuality. They often expect their kids to look and behave a certain way in order to make Mom or Dad proud.

One-up individuals frequently have diminished empathy or have no perspective, and attempts to appeal to them emotionally typically fail. They have an extreme need for validation, and are hypersensitive to criticism, with hair-trigger nervous systems that can be activated during even the most minor conflict, resulting in defensiveness or fits of rage.

Being unskilled at anything tends to cut their sense of worthiness and belonging in the world to the quick, and they tend to be very reactive if called out or when their behavior upsets others. They frequently refuse to admit that they screwed up—especially if the mistake was a big one. Instead, they often project their own imperfections and inadequacies onto others while remaining blind to those flaws in themselves.

In short, as long as things are going the one-up person's way, everything is hunky-dory and their grandiosity leads. But if anything

---

* Read about the distinction between real love and love bombing here: https://lissarankin.com/12-differences-between-real-love-love-bombing.

interrupts their feelings of superiority and dominance, if they fall off their pedestals or experience failure, all hell can break loose.

All of us occasionally face disappointment or mess up. We're human! Things don't always go our way, we make mistakes, and other people don't always cooperate with our agendas. But folks who tend to go one up really struggle when they fall off their pedestal or fail to get their way. They can't handle feeling any amount of humiliation or shame. That's when the gloves come off, and the superstar with the charmed life can flip from charming to insensitive, boundary violating, entitled, or even cruel. If you dare to stand up for yourself against someone who feels out of control when they're not one up, if you set boundaries and/or call out the one-up behaviors that you find difficult to handle, their defensiveness can quickly escalate.

If you try to hold someone grandiose and one up accountable, you'll likely see behaviors intended to shirk accountability and flip the blame. Jennifer J. Freyd, PhD, a research psychologist formerly at the University of Oregon, coined the term DARVO (Deny, Attack, Reverse Victim and Offender) in the late 1990s. Freyd observed that when one-up abusers are confronted, they frequently respond with a predictable pattern: Deny the behavior, Attack the accuser, and Reverse Victim and Offender roles.

Remember, narcissism exists on a spectrum. Some one-up folks aren't outright abusive. It's just that their nervous system can't handle being seen as imperfect, and they don't have the skills, resilience, or maturity to behave more responsibly. Whether this behavior is intentional or not, when you feel like you can't get out from under someone's grandiose one-upping, it can erode your own self-esteem, make you doubt yourself, and take a toll on your nervous system that leads to relationsickness.

By the time you experience the consequences of being one-upped, you may already be financially dependent on the one-up person. You may have been seduced or manipulated into marrying very quickly, giving up your job, having a baby, or becoming business partners before the other person's true colors had a chance to show through. You may feel trapped, confused, bewildered—and even come to think it's your fault the other person is behaving the way they are.

Covert One-Up Behaviors

Some one-up behaviors are such obvious red flags that they may be relatively easy to spot, once you're hip to them. But others are much sneakier. In psychology speak, you might call these the "covert" or "vulnerable" one-up behaviors.

Someone who is covertly one up may be relatively lacking in charisma and charm. The childhood wounding that causes kids to grow up to engage in one-up behaviors doesn't always select exclusively for the most good-looking, intelligent, and talented individuals. Some people who tend to go one up may not be smart enough, beautiful enough, skilled enough, or tall enough to become famous or respected. But that doesn't dim their desire for high performance, power, attention, and validation. It just makes them mad at the world for never giving them the attention they feel entitled to—all while feeling deeply unworthy and insecure just beneath the bravado.

Covert one-up individuals can be hostile and bitter, or needy and pitiful. They may appear superficially humble, but the same grandiosity, arrogance, entitlement, and need to be the center of attention lurk under the surface. Their grandiosity may come out in a more sideways manner, through insulting and mocking other successful people. They have a chronic chip on their shoulder, as if their ship never came in—not because they aren't awesome, but because the world is just too stupid to recognize their greatness.

They may think it's beneath them to have a regular 9-to-5 job, as if they're too special to punch the clock or too brilliant to do menial work. But even if they are given the opportunity to achieve their grandiose dreams, they may lack the discipline, talent, intelligence, or ambition to do so. Some who are more covertly one up may genuinely be discriminated against when it comes to success, but more often they feel too entitled to actually put in the labor needed to climb the corporate ladder or develop a talent or skill. They expect to get special treatment and resent it when they don't. They attribute other people's success to sheer good luck, and blame others for their own lack. They may be chronically unsatisfied, argumentative, hypercritical, and insufferable to be around.

Covert one-up behaviors can also show up as excessive rescuing behaviors. Going one up in this way tends to be observed in caregiving professions, like medicine, nursing, or social work. For one-up individuals in these fields, caregiving or saving lives masks a need for power and control over those they are helping and fuels the belief that they're superior to the more vulnerable people they care for or rescue. Rather than being motivated by true altruism arising from genuine empathy and a desire to serve humanity, they tend to be motivated by pride and the grandiose fantasy that they are special, chosen, and saving the world. They may also spiritualize these one-up behaviors, seeing themselves as saintly, self-sacrificing martyrs.

Covert one-up folks can also get hits of grandiosity and power from people they try to rescue in their personal lives. In relationships, they tend to pair up with people they see as more needy than (and therefore one down from) themselves. This perceived power imbalance between themselves and the person they help is what allows them to see themselves as one up: better, stronger, or less messed up.

If you've seen the wonderful Susan Sarandon movie *The Meddler,* it presents a compassionate character study of this kind of one-up behavior. The main character, Marnie, crosses all kinds of boundaries—first with her daughter and then, when her daughter shuts her down, with total strangers—all in the name of helping. She offers rides to Freddy, who needs transportation to school, and then spends every drive monologuing on and on about her late husband, her daughter, her life in New Jersey, and whatever is on her mind—essentially using him as a captive audience for her own unprocessed feelings while he's trapped and can't get away. She interferes unasked in the life of an ailing woman at the hospital to try to reconnect her with her son. When she overhears that a lesbian couple never got the big wedding they wanted, she offers to throw them a wedding (i.e., control it), so she can get her attention- and validation-seeking needs met by a reception full of people who barely know her but think she's a saint.

Marnie is grieving the loss of her husband, and many of us can be a bit more controlling or attention seeking during a crisis. That's normal. But some people demonstrate this kind of behavior their whole adult lives. They're the ones whose funerals are full of relative strangers grateful for the deceased's generosity, even though the people closest to them are estranged due to their controlling, boundaryless, intrusive behavior.

As long as the people they're "helping" behave gratefully, those who exhibit covert one-up behaviors are happy and feel secure. But most people don't like being controlled. If others express displeasure or rebel against what the one-up person recommends, the gloves come off, and we see the same denial, defensiveness, rage, and projection exhibited by grandiose one-up individuals, previously disguised beneath the superficially loving exterior of the helper. Or these individuals may bury their anger, leading to seething resentment and passive-aggressive behavior toward the very people they claim to love and want to help.

The reason these kinds of one-up behaviors can be so easily overlooked as red flags is because these individuals lead with the mirage of selflessness and are often blind to their own true motivations, genuinely believing they're called to serve—and they may be! Their one-up impulses can be so buried in their unconscious that they don't recognize their own need for power, control, attention, and validation. But however impressive their outer altruism, they cannot hide their controlling tendencies from their closest friends, family, or business colleagues.

When you're dealing with someone covertly one up, the dynamic can feel more slippery and confusing than when you're with someone more grandiose. Instead of meeting your boundaries with loud defensiveness or obvious put-downs, the covert one-up person may posture as the long-suffering victim, sighing heavily, withdrawing affection, or guilt-tripping you for having needs. You may be met with subtle digs, sulking, or a torrent of self-pity that makes you feel like the cruel one for daring to assert yourself. Because the covertly one-up person's superiority comes in the form of martyrdom—"Look how much I've sacrificed," "You don't appreciate me"—it can be hard to call it out.

Over time, you may start walking on eggshells, bending over backward to avoid "hurting" them, and even internalizing the idea that your healthy self-advocacy is somehow selfish or unkind. You may lose touch with your own needs and instincts, get caught in cycles of guilt and over-responsibility, and end up depleted, anxious, full of self-doubt, and relationsick. By the time you recognize the covert one-up pattern, you may already feel emotionally trapped—bound by sympathy, guilt, or an unspoken sense that it's your job to keep the other person from falling apart.

People exhibiting these kinds of behaviors might seem unworthy of compassion; it feels awful to be on the receiving end of such behaviors, and isn't treatment that others should accept. But keep in mind that, whether we're talking about the grandiose one-up style or the covert, these are trauma symptoms. Being in the one-up position often *feels* less stressful to the nervous system than being one down, which is why some trauma survivors gravitate to it. Power—even if it's defensive or inflated—temporarily quiets the terror of collapsed self-esteem and the freak-out of feeling out of control. But this is not the same as true regulation or healing. The grandiose one-up person may look calm, but it's a brittle calm that depends on keeping others down. The covert one-up may appear selfless and helpful, but it's based on needing to be the one in control, and that control is always at risk of slipping away. In both cases, the underlying trauma is still running the show.

WHAT POWER DOES TO THE BRAIN

Berkley Social Interaction Lab director Dacher Keltner is best known for his research[32] on the psychological effects of power. His approach/inhibition theory proposes that the more social power someone has, and the more they acquire power in the world, the more likely they are to act on even the most inappropriate desires without restraint. Once they acquire power, powerful individuals often believe it's okay to act in ways they'd usually deem unacceptable for others. Keltner's lab found that when people feel powerful, they were more likely to break social norms—cutting in line, littering, making risky choices, and even stealing candy set aside for children. Powerful people are more likely to think it's fine for them to break the rules they think others should follow—in other words, that there are two sets of rules: one for them, and one for others.

Power also increases focus on the self and diminishes focus on others, physically weakening empathy networks. In studies by neuroscientist Sukhvinder Obhi,[33] researchers primed participants to feel powerful by assigning them leadership and decision-making roles and asking them to reflect on times when they had more power, then had them observe another person's actions while their brain activity was recorded. Those power-primed individuals then showed reduced mirror neuron activity in fMRIs of the brain and less neural alignment compared to controls. In other words, feeling powerful led to less empathy for others.

Behavioral research from Keltner's team similarly showed that powerful individuals experienced less distress and compassion when witnessing someone else's suffering. Keltner describes how power alters behavior, empathy, and impulse control as the "power paradox": The very skills that help people gain power—empathy, generosity, cooperation—tend to erode once power is attained. This is why disempowering experiences, like failing to achieve a goal, getting sick, or having your partner divorce you, can humble someone back toward greater empathy, checking their power. With no checks and balances on power, as when a partner fawns instead of holding someone powerful accountable, the risk of abuses of power in relationships can increase.

If you've been one down and overpowered, a little empowerment can tempt us to switch power roles, because we feel better when we become the one with the power. But it's crucial to remember that true, enduring power is best maintained not through controlling and one-upping other people, but through caring about others, cultivating empathy, altruism, and gratitude, while also caring equally about yourself: your safety, your health, and your own precious needs.

BEING ONE DOWN IN A RELATIONSHIP WITH A ONE-UP PERSON

One-down status in a relationship is, in and of itself, a major stressor. Walking through life feeling "less than" keeps the nervous system on high alert, and that dysregulation alone can take a toll. It also often drives fawning behaviors, like appeasing, overgiving, or erasing yourself, even when there is no real threat in the present moment.

Being one up can also be stressful. The pressure to be flawless, maintain control, and shoulder excessive responsibility can wear down even the most grandiose nervous system. But our research and many people's lived experience suggest that being stuck one down, especially in a relationship with someone who dominates, exploits, or bullies you, is usually even more damaging to long-term health. The behaviors of people who go one up in relationships can cause a great deal of nervous system dysregulation in anyone who tries to get close to them. The bewildering combination of love bombing and generosity they exhibit; the ecstatic feelings and admiration we may feel toward them; and the gaslighting, meanness, and disorientation we may experience when we try to stand up for ourselves are often more than our nervous systems can handle. Likewise, when we're overloaded into overwhelm or pushed into dissociation, the impact on our physical bodies can be extreme. Trying to be close to someone who behaves this way can cause both mental health issues and a full-on physical health breakdown.

People who engage in a lot of one-up behaviors typically have unrealistic expectations of others. They may expect their partner, family members, or friends to meet impossible-to-attain standards of perfection, or engage in a lot of caregiving behaviors toward them, then act put upon or feign incompetence if the other person expects the favor to be returned equitably. People who prefer the one-up role tend to choose fawning types in relationships, either consciously or unconsciously. Because one-up folks typically think they're better than the people who fawn them, the power imbalance and inequality in the relationship often don't register to either party as unfair. It's what they both expect. If your childhood trauma causes you to feel intimidated by those you see as one up, you may just jump when they say jump, without pausing to consider whether it's in your best interest to accommodate what they want. Over time, both the stress of these entitled expectations and the energy required to fulfill them can put people who are one down in these kinds of relationships at risk of relationsickness.

We'll talk more in part two about how to stop fawning and enabling, and how to protect yourself and others from going one down or one up, in order to treat relationsickness. For now, we just want to raise your awareness of the relationships where you tend to go one down, and help you stop thinking that's healthy and normal, so you can start preparing to make changes in your relationships. As Terry Real says, "If you are in a shame state, bring yourself up. If you're being grandiose, bring yourself down. If you are boundaryless, pause and reset your boundary. If you are walled off, take a deep breath and get back into engagement." It takes two willing people to create real change, but you can start by changing yourself.

NOT ALL UNBALANCED RELATIONSHIPS ARE CREATED EQUAL

If you've recognized yourself in some of the unbalanced power dynamics we've just described, it may stir up some big feelings. Realizing you've been in a one-down position can feel shocking, disorienting, bewildering, even devastating. You might suddenly be seeing someone close to you as the villain of your story. You may be wondering whether the only path to health is to walk away.

But before you leap to any conclusions, we want to invite in some nuance. Many relationships that struggle with power imbalances and inequities are not doomed to stay that way. In spite of what you might hear from internet influencers, not every one-up person is malicious or irredeemable. Many are simply operating out of their own trauma responses, without the skills or nervous system resilience to relate differently. That doesn't excuse the pain their behaviors have caused or let them off the hook of accountability, but it does open the door to a more compassionate, complex, and trauma-informed view of them.

Let's not forget that unbalanced relationships are not always relationally unhealthy, and not all unbalanced relationships are abusive. It can be helpful to think about unbalanced relationships in degrees, as the following chart depicts. Any unbalanced relationship can lead to relationsickness, but the more unbalanced—and abusive—it is, the higher the risk.

DEGREES OF UNBALANCED RELATIONSHIPS

LEVEL 1	LEVEL 2	LEVEL 3	LEVEL 4
Caregiver/ care receiver dynamic, without any other significant power imbalances	One-up/one-down power dynamic, without significant coercive control or criminal behavior	One-up/one-down power dynamic, with coercive control, without other criminal behaviors	One-up/one-down power dynamic, with coercive control, with other criminal behaviors

Level 1 Relationships

Relationships where the balance between caregiving and care receiving is unequal, but with no other unequal power dynamics, fall in Level 1. Both people are basically good hearted and well intentioned, but one of them is contributing more than the other. Maybe one person is disabled and cannot split adult responsibilities 50/50. Or one person is neurodivergent, with autism or attention-deficit/hyperactivity disorder (ADHD), and struggles to function at the same level of efficiency and competency as the other person, who is neurotypical. Whatever the reason, the responsibilities for financial providing, home and child care, maintaining the social network and community, and emotional nurture fall too much on one person's shoulders, leaving them stressed, overburdened, and potentially relationsick.

In Level 1 relationships, one person is overfunctioning without receiving enough care, not because of someone else's one-up behaviors—the other person feeling entitled to take advantage of their generosity, for instance, or the other person's selfishness, lack of empathy, or malice—but simply because the caregiver isn't getting the support they need and deserve.

Maddy is a good example. Her husband developed Alzheimer's when he was quite young, and her son had severe autism, requiring 24/7 caregiving. Maddy was also a therapist, trying to attend to the traumas of others without enough support for herself. We see this commonly among people who work as full-time caregivers—therapists, nurses, doctors, social workers, and schoolteachers—and are also expected to do a lot of caregiving at home.

While mismatched Level 1 relationships are nobody's fault, they can still contribute to exhaustion and illness. The body doesn't care *why* it isn't getting enough rest, support, and help—it just knows that it isn't. That said, the risk of relationsickness is generally lower in a Level 1 relationship than in higher levels. Here, the strain often comes from caregiver burnout or external pressures, rather than from the constant internal stress of being chronically one down. In fact, caregivers may even occupy the one-up position relative to the person they're helping, which means they aren't living under another person's thumb in the same way. By contrast, when a relationship involves intimidation, exploitation, betrayal, abuse, or other dynamics that trigger fawning responses, the stress is twofold: the outer stressors of imbalance plus the inner stress of feeling overpowered. This combination places the body at much higher risk of breaking down.

The sick people we interviewed who were in Level 1 relationships often knew the pressures on them were unfair, but they felt helpless to change the dynamic. This sense of helplessness often led these overfunctioners to become critical and passive-aggressive because of caregiver burnout, acting out covert one-up behaviors out of sheer exhaustion.

People like Maddy love and empathize with the people they care for, and feel loved by them, even though the relationship dynamics aren't reciprocal. They typically still get time in the ventral vagal parasympathetic state (as discussed in chapter two) with those they caretake. They feel loved, appreciated, and purposeful, even though they're exhausted. This may convey some protection against relationsickness, compared to the other levels.

Caregiver burnout is a legitimate risk factor for relationsickness, but what we want to focus on primarily is the even higher risk of relationsickness for those who are one down in higher-level power imbalances, like those in Levels 2, 3, and 4 relationships.

A WORD ABOUT NEURODIVERGENCE AND RELATIONSHIPS

When it comes to people with ADHD, autism, learning disabilities like dyslexia, or trauma-related nervous system differences like the kind that accompany complex PTSD, relationship balance can be challenging. To make things even trickier, the trauma associated with growing up neurodivergent can compound this.

Because our culture is built to support neurotypical folks, neurodivergent people often wind up feeling systemically disempowered, even when caregivers are doing their absolute best to empower them. Some neurodivergent folks grow up feeling lesser than and not good enough, and as a result tend to go one down in relationships. For others, neurodivergence may have made them exceptionally gifted—musically, academically, or in business—which made them feel superior to others, and so tend to go one up. As a result, neurodivergent individuals in unbalanced relationships can be either the person fawning or the one expecting fawning.

Simply living as a neurodivergent person in a world designed for neurotypical folks can also cause trauma that dysregulates the nervous system. Neurodivergent children may feel pressure to "mask," or cover up behaviors or traits that others deem weird, different, or unlikeable. This pressure can stress the nervous system and lead to fawning behaviors.

Further, neurodivergence is associated with an intense sensitivity around feedback and criticism, often referred to as rejection sensitivity dysphoria (RSD). On its surface, RSD can look very similar to DARVO, causing some neurodivergent people to get mistakenly labeled as narcissistic, but there are subtle yet important differences. DARVO protects a fragile, shame-based ego by deflecting accountability and maintaining control or dominance in the relational dynamic. It's usually strategic (though often unconscious), an automatic reflex to preserve a grandiose or "good" self-image. RSD, on the other hand, is a reflexive nervous system response to perceived rejection, activating trauma rooted in chronic invalidation or social exclusion. The inner world of someone exhibiting RSD behaviors reveals sincere pain and fear of losing belonging, not entitlement or superiority. DARVO is about protecting image. RSD is about protecting connection.

All of these issues potentially affect power dynamics in relationships where one or both people are neurodivergent. Although many neurodivergent folks are not disabled, unable to participate in an equal relationship the way someone with dementia might be, their ability to share tasks and responsibilities equally still might be impaired. A well-intentioned neurotypical partner with an ADHD spouse, for example, may wind up doing the executive functioning for them both, bearing the brunt of the mental load and winding up resentful, burned out, and relationsick. They may also end up engaging in one-up behaviors, like criticizing, insulting, and otherwise verbally abusing their neurodivergent partner.

The treatment for relationsickness caused by this kind of unbalanced relationship is beyond the scope of this book, requiring more delicacy and nuance than we'll be able to adequately address. But the tools and practices we teach in part two can still help. It can also be useful for the neurotypical partner in mixed-neurotype relationships to remember to appreciate the positive qualities that drew them to the other person in the first place, to avoid demeaning, disempowering, or otherwise treating their partner like they're "less than" and one down. And just as the relationsick caregiver of a disabled person might need extra help, to take some of the burden off them so their bodies can heal, the neurotypical partner of someone neurodivergent may need additional support to compensate for the invisible labor of the extra executive functioning.

Our hearts go out to those mixed-neurotype or neurodivergent couples who struggle to try to find balance and share power equally.

Level 2 Relationships

In a Level 2 unbalanced relationship, one person is generously overgiving, like the giving tree, and the other, like the boy, is acting entitled, narcissistic, or maybe just opportunistically exploitative. This is not necessarily because the latter has malicious intent but rather because they are simply conditioned to believe that some people matter more than others and deserve special treatment. Factors causing this include socioeconomic privilege, patriarchy, racism, ableism, or because they were indulged or had their egos inflated as children and grew up demanding and entitled. For example, maybe because they are the primary breadwinner, they think paying the bills is enough of a contribution to compensate for neglecting the other person's needs in other areas.

Those who develop relationsickness from a Level 2 relationship often devoted themselves to someone who did not *need* to receive more care than they gave due to illness, disability, or neurodivergence, but nonetheless still felt entitled to it. (It's also possible to have a Level 2 relationship with someone sick, disabled, or neurodivergent, of course. Disabled people can act out one-up behaviors separate from their disability or neurodivergence, and having a disability is not an excuse for expecting someone else to overgive.)

It takes two to participate in a Level 2 relationship. Some of the sick people we interviewed had been justifying the inequality in their relationship with a variety of different defenses, distorted beliefs, and ways of thinking. They often viewed the one they'd been giving to as "superior" in some way. Sometimes they thought they weren't good enough to be in an equal, balanced relationship with someone so smart, successful, good-looking, talented, or rich, and so had to overgive to keep them. Other times, they overgave to compensate for some perceived inner defectiveness, unworthiness, or unlovability, taken on because of relational trauma. Or they convinced themselves they were needless and wantless or that the other person's needs mattered more.

Regardless of the reason, the result is the same: The one-down person winds up burned out from overgiving and traumatized by the devaluation and neglect of their needs. And their body pays the price.

Unlike in Level 1 relationships, the person who does more of the taking in Level 2 relationships usually has narcissistic tendencies. They function as if they believe they are more valuable, deserving of care, and special than the one-down person. The one-down person tends to fawn and may be more classically codependent. They enable the one-up person to get away with treating them as less than, sometimes because they don't know they have the right to receive more.

Although Level 2 relationships can exhibit mildly abusive dynamics and may involve volatile conflicts, if an unbalanced relationship is outright abusive, or if postconflict repair is always out of reach, it's not Level 2. If the one-up person is so controlling that the one-down person has lost all autonomy and agency, or if the one-down person is a victim of criminal abuse, like assault, rape, or theft, it's not a Level 2 relationship.

Level 3 Relationships

Relationsick individuals in Level 3 relationships are often victims of coercive control, a pattern of emotionally abusive behavior used to dominate and manipulate another person, typically in an intimate or familial relationship, but sometimes in a cult, spiritual group, therapy dynamic, or workplace. This type of abuse often gets missed if there's no physical component, and while it is illegal in some parts of the world, it remains legal in most.

Coercive control can be perpetrated by an intimate partner; parents; an overbearing mentor, healer, teacher, or leader; or a demanding *Devil Wears Prada*–worthy boss. Often, one person sits at the top of the power hierarchy and demands a different set of rules for themselves (and their inner circle) than for everyone else. Whether it's a cult of two in a romantic relationship, a cult of four in a family, or a cult of one hundred in a commune, anytime one person coercively controls the psyches (and lives) of one or more other people, the bodies of those one down are likely to bear the burden.

In relationships, the coercive controller dominates their victim through a mix of manipulation, intimidation, degradation, gaslighting, and control over basic freedoms—making it very hard to leave. These relationships often start with charm, promises, and connection. But over time, through small concessions, the victims find themselves far from who they once were—isolated, self-doubting, and entirely under someone else's influence.

Many celebrity lawsuits played out in the public eye demonstrate what this kind of coercive control can look like. For example, in her 2023 lawsuit against Sean "Diddy" Combs, singer Cassie Ventura described years of coercive control disguised, at first, as love and opportunity. She alleged that he used intimidation, manipulation, and physical violence to keep her in a cycle of dependence, dictating where she lived and what she wore, and even pressuring her into unwanted sexual encounters. Britney Spears's conservatorship under her father is another high-profile example. Court testimony and reporting showed that her father oversaw her finances, medical care, and personal choices down to what she ate and whom she saw, leaving her stripped of autonomy. Both stories illustrate how coercive control can unfold in plain sight, hidden under the guise of protection, love, or guidance, until the victim's freedom is almost entirely erased.

Victims of coercive control often fawn their abusers rather than protesting the controlling behavior, pretzeling themselves to please the other person in hopes of winning better treatment, because they feel trapped in the relationship, confused and powerless, but also attached to the person who is abusing them. This degree of chronic nervous system dysregulation can devastate their health. Coercive control is nearly guaranteed to lead to medical problems, such as headaches, gastrointestinal distress, insomnia, chronic pain, or gynecologic problems, not to mention complex PTSD and other psychiatric conditions like dissociative disorders, anxiety, and depression. Over time, it can also bring on cancer, heart disease, autoimmune conditions, and more. While physical abuse may leave visible wounds, coercive control works like an invisible poison, eroding the nervous system and immune system, causing chronic inflammation, and affecting one's overall ability to heal and thrive.

Sadly, our medical, legal, educational, and law enforcement systems often overlook patterns of coercive control and so miss or minimize abusive situations that, though invisible and legal, still cause immense harm.

Level 4 Relationships

At the most severe end of the spectrum are Level 4 relationships. Here, the coercive control of Level 3 relationships becomes an umbrella for criminal offenses like domestic violence, child abuse, rape, kidnapping, theft, labor trafficking, fraud, and more. An increasingly common variation of Level 4 relationships are the "sweetheart swindlers" who employ coercive control to prey on the vulnerable, the elderly, the lovelorn, and the wealthy, conning them out of their life savings.

If you google "Sweetheart Swindler 20/20" you can watch a harrowing true crime story about Ralph Raines Jr., multimillionaire heir to his family's Oregon tree-farm fortune. In 2004, Ralph, a secluded bachelor who longed for companionship, met a charismatic "psychic" named Rachel Lee, who gradually inserted herself into his life—first as life adviser, then as confidant, then as bookkeeper and decisionmaker. Over the next decade, she manipulated him into handing over power of attorney of his financial affairs, convincing him she could secure what he most wanted: love, family, and a child.

Rachel and her accomplices orchestrated an elaborate deception: a "wife" who was really Rachel's teenage daughter, Porsha Lee, in disguise; a purported child named "Giorgio Armani" whom Ralph believed was his own; and millions of Ralph's dollars siphoned into exotic vacations, luxury cars, and properties.

By the time law enforcement intervened, after suspecting that the Lee family was preparing to harm Ralph, his fortune, once estimated at more than $15 million, was only a few hundred thousand dollars. Rachel, her longtime partner Blancey Lee, and her sweetheart-swindler daughter Porsha all went to jail—while Ralph continued to defend them, despite the financial ruin and emotional betrayal. He still viewed his "wife" and "child" as real.

The Ralph Raines case is a classic example of a Level 4 relationship. Victims in the most severe Level 4 relationships may not only fawn their abusers but also defend and protect them if others try to hold them accountable for the abuse. This psychological response, in which a victim develops feelings of trust, attachment, and even loyalty toward their abuser or captor as a survival strategy, is fawning in its most extreme form.

Level 4 relationships often involve someone who meets the criteria for the "dark tetrad":[34] malignant narcissism, sociopathy, Machiavellianism, and sadism. This toxic combination of obsession with power, antisocial and often criminal behaviors, lack of empathy, a distorted view of reality, manipulation, and sadistic pleasure derived from hurting others leads to a very high risk of relationsickness. Victims of this kind of abuse are very vulnerable to developing the worst kinds of physical diseases, not to mention severe mental health issues.

Victims in Level 4 relationships usually have a high degree of relationship trauma that preexists their current relationship. Those who grew up in households with severe relational trauma, such as chronic childhood abuse or neglect, a parent with an untreated personality disorder, or long-term exposure to domestic violence, may be unconsciously drawn to abusive power dynamics because they feel familiar. People with these histories may have been conditioned to normalize control, fear, intimidation, and inconsistency in relationships. Having learned early on to survive by appeasing volatile caregivers, they are often more susceptible to gaslighting, isolation, and the slow erosion of boundaries that characterize criminal levels of coercive control.

HOW TO RECOGNIZE A MALIGNANT NARCISSIST

While most of us indulge in one-up or one-down behaviors occasionally, malignant narcissism is a different, darker beast altogether. The malignant narcissist might start out with garden-variety one-up behaviors, but then quickly escalate to dangerous levels of coercive control that automatically put a close relationship with a malignant narcissist into the Level 3 or 4 category.

These individuals are often cold, calculating, aggressive, paranoid, and deeply manipulative. While someone merely one up and grandiose might be like a German Shepherd that licks you one moment and bites you the next because you stopped petting them, the malignant narcissist is more like a pit bull tortured into becoming a killer. When they target you as prey, it's with the intensity of a true predator set on domination and destruction.

Malignant narcissists operate with a willful disregard for the emotional, physical, and psychological safety of others. They tend to exploit the people closest to them, leaving a trail of psychological and sometimes physical or financial wreckage. They frequently justify their actions, seeing themselves as above the rules that apply to everyone else, and behave in ways that are immoral, unethical, or even criminal: lying, cheating, stealing, assaulting, intentionally ruining others, or manipulating them without remorse. Many struggle with addictions—to substances, sex, gambling, shopping, work, or domination itself.

They can be master manipulators. Like the fraudsters you see in true crime documentaries—the startup con artists, the romance scammers, the cult leaders—they often present as charming, persuasive, and charismatic at first. But the charm is just a smokescreen concealing a deeper agenda of control and exploitation. They're also prone to deep paranoia and projecting their own bad behavior onto others, accusing those close to them of cheating while they're having multiple affairs or blaming business partners for theft even as they're the ones embezzling. It's as if they assume everyone else is as dishonest and manipulative as they are.

Malignant narcissists—and also their victims—often fail to recognize their abuse. Even when presented with evidence in court that they are hurting others, malignant narcissists may be unable to see or admit what they're doing. Likewise, even when presented with evidence that they are the ones being preyed upon and abused, victims of malignant narcissists may struggle to see it. Instead, they may double down and refuse to admit what's real.

In the victim's case, they may unconsciously suppress awareness of the betrayal to cope with the devastation of being betrayed by someone they love as a way of preserving what they see as an essential relationship. This can be agonizing for those who are trying to get justice or help someone leave an abusive situation, like those who were trying to help Ralph Raines. And this denial, this betrayal blindness, can be nearly impenetrable, taking years to unravel.

It's important to realize that anyone can fall under the spell of a coercive controller. It has nothing to do with intelligence, education, or strength of character. Anyone can be drawn in. The mistake victims make is trusting someone who turns out to be dangerous. And that is not a shameful mistake. The shame belongs to the abuser—not the victim.

No one consents to being abused. Even if you said yes to certain things, stayed too long, or accommodated too much, that's not consent—that's a response to manipulation, conditioning, and fear. Abusers never begin a relationship by telling you they're going to destroy your self-worth, bankrupt you emotionally or financially, take full control of your life, or leave you relationsick. Instead, they offer you love, belonging, purpose. And then, little by little, just like the boy in *The Giving Tree*, they begin to take everything.

Please know that, if you are in a relationship with a malignant narcissist, you don't owe empathy to someone who is actively destroying you. Yes, these individuals are often profoundly wounded. But it is not your job to understand and redeem them. Your job is to protect yourself, recover your freedom, and restore your health.

AM I BEING COERCIVELY CONTROLLED?

These questions are not intended to be a diagnostic tool, but rather a flashlight in the dark—a gentle guide to help you reconnect with your inner knowing and tune in to whether patterns of coercive control may be affecting your health, safety, and sovereignty. Please read slowly. Breathe between each question. Answer "yes" or "no" based on your own lived experience—with self-compassion and without judgment.

1. Have aspects of my day-to-day life been tightly controlled—like when I sleep, what I wear, where I go, what I'm allowed to do, or who I see?
2. Have I been denied or had access restricted to basic necessities like food, clothing, medical care, or shelter?
3. Has someone tracked my movements, phone calls, texts, emails, or online activity—either overtly or secretly (including through spyware or shared devices)?
4. Have I been repeatedly belittled, shamed, or made to feel small, worthless, or broken, such that my self-confidence has eroded over time?
5. Have I been denied access to money, pressured to give up my work, prevented from making my own money, or manipulated into being financially dependent against my will?
6. Have I been forced to work, while access to the money I earn has been taken away from me (for example, turning over power of attorney when you're still competent to manage your own money)?
7. Have I felt scared to push back, protest, rebel, or leave the relationship due to threats (verbal or physical) aimed at me or my loved ones, pets, or property?
8. Have I been made to doubt my own memory, sanity, or perception of reality?
9. Have I been coerced into fulfilling rigid roles based on gender (e.g., submissive wife, breadwinning husband, or stay-at-home mother)?
10. Have children or pets been threatened, manipulated, or used as leverage to control me?
11. Have I lost my sense of autonomy—struggling to make independent decisions or trust my own judgment?
12. Has anyone manipulated me by love bombing me one moment, then insulting me the next?

13. Have I developed anxiety, depression, panic attacks, or physical symptoms that worsened in this relationship?
14. Have I withdrawn from friends, family, or community because of fear, shame, humiliation, or pressure?
15. Have I sacrificed my own needs, authenticity, preferences, and safety in order to try to make someone who seems unpleasable happy?

For each question where you answered "yes," give yourself 1 point. Tally your score out of 15. Now reflect gently on where you fall:

0–3: Early Warning Signs

You may not be in an overtly coercive relationship, but you may be experiencing or engaging in some boundary-blurring or self-silencing behaviors. Ask yourself: Are there places I feel I must shrink to stay safe or loved? This may be a time to strengthen your voice, rebuild your support network, or seek guidance from a trusted therapist.

4–7: A Pattern That Deserves Your Attention

A score in this range suggests a pattern of control, fear, or manipulation that may be affecting your sense of self and safety. You might be accommodating harm without realizing it or minimizing red flags to maintain peace. Your nervous system may be in a chronic state of stress, leading to fawning. This is a time for deep self-trust. Your discomfort is data—not drama. Consider sharing your answers with a trauma-informed therapist, support group, or trustworthy friend who really sees you.

8–11: High Likelihood of Coercive Control

You may be living in an environment where your autonomy is systematically undermined—physically, emotionally, financially, and/or spiritually. You may feel trapped, confused, or like you're "losing yourself." The toll on your health may be significant. Please know: You are not lost. You are not weak. You are not alone. Consider reaching out to a domestic violence advocate, therapist, or legal support resource—even if you're not sure you qualify. Your body might be saying otherwise.

12–15: Very High Likelihood of Coercive Control
This score suggests a highly dangerous power imbalance that may be impacting every part of your life—mental, physical, emotional, and spiritual. If you feel entrapped, there's a reason. You may be experiencing what's often called intimate terrorism—a form of abuse that can exist even without physical violence. Please consider connecting with a domestic abuse organization, mental health professional, or legal advocate. Safety planning may be an important next step.

If your score was high and your heart is racing, take a break to recalibrate your nervous system. Remember, there is no rush, no shame, no test to pass. You didn't deserve this. It's not your fault. You don't have to keep adapting to what harms you. You are worthy of love that honors your wholeness and health, not love that demands your erasure.

If you are being coercively controlled, even if you're not being violently abused, you can call the National Domestic Violence Hotline in the United States, 1-800-799-SAFE (7233); the National Domestic Abuse Helpline in the United Kingdom, 0808 2000 247; or the national domestic, family, and sexual violence line in Australia, 1800RESPECT.

RELATIONSICKNESS IS DOSE DEPENDENT

Some unbalanced relationships have nothing to do with childhood trauma and are the result of an unexpected change of circumstances: a car accident that leaves one partner disabled, a loved one who gets early

Alzheimer's, or a chronic illness that makes it harder for one person to carry their weight equally, leading to a Level 1 relationship. But more often than not, unbalanced relationships *start out that way,* even though it might not be obvious at first.

Remember imagos? People who feel safer and happier when they're in a one-up role, like those who were overpowered in childhood and decided *never again* or those who experienced falsely empowering abuse, often seek out partners they think they can rescue or control—who will be a submissive doormat grateful for the rescue or who don't complain about doing more than their fair share because they don't feel worthy of reciprocity. Someone who tends to go one-up in relationships may not even be attracted to someone with good boundaries, the ability to assert themselves, an understanding of their own value, or healthy self-protection.

Similarly, someone who feels safer when they're one down, perhaps because of disempowering abuse in childhood, may consciously or unconsciously be looking for someone powerful and competent who can help them feel less overwhelmed by adult responsibilities, like earning the money, handling the finances, and making most of the decisions. They may feel more comfortable handling lower-stakes domestic tasks, like housekeeping or errand running, while deferring to someone else on more important life choices, like choosing where to live, making health-care decisions, or planning retirement investments—essentially giving someone one-up permission to control them.

In extreme cases, childhood trauma can flip our sense of safety upside down, so that our nervous system registers danger around healthy, well-boundaried people and safety around people who are controlling and emotionally or physically dangerous, leaving us vulnerable to Level 3 and 4 relationships. It's crucial to understand that relationsickness is dose dependent: The higher the level, the more relationsick we are likely to become, and the harder it will be to get well. No matter how much we try to engage in health-inducing behaviors, as long as we're at the mercy of an unbalanced relationship, our bodies may struggle to keep up with the repair of daily bodily wear and tear necessary for long-term, symptom-free health.

While an unbalanced Level 1 relationship may stress and burn out the caregiver, and while additional caregiver support might be needed in order to prevent or treat relationsickness, a Level 1 relationship does not distress the nervous system and impair the body's natural self-healing mechanisms as much as being overpowered, devalued, coercively controlled, or otherwise abused. A caregiver in a Level 1 relationship may be exhausted, overwhelmed, and strained by the mental and physical load of overfunctioning, but they still know they are loved, appreciated, and valued by those they care for, who usually feel awful that they're unable to carry their weight equally.

That's very different from a Level 2 relationship, in which one person feels entitled to the other person's overgiving, gets angry when not being waited on, expects to override the other person's consent, and doesn't think there's anything wrong with behaving that way. And it doesn't even begin to compare to a Level 3 or 4 relationship, in which one person is being coercively controlling or criminally abusive. While all of these levels of relationships are unbalanced, they affect the nervous system and the body in vastly different ways, largely because of the emotional impact of being treated as "less" if you're in a Level 2, 3, or 4 relationship.

Regardless of why we end up in an unbalanced relationship, the good news is that Level 1 and often Level 2 relationships can be rebalanced, in order to support healing relationsickness. We'll focus on how in part two. But first, let's talk about how our belief systems may keep us from protesting relational inequality, calling out one-up power dynamics, standing up for ourselves in the face of abusive relational patterns, and otherwise encouraging us to justify staying in relationships that may make us relationsick.

CHAPTER 6

Indoctrination and Spiritual Bypassing

Morality is doing what's right, no matter what you are told. Religion is doing what you are told, no matter what's right.

—H. L. Mencken

While this book was originally inspired by the radical remission survivors from our research, the kinds of relational trauma that lead to relationsickness, and the belief systems that cement them in place, are very personal for Jeff, the coauthor of this book.

Jeff grew up on a farm in Indiana, in a house where chores were done early, the Bible sat open on the kitchen counter like a command, and nightly Christian readings were followed by kneeling by their dinner chairs for long, droning prayers. Jeff's mother followed her church's interpretations of the Bible's teachings like she was steering a ship through a storm.

But it wasn't just the Bible she followed; it was also Bill Gothard, founder of the Institute in Basic Life Principles (IBLP). Gothard's teachings were treated as gospel in Jeff's house, even more than the scriptures themselves. Gothard had a formula for everything: how to raise children, how to handle sin, how to be a godly man, and especially how to break the will of children in order to keep them in line.

By the time Jeff was six, he knew how to sit still as stone in church with a smile plastered on his face, even as his stomach was in knots. He knew that boys obeyed their parents, and mothers were supposed to obey their husbands, even though his iron-fisted mother seemed to be the one who wore the pants in the family.

Maybe Jeff's mother believed with her whole heart that she was protecting her boys, that she was saving their souls from the ruin of willfulness. But those teachings hollowed her children from the inside out. They were designed to separate children from their bodies and from their natural instinct about right and wrong, to install an inverted morality of obedience and conformity, rather than a morality built on dignity, justice, or the belief that all human beings have equal value. Having feelings, opinions, or your own perception of reality was dangerous and ungodly. Good little boys and girls bowed to whoever dominated, keeping any sense they had that something was "off" to themselves.

During the normal stages of childhood development when children practice setting boundaries, saying no, and asserting themselves, Jeff was beaten by both his mother and his father, trained to fawn—to please, submit, comply—or else face physical and emotional consequences. Otherwise, they told him, he would bring shame to the family and burn in the endless fiery flames of eternal damnation. Questioning authority was framed as rebellion against God Himself. Self-sacrifice was seen as holy. In IBLP's teachings, martyrdom isn't a tragedy—it's a goal.

Along the way, Jeff internalized the idea that his body was not his own, and that his unique thoughts and feelings were a threat. So when physical, emotional, or other lines got crossed, when things got dark or confusing, he didn't fight or flee. He performed. Until he started dissociating and couldn't concentrate anymore, he wowed the teachers, got straight A's, and won the spelling bees. He also got quieter, shyer, and more obedient. He tried his best to become the good son, the respectful Christian boy, and later, the dutiful husband. He wore the mask so well, no one ever thought to look behind it and wonder who he really was. Because he was trained not to draw attention to himself, he told no one when at age sixteen he had severe chest pain in the basement of his house, later diagnosed (when an EKG showed the resulting permanent changes) as a heart attack. He also developed chronic, debilitating back pain.

When, as an adult, Jeff reclaimed the parts of himself that had been taken from him and demanded his parents admit the violent abuse they'd put him through, they refused. Instead, they called him a liar and shunned him. And for many years, Jeff's three siblings, too, sided with his parents, choosing to pretend that none of the abuse had ever happened, even though for years they had witnessed Jeff getting singled out for the most extreme violence. Their own childhood indoctrination led them to fawn and side with his—their—abuser, rather than empathizing with and standing up for Jeff as victim.

Then, thirty years after Jeff had been cut off from the family, his younger brother David finally reached out to him and said, "Brother, I believe you about the abuse. That *did* happen. And it happened to me too after you left home."

David decided that, rather than continuing to play along with the charade that they had all grown up in a happy, healthy, loving Christian home, he wanted to initiate a repair process that required holding their mother and father accountable for their abuses. He wrote a seven-page victim impact statement letter, detailing the specifics of some of the abuses committed, most of it perpetrated upon Jeff, with David and their sisters as horrified, terrified witnesses. Then he sent the statement to the whole family.

David's repair attempt was ignored, as if it simply hadn't happened. Instead, the rest of the family ramped up both their "PRAISE JESUS!"

and holy hallelujahs, as well as the denigration and assassination of Jeff's character.

During her rare moments of acknowledging that she and her husband may have sinned, Jeff's mother put the burden of forgiveness squarely on those she abused. As falsely empowered one-up folks tend to do when confronted with harms they've caused, she became hostile and accusatory, pressuring Jeff to just forgive and forget. Let bygones be bygones. Put it all in the past, and stop holding grudges. Be a good Christian!

In an effort to both support David's letter and defuse the family shame that he thought was causing the defensiveness and denial, Jeff wrote his own letter. But rather than holding his mother to account and backing up David's victim impact statement, he effectively short-circuited the opportunity for any repair or healing.

Jeff found himself feeling compassion for the self-loathing he believed his mother must have felt toward herself—why else would she have projected it so strongly onto him? He wanted to ease the burden of shame for the whole family and remind them of their essential goodness, partly so they would be less defensive and more willing to take responsibility for what they had done. "Ultimately, I believe that we were all brought together for a beautiful reason," Jeff wrote. "Each person brings something of value in this family, whether we easily see that or not. It's up to us to decide what we are made of and see if we are willing to heal this. I suggest that we put the past behind us. All of us are imperfect."

Jeff's letter suggested that accountability be shared by everyone in the family, as if the offenses were somehow equal, claiming that everyone had messed up and everyone was also beautiful, holy, and worthy of love, without acknowledging that the mistakes of his parents were criminal offenses and the understandable reactions of their victims were not. Rather than having David's back and joining together to hold their mother to account, he repeated the same indoctrinated religious teachings about forgiveness that too often place the burden of reconciliation only on the victim. It was those very forgiveness teachings that for too long had prevented him from confronting people who crossed his boundaries, holding abusers to account, seeking justice when he was entitled to it, and keeping himself safe from those who wished to harm him, including criminally.

Though Jeff had hoped to help the family heal, in the end he added to the problem rather than helping facilitate repair. His response enabled his mother and let his violent father and other family members off the hook. In other words, Jeff did what so many victims of one-up and boundaryless parents do: He fawned his abusers.

But he was also doing something else: *spiritual bypassing.* Spiritual bypassing is the tendency to use spiritual beliefs, practices, teachings, or language to avoid facing the raw, messy, and often painful terrain of human experience. It's what happens when we try to transcend or skip over the uncomfortable emotions—grief, rage, fear, shame, jealousy, disappointment—and avoid holding abusers accountable, all in the name of being "unconditionally loving," "high-vibe," "non-attached," or "enlightened."

HOW RELIGIOUS BELIEFS CAN ANCHOR IN OPPRESSION

You don't need to be indoctrinated into disempowering cultic religious belief systems, the way Jeff was, to fawn as a stress response—to reflexively say yes, avoid conflict, people-please, and overgive. Nor do you need to be religious to bypass seeing and repairing past wrongs, like Jeff's family did. But if you add religious indoctrination on top of a history of disempowering abuse, and spiritual bypassing on top of conflict avoidance and a tendency to avoid holding abusers accountable, you get a recipe for ongoing trauma.

Why? Many religions have belief systems built into them that are designed to protect perpetrators by shaming and blaming victims, causing them to point the finger at themselves and let their abusers off the hook. This enables ongoing abuse without accountability, embedding systems of oppression and empowering abusers to get away with even the most violent crimes.

Those of us subjected to religious indoctrination were raised to believe that unconditional love for others—love without bounds, without limits, and without boundaries—is the way to be a good and godly person. We grow up being told that if someone hurts us, we should forgive and forget, an indoctrinated belief that pressures victims to forgive quickly, without requiring the perpetrator to admit wrongdoing, express remorse, be held to account, or make amends. Victims are told that if they can't "move on," they're in sin or spiritually immature. Forgiveness ends up equated not with the natural release of resentment after repair, but with premature reconciliation and the kind of silence that bypasses justice and deepens the victim's trauma.

Many religious teachings also sanctify suffering, elevating martyrdom as a spiritual virtue and turning stoic endurance of abuse into a badge of holiness. This encourages victims to spiritualize abuse ("God is testing me," "This is my cross to bear"), rather than seek protection, justice, or healing. The assertion that God ordains all things, including your trauma, protects abusers by spiritualizing their actions. It also muddles morality, twisting the moral compass of believers to enable perpetrators and blame victims for not being forgiving enough. It encourages dissociation in the victim, prevents relational repair and accountability, and delays healing. When indoctrinated kids' impulse to protect themselves is met with "Everything happens for a reason," they grow up with learned helplessness, like the rats that couldn't stop the shocks no matter what they did.

Another common form of indoctrination is to frame submission, surrender, and obedience to the will of the spiritual leader or the head of the family as spiritual virtues, prioritizing unquestioning compliance with church or family authority over safety or personal autonomy. This teaches kids that standing up for yourself is rebellious, prideful, or sinful. Especially in patriarchal religious traditions, which teach that spiritual power lies in the hands of men, those unlucky enough to be women and children are discouraged from setting boundaries or challenging men's will, behaviors, or decisions—because to do so would be to go against the will of God. This teaches them that obedience is equal to righteousness, even if they're getting abused.

When kids raised like this grow up, these kinds of teachings interfere with relational recovery and can actually make unhealed trauma from childhood worse as the years go by, leading to what psychologists call "traumatic reenactments," where we play out our childhood wounding in our adult relationships. When someone is hurting us, the healthy response is to say "Ouch!"—to confront them and hold them accountable for the pain they have caused, even if they try to shirk accountability—and to stand firmly in our boundaries and in our self-worth. But these indoctrinated spiritual beliefs numb us to our healthy anger and shatter our boundaries, shutting down our desire and ability to stop other people from hurting us. They allow us to avoid confrontation and bypass the acknowledgment and release of uncomfortable emotions like anger, disappointment, and brokenhearted sadness that real relational recovery requires—all while anesthetizing us into believing that tolerating the mistreatment makes us good and noble people.

Instead of honoring the full arc of our grief or allowing our sacred anger to rise in defense of our dignity, we skip ahead to forgiveness. We hide behind mantras, affirmations, or pithy spiritual platitudes rather than tending to our own wounded, scared, or hurting selves. Instead of calling out imbalances or abuse in relationships for what they are, we meditate or pray about them, without saying a word to the person who is hurting us. Or we do yoga to numb out, rather than listening to our own pain or going to therapy. We mistake spiritual detachment for enlightenment. To quote Robert Augustus Masters, it's "conflict avoidance in holy drag."

To make the body ripe for optimal health outcomes, we have to deconstruct old indoctrinated beliefs and install new, healthier ones. Love protects, not enables. Forgiveness is not the same as reconciliation or restitution. Truth-telling and calling out abuse are not a betrayal or a sin; they're your birthright. Anger can be sacred and holy when it's used in self-defense or to protect the vulnerable, including yourself. Defending yourself from abusers does not mean you're less spiritual; it means you're healthier than those who excuse mistreatment or settle for less than the dignity, justice, and protection from abuse we all deserve.

We must be on guard for and avoid misusing spirituality as a way of bypassing justice-seeking and relational repair. Spiritual bypassing won't reverse relationsickness; it may even make it worse. While spiritual bypassing can feel safe and be socially rewarded, especially in spiritual communities, it often leaves our inner child abandoned, our nervous system dysregulated, our fawning behaviors untouched, and the trauma that causes fawning unhealed.

True healing means going toward the pain, not around it. It means being brave enough to feel what hurts, to be present with what's real, and to allow your wholeness—not your performance of peace or your dispassionate equanimity—to lead you home.

WHAT IS INDOCTRINATION?

Left to our own natural instincts, we tend to recoil from those who hurt us. Just like we pull our hand back when we touch a hot stove, we may move ourselves away, say "Ouch!" or "Stop!" and do what we can to protect ourselves from getting hurt again. To stay close to someone who causes us a lot of emotional or physical pain, rather than listening to those instincts and insisting that they stop, we typically have to be indoctrinated, intimidated into compliance, or both.

What does it mean to be indoctrinated? It's the process of repeating an idea or belief to someone, often in childhood but also in adulthood, until they accept it without criticism or question. Indoctrination interferes with critical thinking, healthy skepticism, good boundaries, and other self-protective behaviors. Any set of ideas or beliefs can be indoctrinated: religious or New Age spiritual beliefs, beliefs around gender or race or disability, ideas about sexuality, and more. Oppressing groups indoctrinate oppressed groups with ideas about culture and society and how one should or shouldn't show up in it as a way of shutting down their healthy protest, teaching them to enable their own oppression by silencing themselves, even when something doesn't feel right.

Many cultural belief systems indoctrinate children out of their natural authenticity, wholeness of emotional expression, and inherent self-protection. The message of *The Giving Tree* is just such an indoctrination, suggesting that it's noble and good to give until you're a sick or dead stump.

Sometimes this indoctrination is gendered. Girls grow up learning that their value lies in their appearance, that they have to be nice, polite, and pleasing to be acceptable ("Little girls hold their temper"). Their role in life is to nurture others, even at their own expense. They must protect others from their sexuality, to avoid tempting anyone, and to avoid being "too much." They internalize beliefs like "I'm only valuable if I'm beautiful," "If someone crosses my boundary, it's my fault," and "My needs are secondary."

Boys, on the other hand, learn that they must be tough ("Big boys don't cry") and must not feel or express emotions. They must win at all costs, regardless of what it takes to do so. Anger in boys may be acceptable, but sadness and vulnerability are not, and they must always know what to do and never ask for help. They internalize beliefs like "I'm only worthy if I'm successful or in control," "I have to earn love through performance," and "My power is tied to dominance, not connection."

Because of these indoctrinated beliefs about gender, girls may develop people-pleasing, fawning, or self-abandoning patterns, especially in the face of trauma, while boys may develop emotional repression, entitlement, a need to be in control, or dissociation from their inner world. Both genders may become disconnected from their authentic selves in order to be loved, accepted, or safe.

Families can indoctrinate their own beliefs, like putting on a front to protect the family image ("Don't air the family's dirty laundry," "We don't talk about that," "What will the neighbors/church/family think?").

Children then learn to keep secrets, disconnect from their feelings, and perform emotional harmony instead of embodying authenticity. They learn that it's not okay to mess up because it'll bring shame to the family, and that they are only acceptable or lovable when they make the family proud. These kids grow up believing their worth depends on performance, comparison, or approval, leading to anxiety, people pleasing, and burnout.

Families can also shatter a child's boundaries with belief systems that prioritize obedience over boundaries ("Because I said so," "Children should be seen, not heard," "Respect your elders, no matter what"). These teachings train children to override their natural instincts about what's right and wrong, mistrust their inner authority, and allow harm in the name of "respect."

One-down behaviors are often codified in family belief systems. Kids learn that they are responsible for how others feel and that it's selfish to do anything other family members might not like. They learn to neglect their needs in order to manage others' emotions, creating patterns of fawning, overfunctioning, and toxic loyalty. Some of these family belief systems hinge on a sense of guilt and duty, which also interferes with healthy boundaries ("Family comes first," "You owe us—we sacrificed everything for you," "You can't trust outsiders"). These beliefs trap adult children in obligation and emotional fusion with parents or siblings, at the expense of their freedom, well-being, and personal agency.

Which brings us to why understanding fawning as a survival strategy can feel so confusing at first, and why understanding indoctrination and how it works is so important to stopping fawning as a part of healing from relationsickness. Because of religious, cultural, or familial belief systems that anchor in and normalize fawning and enabling behaviors, these behaviors might not feel like a trauma response to the person who is fawning. Instead, they feel normal.

Many individuals oppressed by either a coercively controlling family system or an authoritarian belief system like white supremacy or patriarchy are so conditioned to fawn those higher on the hierarchical totem pole that they experience fawning as automatic and right. They may have even normalized fawning so much that they judge others who *don't* fawn as meaner or less compassionate, mature, or spiritually developed. Their indoctrinated beliefs lead them to police themselves into compliance. Once the indoctrination is complete, nobody on the outside is needed to ensure compliant behaviors. To heal from relationsickness, you have to deconstruct these indoctrinated beliefs to make space for new, healthier beliefs, like, "My needs and safety matter, and I deserve to be protected," "I am entitled to justice," and "It's healthy to care for myself rather than martyring myself for someone else."

Although all of us are vulnerable to many different kinds of indoctrination as we grow up, we've chosen to talk specifically about religious and spiritual indoctrination, and the spiritual bypassing that results, because it so deeply affected us both and came up so often among the radical remission survivors we studied. When these survivors mentioned what kept them from changing how they showed up in relationships *before* they got sick, they often explained that it was religion or some distorted form of spirituality that interfered with their ability to protect themselves.

Maybe you were lucky and nobody confused you or overrode your natural spirituality with any distorted spiritual or religious indoctrination. But since 85 percent of the population identifies with one of the world's religions, and many of the rest identify as "spiritual but not religious," it's statistically likely that some religious or spiritual indoctrinated beliefs have lodged in your consciousness in ways that might interfere with your healing and recovery. Healing requires holding people accountable when they hurt you, which spiritual bypassing belief systems don't allow. By contrast, believing you are worthy and deserving of protection and safety can facilitate real healing, recovery, and, potentially, better health outcomes.

ASSESSMENT

INDOCTRINATED THINKING PATTERNS THAT CAN PREVENT HEALING

Do any of these indoctrinated beliefs sound familiar? Acknowledge that they might be distorted thinking patterns and be willing to challenge them.

- [Fill in the blank: Saying yes/giving up boundaries/tolerating abuse] is the only way I can be part of a family.
- The way I am being treated is as good as it gets.
- I'm not [good/smart/special/pretty/rich/young/successful] enough to deserve someone kinder.
- There are two sets of rules in my [relationship/family/workplace/spiritual community].
- This person's abusive behavior is my fault. I caused them to do it.
- Boundaries are selfish and controlling.
- Men aren't allowed to have vulnerable emotions.
- Women aren't allowed to be angry.
- Saying no to this person means the relationship will end.
- My soul chose this person to help me [evolve/become more enlightened/learn to love unconditionally].
- I'm expiating karma from a past life.
- I'm earning myself a better reincarnation.
- This person is my twin flame and our relationship is supposed to stretch me spiritually.
- This is what God expects of me.
- It's my responsibility to heal this person.
- Expectations (or attachments) are the cause of all suffering and should be abandoned.

JEFF'S EXPERIENCE WITH RELIGIOUS INDOCTRINATION AND SPIRITUAL BYPASSING

For most of his life, Jeff had no idea how severely the religious indoctrination from the high-control family and fundamentalist church he grew up in had impaired his ability to protect himself in relationships. Although he believed seminary had been the most important part of his preparation to become a physician, by giving him a person-centered way of being with patients, he also appropriated that training in a way that cemented the indoctrination. Not only was he severely traumatized in ways that led to fawning behaviors; his religious indoctrination bolstered his certainty that tolerating abuse was the mark of a man of God. Even after he left the church behind, beliefs that encouraged spiritual bypassing, rather than pursuing the self-protection and justice necessary to heal from trauma, lingered.

For many years, Jeff used every possible spiritually bypassing belief he could to justify not holding people who mistreated him to account, never recognizing that those beliefs were really a cover for extreme conflict avoidance, arising from the child abuse he'd endured. Not until he woke up to how all those indoctrinated beliefs had devastated his life did his real recovery finally began.

To begin his healing, Jeff had to go back into the memories of abuse he'd buried deep within. He remembered his father beating him with that 2 × 2 piece of lumber, all while apologizing to Jeff for doing so when he knew Jeff was innocent. He remembered how, for many years, his mother would allow him to shower or bathe only once a week (a problem, since they lived on a farm, where he finished many days covered in grime). The bathroom door was never allowed to be locked, to ensure Jeff was complying with the bathroom rules, and she would watch him both bathe and go to the toilet until he was seventeen. His showers were timed, and when using the bathtub, the water wasn't allowed to warm up first and needed to be turned off before reaching the back of the tub, meaning he was always freezing while bathing.

For Jeff and his brother, there were no happy, nurturing, or comforting moments, no bedtime stories or cuddles—only a constant preoccupation with God and His threats. As children, Jeff's sisters got to sit on their parents' laps when they were scared or lonely. But if he or his brother came out of the bedroom at night, expressing fear because of a thunderstorm or bad dream, they were told to stop crying immediately, or they would be beaten. As his brother reminded him years later, "It was oral thermometers for the girls and rectal thermometers for the boys."

Jeff was the oldest child and the most spirited among his siblings. He initially rebelled against his mother's coercive control and domination, but was scapegoated for his attempts to break free of the abuse. She used fundamentalist Christian teachings and beliefs like "Spare the rod and spoil the child" to justify controlling Jeff's every move in an attempt to break his strong will and silence his protests. The responsibility of Christian parents, his mother believed, was to break the will of children so that they would grow up to become dutiful, obedient followers of Christ. She demanded instantaneous obedience from her boys, and would not tolerate having to ask two or three times. She wanted them out of their chairs and complying before she finished her sentence, or face the consequences.

Jeff was frequently reminded that this mandate to obey was not coming from his mother, but from God, and that the consequences for rebellion were steep both in this life and the next. She made it crystal clear that a rebellious spirit would spend never-ending eternity in the unquenchable, agonizing fires of hell.

Jeff internalized early on that, to survive, he'd have to white-knuckle his way through life on his own. He had no one he could tell about what was going on behind closed doors in his allegedly Christian home, so he battened down the hatches, learning to avoid conflict, suppress his desire for justice, and ignore his rage. And it wasn't until late adulthood, when he lost everything via criminal theft to someone close to him, that he was forced to see what until then he had not been able to: that the childhood trauma he thought he had left behind festered beneath the surface, leading him, in his adult relationships, to exactly recreate what remained unhealed.

In the process, Jeff came to realize that the profound equanimity he was known for was actually dissociated numbness. What he thought was a capacity to love unconditionally was a vulnerability to exploitation. What he thought was a vitality capable of carrying a workload that would make others crumble was also workaholism and intimacy avoidance.

He no longer had access to emotions like anger or grief, he realized. His response to being hurt or exploited by others was not to seek justice, by holding people who had behaved abusively to account, but to pride himself on how easily and quickly he was able to forgive and let others off the hook. The beliefs he'd been indoctrinated with as a child were still preventing him from taking the steps necessary to heal.

When Jeff told Lissa about the theft he experienced, she asked him why he didn't call the cops. Yet at the time, Jeff hadn't even thought to. Why? Because the Sermon on the Mount taught him that if someone slaps you on one cheek, the spiritual, loving thing to do was to turn to them your other cheek. If someone sues you to get your coat, you're supposed to give them your cloak as well. The fundamentalist Christian beliefs he grew up with meant Jeff struggled to say no to anyone who wanted something from him, no matter how entitled, exploitative, or demanding they might be.*

---

* Another reason Jeff never sought aid from law enforcement or lawyers was Bible verses like the one that instructs followers of Jesus to avoid the secular courts: "Furthermore, how dare you take a fellow believer to court! . . . Wouldn't it be better to accept the fact that someone is trying to cheat and take advantage of you, and simply choose the high road? At times it is better to just accept injustice and even to let someone take advantage of you, rather than to expose our conflicts publicly before unbelievers" (1 Corinthians 6:1–8). Far too often, churches or other religious groups use biblical admonitions or spiritual teachings like this as a way

Instead of teachings that hold perpetrators to account, followers are instructed to forgive "seventy times seven," with no caveat for whether the perpetrator is remorseful or changes their behavior going forward. The Bible also has multiple verses that promote loving without conditions,* without acknowledging that letting someone into your life should absolutely be conditional upon whether they are safe to have so close. Although plenty of religions teach adherents to love others in the same way they love themselves, sects like fundamentalist Christianity that demand obedience and conformity tend to emphasize or actively teach loving others *more* than oneself, which puts followers at risk of enabling others in ways that might lead to harm or self-neglecting to the point of relationsickness.

Because the Bible discourages empowerment with messages like "the meek shall inherit the earth," Jeff found himself giving his power away to anyone who asked for it—sacrificing not just his coat, but also money, career favors, even homes, all in the name of being a good, loving, "spiritual" person. He had a lot of things people wanted, and this indoctrination made him an easy target.

Part of the reason indoctrinated beliefs like these persist, even when they hurt the person holding them, is because these beliefs allow people who are mistreated to feel like good and spiritual people, rather than like victims. Indoctrinated beliefs can feed grandiosity, making us think we're smarter, wiser, more enlightened, more righteous, and generally morally superior to those who don't hold them.

As Terry Real explains, "The emotion driving both shame and grandiosity is contempt." Contempt turned inward creates shame, while

---

of not holding abusive leaders in the church accountable for all manner of abusive behaviors.

* Philippians 2:3-4: "Do nothing out of selfish ambition or vain conceit. Rather, in humility value others above yourselves, not looking to your own interests but each of you to the interests of the others"; 1 Corinthians 10:24: "Let no one seek his own good, but the good of his neighbor."

contempt turned outward creates grandiosity. For people with a tendency to have contempt for themselves because of childhood trauma, flipping that contempt toward other people they deem "less than" can give them a hit of grandiosity that counterbalances feelings of shame.

This can feed one-up behaviors in relationships, including all kinds of boundary violations in the name of missionary zeal—behavior Jeff saw in his mother, who used her own indoctrinated beliefs about breaking the will of children to justify her abuse. But it can also reward one-down behaviors, as it did with Jeff. His pride in his ability to forgive and unconditionally love those who hurt or betrayed him, no matter how extreme the abuse, mitigated the shame he felt for "allowing" others to hurt him to begin with.

Beneath the certainty in his own spiritual superiority, Jeff believed he was not entitled to basic human rights or the privilege of justice. And it wasn't until he was knocked off his spiritual high horse by being called out for those belief systems that he was able to let go of his spiritual bypassing, seek justice, and start healing his relational trauma.

HOW BEATING A CHILD IMPACTS THEIR MORALITY

We'd all like to believe that, if we were non-Jews in Nazi Germany, we'd have been the kind of people who would hide Anne Frank. But it turns out that, during the Holocaust, less than one-half of 1 percent of people who could have risked their lives to hide or aid the Jews actually did so.[35] What made rescuers of the Jews different from those who went along with the Nazi agenda, thus becoming enablers of human rights atrocities? As it turns out, it was the kind of home they were raised in.

In Samuel and Pearl Oliner's extensive research, summarized in their book *The Altruistic Personality*, people who rescued Jews were significantly more likely to have come from close, loving, and supportive families where parents emphasized reasoning and explanation, rather than physical punishment. These were family environments where accountability was important, but discipline was light and focused on fostering empathy, trust, and learning the difference between right and wrong.

Nonrescuers, on the other hand, were significantly more likely to have come from families that used physical punishment, emphasized obedience and conformity, and prioritized compliance with the demands of authority figures. These families were more authoritarian and hierarchical in nature, aligned with the idea that "might makes right." What was called "morality" was what the authority figure said was moral. Corporal punishment was not only significantly more prominent but also more likely to be experienced as harsh, abusive, malicious, and beyond what fitted the wrongdoing.

Because of all this, these children tended to grow up confused about power, with an operating system and world view that was driven by fear and an obligation to please authority figures, or become one, rather than by real ethics, integrity, and morality. These kids developed an upside-down moral compass, which caused them to turn on their Jewish neighbors rather than help them. The result is an upside-down "morality" that fawns and kowtows to power, even if doing so means hurting other people, including not trying to help them.

IT'S NOT JUST CHRISTIANITY

We don't mean to pick on the Protestant faith. But since Jeff was raised in the IBLP cult and then went to Princeton Theological Seminary, which is Presbyterian, and because Lissa was raised with three Methodist ministers in the family, it's the religion we've had to personally deconstruct the most. The same issues are at stake in any number of indoctrinating religious sects or cults. In addition to using teachings from the Judeo-Christian Bible, people we've known—ourselves included—have justified passivity, fawning, enabling, and overaccommodation of abusive people with spiritual teachings from Islam, Buddhism, Hinduism, and the Christian mystics, as well as with New Age spirituality, Helen Schucman's *A Course in Miracles*, the power of positive thinking, and the law of attraction. All of these belief systems can disable one's natural self-protection just as powerfully as biblical faiths.

Lissa had no clue how much she'd been fawning and enabling since preschool until she had an epiphany on July 4, 2014—her country's Independence Day. She had just come out of a relationship with a one-up lover she'd gone one down to. He'd betrayed her trust and crossed all of her explicitly stated boundaries; nonetheless, she had managed to salvage a friendship with him. Doing so had required employing every indoctrinated belief she'd ever taken on about love, forgiveness, and what it means to be a good and spiritual person. She found herself thinking, *I deserve a PhD in unconditional love. If I can love and tolerate even this abusive asshole, I have officially graduated from Love School.*

Then, as quickly as that first inflated thought came, a loving, compassionate voice crashed into her awareness. The voice said, *Sweetheart, you are only halfway up the mountain. You have proven you can extend compassion to the perpetrators of abuse. But you are just starting kindergarten when it comes to extending the same kind of unconditional love to yourself.*

Fireworks were going off at the Fourth of July party she was attending, but she felt like a bomb had just been dropped on her. In that moment, she felt flooded with grief as she realized how much hurtful behavior, abuse, and betrayal her fawning and enabling behaviors had allowed to continue unchecked, with no accountability and few, if any, consequences for the perpetrators. All this time, she had thought she was learning unconditional love. But she'd confused love with neurotic tolerance, boundarylessness, and premature forgiveness. She'd been betraying herself by not standing up to protect her own safety, rights, and values.

Lissa had been a civil rights activist since college, fighting for human rights for her adopted BIPOC sister. But she'd never thought to protest when others violated *her own* human rights. She felt a rush of love for her own tender-heartedness and naivete, vowing that things were going to change, starting now. But she also felt terrified by that vow.

Lissa realized that, as a child, she never knew that consent was something she had a right to grant or withhold. She had not been asked whether it was okay to share her private secrets in the family's annual Christmas letter or go to church three times per week. Nobody asked her whether she actually chose to save herself until marriage; she was ordered to do so. When her mother imposed rigid and unfair restrictions on her freedom and autonomy in order to make sure she toed the line of her mother's choosing, and Lissa appealed to her father, he just said, "Your mother's in charge."

Since rebelling against injustices she experienced had gotten her nowhere, she'd stopped even trying to say, "Stop. No. That's not fair." Instead, she used spiritual beliefs to justify trying to expand her heart to love people who mistreated her rather than calling out the injustice and demanding better treatment. She sincerely thought these abusive people were her spiritual teachers, testing her, pushing her to become more spiritually advanced. She believed they were teaching her greater tolerance, patience, and equanimity, so she could grow her capacity for the ultimate spiritual value—unconditional love.

A few days after her July 4 epiphany, synchronicity led Lissa to encounter former cult-leader-turned-psychologist Robert Augustus Masters's book *Spiritual Bypassing*. She felt called out—in a good but uncomfortable way—by a chapter describing a kind of naïve compassion rooted in the belief that we're all doing the best we can. She could see in herself how this caused her to cut people far too much slack, making excuses for other people's behaviors because "their trauma made them do it." Since all trauma deserves our compassion, she'd believed, it was therefore the right thing to forgive abusive treatment, rather than call it out. She'd never thought about how this justified her conflict avoidance and gave her an excuse to avoid protesting mistreatment, setting and enforcing firm boundaries, and demanding justice where it was due.

Lissa was afraid of her anger, afraid of confrontation, afraid of not coming across as a good, kind, loving, noble person. She hadn't realized that her "conflict avoidance in holy drag" wasn't born of love, but of fear—the fear of upsetting people, of getting blamed for being "unspiritual" if she pushed back. In other words, it wasn't love, it was fawning.

When you're under the spell of that kind of indoctrination, it's very challenging to break out from under it, because it can make us feel very good about ourselves. But basing our self-esteem on tolerating the intolerable and martyring ourselves in the name of unconditional love leaves us with a precarious sense of our own worth and value that can harm our mental and physical health.

As Masters writes, "When we mute our essential voice, our openness is reduced to a permissive gap, an undiscerning embrace, a poorly boundaried receptivity." This kind of naïve compassion "confuses anger with aggression, forcefulness with violence, judgment with condemnation, caring with exaggerated tolerance, and more tolerance with spiritual correctness."

Lissa hadn't had language for what she'd been doing before. She'd just called it "unconditional love." But it was really naïve compassion, justified by spirituality but lacking in guts, that bypassed accountability, justice, and health-protecting boundaries.

SPIRITUAL BELIEFS THAT BYPASS ACCOUNTABILITY AND JUSTICE

"Forgiveness sets you free."

How it bypasses: Pressures survivors to forgive before they're ready, often skipping the crucial steps of grieving, confronting harm, holding perpetrators of abuse to account, and/or setting boundaries. It can be used to let perpetrators, including religious leaders and spiritual teachers, avoid responsibility or consequences.

“Everything happens for a reason.” “You attracted this into your life.” “Your soul chose this.”
How it bypasses: Turns real trauma into a spiritual lesson too soon, minimizing suffering and preventing empathy or justice. It can imply that the victim somehow needed or chose the harm, thus placing the blame on victims.

“Choose peace and love, not fear.”
How it bypasses: Implies that fear, and related emotions like anger, disappointment, jealousy, and grief, are “low vibration” or unspiritual, invalidating survivors’ real, valid emotional responses, silencing outrage that might lead to justice or protection, and encouraging people to avoid “drama,” conflict, or legal action. Peace often comes after truth-telling, accountability, and boundaries, not from avoidance.

“Don’t judge others.” “Stop polarizing.”
How it bypasses: Shuts down discernment. Perpetrators are shielded by calls for nonjudgment and ending divisiveness, while survivors are criticized for “calling out” abuse or naming what happened.

“Let go of your story.”
How it bypasses: Dismisses the survivor’s narrative as an ego attachment or identity trap, invalidates lived experience, and prevents the integration that comes from telling one’s story and having someone believe and validate it.

“Focus on the positive.”
How it bypasses: Shames survivors with toxic positivity for expressing pain, rage, or grief—essential steps toward healing.

"Just meditate on it."
How it bypasses: Turns inward what should be addressed outwardly. While mindfulness can be healing and meditation can help you calm your nervous system, using it in place of dealing with your trauma, naming harm, or pursuing accountability implies that silence is the path to peace, not justice.

"Be here now."
How it bypasses: Disconnects survivors from the origin of their pain and short-circuits meaningful processing or repair by discouraging exploration of past trauma. It also denies that "now" is actively traumatizing for some victims.

"Your abuser is your greatest teacher."
How it bypasses: Even if people grow through trauma, that doesn't mean the abuse was good—or that the abuser deserves reverence. Survivors shouldn't be asked to spiritualize their pain.

"Let go of attachment."
How it bypasses: Discourages a survivor's legitimate desires for justice, acknowledgment, and/or safety. It can minimize trauma as mere ego clinging.

THE BABY IN THE SPIRITUAL BATHWATER

Does this mean religion, spirituality, and certain beliefs like these are always harmful? Absolutely not.*

---

* If you're looking for further reading to help you deconstruct which part of your own beliefs are helpful for your healing, and which are not, Lissa offers her own interpretation in the book *Love Bigger: An Exploration of Spirituality Without Spiritual Bypassing*, which she released on Substack (LissaRankinMD.Substack.com).

We sincerely believe a genuine, trauma-informed, non-bypassing spirituality can promote healing and make the body ripe for miracles. Spiritual practices like meditation can calm the nervous system, foster secure attachment inside and out, increase nervous system resilience, and improve stress physiology so the body can heal more efficiently. And spiritual beliefs that focus on the innate wholeness of human beings, rather than our brokenness, can bolster self-esteem in those who go one down, and foster greater empathy, accountability, and care in those who tend to go one up.

After years of interviewing radical remission survivors, we were both moved by how often they credited their cure with making contact with the part of themselves that was already whole and complete, beyond the warp and woof of time and space—that aspect of our being that can't be damaged by trauma and knows our worth and value. And when they did so without bypassing their traumas, when they began allowing their spirituality to help them heal instead, the health changes could be startling. Especially when they did this in a community of likeminded spiritual seekers, who were also committed to healing and not bypassing, those changes were often amplified.

The challenge is to retain these positive benefits without using spirituality as an excuse to tolerate unequal relationships, silence healthy protest, justify conflict avoidance, and let people who mistreat us off the hook. When we see others only through the lens of unconditional love and acceptance, it interferes with our ability to spot those who do not wish us well and advocate for ourselves when we are mistreated. As the cartoon horse BoJack Horseman said, "You know, it's funny. When you look at someone through rose-colored glasses, all the red flags just look like flags."

It has been a long, slow process for the two of us to deconstruct what is and is not aligned with our values—which spiritual beliefs and ideas we're going to keep and which ones we're tossing out as oppressive. We encourage you to dive into the depths of your own spiritual beliefs and find *your* "babies in the bathwater." Which beliefs are your "babies," helping you heal, nourishing and uplifting you, and supporting your growth? What "bathwater" beliefs anchor in conflict avoidance and prevent you from standing up for yourself and others, and are better left behind?

Healthy spirituality does not demand that we fawn in order to look or act or be seen as spiritual. It celebrates reciprocity in relationships, honors our right to good boundaries, rewards healthy confrontation, and gives us back the healthy anger that protects us. Mature spirituality does not ask us to value someone else over caring for ourselves. Instead, it helps us find a balance between self-care and care for fellow humans, between compassion for ourselves and compassion for others. It doesn't ask us to make excuses for when we're being treated unfairly, as when relationships are unbalanced or outright controlling or abusive.

Mature spirituality is not the naïve compassion of spiritual bypassing that lets abuse perpetrators off the hook, but rather the trauma-informed compassion that does not exclude any human being from being treated with dignity and respect—including you.

ASSESSMENT

AM I SPIRITUALLY BYPASSING?

Check yourself for the following behaviors or beliefs, characteristic of many spiritual bypassing belief systems:

- Do I use my spirituality to justify conflict avoidance when confrontation is necessary and healthy?
- Am I averse to any emotion deemed "negative" or "not spiritual," especially anger or jealousy?
- Do I practice "toxic positivity" to the point of inauthenticity in situations where anger, grief, jealousy, disappointment, or sadness would be more appropriate?

- Do I put the burden of forgiveness squarely on my own shoulders, forgiving others even when they're not remorseful, willing to be held accountable for mistreating me, or on board with participating in real repair?
- Do I tolerate being controlled or having my consent overridden in the name of being loving, kind, tolerant, easygoing, or nonjudgmental?
- Do I emphasize niceness or unconditional love to the point of not being able to take a clear stand or protect myself from others?
- Do I ever blame people who are suffering from legitimate victimhood (including myself) using beliefs like "Your soul chose this," "This is your karma," or "Anything you don't like in others is a projection of what you don't like in yourself"?
- Do I have difficulty staying grounded in reality, tending to talk a lot about spirituality or other "dimensions"? Do I spend hours each day engaging in spiritual practices while neglecting painful or difficult earthly realities that need my attention and activism?

BREAKING OUT OF SPIRITUAL BYPASSING

Years after Jeff sent his family the letter full of spiritual bypassing in response to his brother's attempt to get justice and repair, Jeff wised up to his spiritual bypassing tendencies. Through therapy, he began to deal with the fear of confronting his family about what actually happened; started getting in touch with his helplessness, grief, and rage; and committed to the long, slow process of deconstructing his indoctrinated belief systems—a process that is still ongoing.

As the scales fell off his eyes, he realized there weren't really two sets of rules, one that applied to other people and another that applied to him. There was just indoctrination pushing down trauma. But the truth is like a beach ball held under the water. You can try to suppress or hide the truth, but it will press inexorably to the surface, until, finally, it explodes into awareness.

Six years after that first letter, and three years after his sister Diana had died from cancer, Jeff finally wrote a more truthful letter to his family. This time, rather than using spirituality to minimize and dissociate from the real abuse he suffered, and rather than fawning his mother and parroting the coercive and cruel perspectives she taught him, he confronted his family with the painful truth of the impact of their abuse on his life and invited them into a real healing process, if they were finally willing to admit wrongdoing.

When it comes to dealing with perpetrators of abuse and seeking justice, as much as we might value compassion and feel tempted to skip straight to forgiveness, we must not bypass the steps of attempting to hold perpetrators of abuse to account, enacting consequences for those behaviors, and setting clear, firm boundaries. Yes, hurt people hurt people, and all trauma deserves our compassion. But if we don't hold highly narcissistic abusers to account, we are enabling them to do more harm—and not only to us.

When we break out of the trance of indoctrination, we are often horrified to realize that, by propagating spiritual bypassing beliefs and practices, we have not only allowed ourselves to be mistreated but also unintentionally hurt others. This can feel shattering, especially when we identify with spiritual values around being loving and kind toward others. Realizing that we have not always been as kind or loving as we believed—to ourselves or others—can lead to a painful inner fall from grace.

The good news is that a true spirituality catches us right where we fall from the grandiosity of our identification as a "good," "righteous," or "spiritual" person. Just when we might be tempted to collapse in shame, we are met in the temples of our own hearts by the unconditional love inside. Just when we might feel the startling sting of regret and remorse, we are cocooned and compassionately held by a love that accepts us and holds us in sacred space, no matter what.

We don't wish to take away any spirituality that supports optimal health, good ethics, compassion for yourself and others, and genuine altruism. Keep what helps! But we feel strongly that any healthy spirituality must abide by the sentiments of Harvard physician and anthropologist Paul Farmer, who said, "The idea that some lives matter less is the root of all that is wrong with the world." If a religious or spiritual belief inflates you at the expense of someone else, if it parrots bigoted discrimination against marginalized groups, if it causes you to submit to abuse without holding your abuser accountable, or if it glorifies martyrdom and enables perpetrators, we strongly believe it should be thrown out with the bathwater.

DECONSTRUCTING YOUR INDOCTRINATED BELIEFS

Whether your indoctrination comes from religion and spirituality, family beliefs, patriarchy, white supremacy, or any other kind of oppressive system in which some people matter more and others matter less, it's hard to change behaviors until you identify the belief systems and ways of thinking that anchor fawning and enabling into place. Here's how you can get started on your deconstruction process, so you can fawn and enable less, protect yourself more, and help your body have a better chance of getting well:

1. **Recognize that your beliefs might be preventing growth, healing, connection, and safety, and acknowledge the need to reconsider them.** Notice any resistance you feel even questioning whether you might have been indoctrinated. Accept that questioning beliefs is a natural and courageous process and you're not a bad person just because

you've taken on beliefs that turn out to be hurtful, false, or oppressive. Remember, sometimes it's not either/or. Spirituality can help you grow at one level but undercut or hurt you at another.

2. **Take an inventory of the beliefs you use to justify fawning and enabling.** List the beliefs you suspect contribute to these behaviors, exploring where these beliefs may have originated (family, culture, religion, education, media, etc.).
3. **Challenge each belief through critical thinking.** Is there any evidence this belief might not be fully accurate, helpful, healthy, or kind—to yourself or others? Is this belief limiting or false? Might it be leading you to tolerate abuse? Seek out alternative perspectives and viewpoints. Ask yourself the following questions:

    Who benefits from me believing this?
    Is this belief preventing me from standing up for myself or holding someone else to account?
    Is this belief causing me to harm others?
    Does this belief align with my personal values, or have I had to pretzel my morality in order to keep believing this belief?
    Can I think of even one example that invalidates or disproves this belief?
    Is my embarrassment at possibly being misguided preventing me from questioning or changing this belief?
    Am I afraid of losing or angering people I love if I question or change this belief?
    Is this belief aligned with fundamental human rights for all human beings?

4. **Learn about the mechanics of how indoctrination happens.** Read books, listen to podcasts, or attend conferences

and workshops that educate you about indoctrination and help support deconstruction. (We've included our list of recommendations in the resources section.) Seek out safe communities where other people who have been indoctrinated are deconstructing their old programming and getting curious about belief systems that are more compatible with optimal health, healing, social justice, and self-protection.

5. **Keep the "baby," toss the "bathwater."** Experiment with adopting alternative beliefs or practices that are more health inducing and nervous system regulating, keeping an open but discerning mind and understanding that a new world view may need to evolve over time. For example, maybe you'll keep your yoga or meditation practice, but you'll throw out some of the beliefs your yoga or spiritual teacher installed, like how you might manifest scary things in your life if you put your energy into going to a political protest or how your disease is the result of focusing on some negative emotion.
6. **Consider working with a therapist who specializes in deconstruction, trauma recovery, and life beyond oppression.**
7. **Grieve what you may have lost because of your old beliefs.** Some of your old beliefs might have provided you with comfort during a time when you might have needed it, but you might also have lost your health or years of your life in an abusive relationship or oppressive spiritual community because of them. Stay compassionate with yourself through your grief. You can't do better until you know better.

For more support around healing from indoctrination, listen to the *indoctriNation* podcast with trauma therapist Rachel Bernstein wherever you listen to podcasts.

CHAPTER 7

Can I Get Healthy and Still Keep My Relationships?

> *Some relationships are medicine. Others are poison. Learn to discern the difference.*
>
> —Lissa Rankin, MD

Amelia was diagnosed with rheumatoid arthritis at the age of forty-two. After years of worsening body pain, when conventional medical treatments and dietary changes failed to help her, and daily yoga only slightly improved her pain, she was desperate. Taking the *Becoming Unf*ckwithable* workshop with Lissa helped her realize that her problems went deeper than autoimmunity. She realized she was one down and boundaryless in a Level 2 relationship with someone who was one up and walled off. In other words, she was relationsick.

Her husband, Joe, was initially defensive when she tried to talk to him about her concerns. He hoped she would just drop it and they could get back to business as usual. But business as usual had left Amelia sick.

Amelia wasn't willing to accept her present reality as the new normal. But she also wasn't prepared to leave Joe, whom she loved and whose life was entangled with hers. She tried talking about it with him several times, and each time, Joe shut her down. He denied any merit to what she was saying about their marriage having something to do with her illness. He trash-talked Lissa and accused Amelia of joining a cult. He invalidated Amelia's feelings about their relationship and her illness, and tried to tell her how she should be feeling instead—grateful for all he'd done for her. He criticized her for turning into a bitch and waxed poetic about how sweet she used to be, back when she muzzled herself instead of speaking up about her concerns.

Then he blamed her for ruining the peaceful harmony of their relationship and making their lives full of conflict. Amelia wasn't used to speaking up or confronting Joe, but she recognized the DARVO pattern he was trying to pull on her: Deny, Attack, Reverse Victim and Offender. She called him out on this, and it just inflamed him more. So Amelia called for a time out and asked if they could table their conversation until the next day.

After they both calmed down, Amelia reminded Joe how much she cared for him. She told him she wasn't blaming him for her illness or calling him a bad person. She appealed to Joe's empathy and asked him to try to put himself in her shoes and imagine how hard it was for her to experience this much pain. Even if working on their relationship didn't improve her health, she hoped he would be willing to consider trying to improve their marriage, as a favor to her, just in case it could help.

He started to protest again, but she cut him off.

"No," she said. "I'm a no to you showing up with this energy when I'm making a valid request for my health."

Amelia explained how things might change between the two of them but appealed to his heart when she said, "I'm not against us. I'm for us. This is how I'm fighting not just for my health, but for our marriage."

Joe experienced this new resolve in Amelia as unsettling to their status quo, and he didn't like it one bit. But he could tell she was serious about trying to implement some of the changes she'd learned about in the workshop. He didn't like feeling out of control—but even more than that, he didn't want to lose her.

A year later, after Amelia implemented some of the tools she'd learned and got some help in therapy, her symptoms were significantly improved. Amelia hoped that Joe's joy at her improvement would be enough to motivate their continued relational recovery, but that wasn't what changed things. Although Joe was relieved that her health started improving, what really shifted the give and take in their relationship was when Amelia let go of her perfectionism, gave herself permission to rest more and do less, and simply stopped picking up the slack, even though it meant some balls got dropped and some chaos ensued.

Amelia, no longer willing to overfunction, stepped back, but it took Joe a long time to fully step into the void and meet the needs his wife once fulfilled alone. It was messy at first. He was often cranky and didn't handle things the way Amelia would have preferred. So she had to do her own work to resist stepping in and doing things herself, even when she wasn't feeling well. But when Joe realized she wasn't going to just collapse into her old ways, he stopped whining and started showing up.

The idea of letting go of overfunctioning may feel scary, especially if you've been the one in control. Amelia was anxious too. It's easy to imagine the things that might go wrong when you start outsourcing things to someone who may not be as competent in certain areas as you are. But it's also important to think about the things that might go right. Amelia was able to heal in her relationship, because as she pulled back and created more space for Joe to caretake her, her relationship healed around her. Dear reader, the same thing could happen to you.

IT'S NOT YOUR FAULT AND IT *IS* YOUR RESPONSIBILITY

At this point, we hope you understand how stress affects the body, how past trauma both contributes to chronic stress and makes it more likely that you will end up in an unbalanced relationship—and how both of these things, separately but especially together, can make you sick and get in the way of recovery.

Even when overfunctioning and doing far more than your fair share in a relationship is nobody's fault, you can still burn out, become resentful, stress your nervous system, and increase your likelihood of relationsickness. But in Level 2–4 relationships, overfunctioning is often an expression of fawning—a stress response based on the fear of upsetting someone in a one-up position. In these relationships, fawning is practically expected by the one-up person, who feels entitled to take advantage of their partner's overgiving, even when it makes the other person sick. Unlike the underfunctioning person in a Level 1 relationship, who often feels awful that they can't give their loved ones as much as they'd like, in Level 2–4 relationships the one-up partner typically feels entitled to take more—and may not want that to change, because they are benefiting from it.

The phrase "You break it, I'll fix it" perfectly captures the essence of the unspoken agreement many of us who tend to go one down internalized in childhood and reenact in Level 2–4 relationships: *If you fall apart, I'll hold everything together. If you explode, I'll clean it up. If you suffer, I'll sacrifice myself to make it better.* On the surface, this may look like love—like loyalty, caretaking, devotion—but underneath, it's driven by fear: the fear of abandonment, rejection, or conflict. The fawning, codependent part of us believes its worth and safety depend on managing other people's emotions and dysfunctions. So when someone "breaks" something—emotionally, relationally, or energetically—we automatically rush in to repair it, often abandoning our own needs in the process. True healing begins when we can lovingly witness this fixer energy, thank it for trying to keep us safe, and begin to set it down. Healthy love says, "You break it, you get to fix it. And I trust you enough to let you."

It's stressful to be in relationships that take more than they give, and where you feel like you need to fawn and fix another person's drama.

Even if you're getting other wonderful things out of the relationship, it's hard on your body. All that chronic inflammation and nervous system dysregulation, immune system dysfunction, and inhibition of physiological self-repair takes a toll. Regardless of the level, relationship imbalance is likely to play a role in your potential for recovery.

If reading this makes you feel guilty, as if you should have known better than to let yourself get into a relationship like this, or like you should have realized what was happening sooner—don't. It's not your fault. But now that you know, you have the chance to do things differently by seeing whether rebalancing your relationship could help you feel better.

Have you heard the story of the boiled frog? Common mythology has it that if you put a frog in a pot of tepid water and very slowly turn up the heat, you can boil the frog without the frog noticing it's in trouble until it's too late.* When you're in an unbalanced relationship, especially when there's a significant power imbalance, it's like being the boiled frog—*you may not notice something is wrong until you're already relationsick.*

Just as nobody asks someone if they want to join a cult, nobody starts a relationship by politely asking, "Will you consent to me taking advantage of you until you're a dead stump?" Anyone who thinks they're entitled to exploiting you usually starts by love bombing you with over-the-top expressions of affection and other behaviors that make you feel appreciated and special. Sometimes this is an intentional strategy on their part, but sometimes it is not; depending on their attachment style, it can be a form of reflexive fawning because of childhood trauma.

We're all vulnerable to eating up this kind of attention, but especially so if we weren't given enough unconditional love growing up. It's usually

* In reality, curious scientists have demonstrated that frogs are smarter than that and will jump out of the pot when they get uncomfortable, but it can still be a useful metaphor for understanding why we may stay in relationships that aren't always good for us.

some time before the other person starts making unreasonable requests or entitled demands. But next thing you know, you've lost your apples, branches, and trunk, and are wondering, "How did I end up here?"

We don't want you to wait that long. If you're in an unbalanced relationship that's draining your life force, if entitled people are still expecting you to caretake them while you're sick and not returning the favor, it might be hard to face the reality of what needs to change. But now that you know, you have a choice.

Not everyone who gets to this point decides they can put their heart and soul into healing their relationships so they can try to optimize their health outcomes—and we get that. But if you're curious how you might get started on this relational recovery journey, let us help guide you.

HOW TO HEAL YOUR RELATIONSHIPS

Having done it ourselves, we know very intimately how difficult it is to come to terms with what's happened in the past or is happening currently, so you can make sense of why we accept unbalanced relationships with people who give too little and take too much. We know how ungrounding and confusing it is to deconstruct indoctrinated thoughts, beliefs, and feelings that keep unequal power balances in place. And we know it can be frightening to think about rocking the boat and what might happen to your relationships if you do.

So now what? Assuming we've convinced you that there's a chance your health might improve if you change the way you show up in relationships, what's our radical road map to recovery?

First, let us acknowledge that you might need some interventions that a single self-help book can't provide. Thousands of books have been written about how to improve the health of your relationships, and we won't be able to summarize them all here. You might need to read more books, take more classes, and go deeper into your recovery beyond what this book can offer. (We'll give you our recommendations in the resources section at the end of this book.) You also might need one-on-one trauma therapy or couples therapy to help you heal and improve the quality of your relationships. But we will offer what we can: an overview of the Internal Family Systems (IFS) model, a way to become intimate and compassionate with all the ways your relational trauma may have shaped your psyche and body, and a six-step recovery process to help you discern which relationships can be healed and how to start healing them where you can.

Sometimes this can feel like climbing Mount Everest. The challenge here is that relational trauma inhibits our ability to get what we most need when we have been traumatized—*healthy, mutual relationships.* It damages our ability to trust that other humans are safe for connection and coregulation. And it also makes it harder to learn crucial relational skills.

With few role models demonstrating reciprocal relationships, and no required classes on how to develop, discern, and participate equally in healthy relationships, many of us grow up not knowing how to be in a relationship. Just like any skill, relationships take practice.

Not every relationship can be rebalanced, mostly because some people like being one up and refuse to get relationally healthy, even when they're making someone else sick. The relational recovery guide in chapter nine can help with Level 1 and 2 relationships. Level 3 or 4 relationships, which can be downright dangerous, need professional support beyond what a book can provide. If you think you might be relationsick because of coercive control, with or without violence, we recommend you seek out the experts—therapists, social workers, and psychiatrists who specialize in coercive control, narcissistic abuse, and, if it applies, cult recovery. If you need help getting out of a severely abusive relationship, you may also need law enforcement, lawyers, and shelters. While what we'll teach you in part two will help you know how to relate with more balanced power dynamics in the future, it may not be safe to apply to your current situation.

WHEN IT ISN'T SAFE TO CHANGE

For people in Level 4 relationships especially, we want to acknowledge that it might not be safe to do this kind of healing work until you're out of danger, or at least safe enough to begin to protect yourself differently. Sometimes, fawning is necessary as a life-saving survival strategy—until you can safely escape a dangerous relationship.*

As we prepare to invite you into part two, to learn about ways you might improve your health by changing how you show up in relationships, we want to make it clear that, as doctors and as fellow humans, we do not advise staying in dangerous, coercively controlling relationships. It will be nearly impossible to optimize your health outcomes as long as you're under the kind of intense stress of that level of relationsickness.

If this is your situation now, you can still learn and benefit from reading about the relational recovery road map we've outlined for you in part two. But until you're safe, we don't advise putting these behavior changes into place. It could put you, your kids, your pets, or other people in harm's way—and we don't want you or your family at risk.

IF I STOP OVERGIVING, WHAT WILL HAPPEN TO MY RELATIONSHIPS?

As you're examining your relationships and thinking about what it might be like to make some of the changes we're talking about here, it's normal

* Fawning may also be an ongoing necessity for people traditionally marginalized or excluded from majority-group opportunities; it can help prevent "death by cop" situations for BIPOC men, minimize the risk of deportations for immigrants, and reduce the risk of violence for women in domestic abuse situations.

to worry about how that might affect your relationships. When Lissa was in therapy processing her Level 2 relationship, her therapist was trying to help her understand one-up and one-down power dynamics and boundaries. She told Lissa that, without healthy boundaries, whoever had the most power would inevitably wind up being the one-up person. If Lissa didn't want to be one up or one down—if she wanted to balance the power in her relationships—she was going to have to shore up her boundaries and stand up for her needs.

Lissa's therapist encouraged her to get more courageous about rocking the boat with healthy confrontation, to complain less and make requests to get her needs met more, and to dial down intimacy and close access when someone wasn't interested in cooperating with helping Lissa get her core needs met. The therapist helped her understand how to make apologies and make amends for mistakes and things she'd done wrong in her relationships. She also showed Lissa how to participate in relational repair when inevitable disconnection arises.

Lissa felt overwhelmed by all that good advice—and afraid that, if she followed it, she was going to wind up all alone. If she stopped overfunctioning, set firmer boundaries, and stopped throwing her own needs under the bus to make everything easy for others, would any of her relationships survive?

"You might be right," her wise therapist said. "Some people might be using you and they might lose interest in you once you don't let them exploit you anymore."

Lissa got teary, thinking of all the times she'd cooperated with getting used, believing that was the only way to get love because she'd been raised to be the narcissistic extension of her mother (who treated her well, but only if Lissa let her control her). She hadn't realized how insecure she felt about whether people would like her if the relationship was more equal.

We want to be honest with you. While some relationships will improve through the relational recovery program we'll map out for you here, others will not survive the journey ahead. You won't know which is true of your relationships until you muster up the moxie to try.

It's scary to open the Pandora's Box of your own trauma—and maybe the trauma of the people you're relating with. It feels vulnerable to make requests or set boundaries, when you don't know how someone else is going to respond. And it may require a paradigm shift to realize you're entitled to repair when someone else hurts you, if they want to continue being close to you.

It's possible you're going to make changes the other people in your life are not going to like. Some people might blow up, storm off, accuse you of being controlling, or threaten to abandon or reject you. In extreme cases, they might get violent or threaten self-harm. (If you think you're at risk of violence, if the threat of violence is what's keeping you one down, we want to reiterate that your safety is key. If it's not safe to do this work now, please don't. Please seek professional help.)

It's also possible the people you're relating with will choose to change alongside you. They may not love your boundaries. They may not be thrilled about losing some of the ways you make their life easier. They may roll their eyes at you or make up hurtful stories about what a selfish person you are. But they'll care about you and the relationship enough to enter into relational recovery with you.

IF I START STANDING UP FOR MYSELF, WILL I BECOME A SELFISH PERSON?

We know, when you've spent a lifetime putting others' needs over your own, it's a big ask to suggest you consider your own needs at least as much as you do the needs of others. *Isn't that selfish?* you might ask.

Making your own needs at least as important as the needs of others is not selfish; it's self-loving. But lest you fear that we're going to encourage you to become someone self-absorbed and unlikable, let us assure you that enacting the healing work we'll be teaching you is not about turning kind-hearted, generous people into selfish jerks.

Some personal empowerment programs teach you how to flip from being disempowered and one down to entitled and one up. That's not relational recovery! That's just the other side of the same power-imbalance coin, swapping one-down enabler for one-up controller.

The empowering but balanced medicine in this book is intended to light a fire inside that burns hot but clean, releasing the destructive beliefs you might have been programmed to believe and replacing them with empowering, health-inducing beliefs that can help you heal. This work is about becoming *relational*, not the selfish one up and not the self-denying one down. It's about meeting other people as equals. It's about finding the middle ground where their needs matter *and so do yours*.

Healing your idea of what it means to be a good and loving person, while reprogramming a new, more courageous way of being, will help you live a life your body will love. It can improve not only your health but your relationships, your work, and your family life. It can also improve your activism in a world that needs more brave, badass people with loving, open hearts committed to creating a world where no lives matter less. Remember, you can't help others unless you put your own oxygen mask on first.

HOW RELATIONAL SKILLS ARE LIKE LEARNING TENNIS

We have loads of compassion for how daunting it can be to learn new ways of relating after what may have been a lifetime of selling yourself short to please someone else. We also understand how tough this can be for others you're relating with, who may have grown accustomed to your fawning behaviors and now expect your easy compliance. We don't want you to feel bad about yourself if trying to make the relational changes necessary is messy and hard. That's normal. When you grow up with people who failed to teach you healthy relational lessons in childhood and young adulthood, when you aren't sure *how* to share power or work as a team, it can activate something deep and primally wounded.

If it were the game of tennis we weren't good at, we might go easier on ourselves. We might not berate or loathe ourselves for not knowing how to play, when we were never given a racket or lessons. A beginner who accidently hit the ball into the next court wouldn't deny the ball went out of bounds. They wouldn't start defending their bad tennis or attacking their partner. They wouldn't conclude that they're a complete and utter failure as a human being. Even if they were playing with a tennis pro—*especially* if they were playing with a pro—they'd know it was just a mismatch of experience levels and skill sets, and hopefully feel inspired by the other player's skills. They'd realize that if they put in their ten thousand hours, they might get good at tennis too!

Of course, it's *not* tennis we're talking about, it's how to love and be loved in a mutual, equal, healthy way. And not knowing how to love because we never got taught cuts to the quick of our self-esteem, creating waves of shame, unworthiness, inadequacy, and sometimes compensatory grandiosity. When you only know how to gain admission in a relationship by paying the high price of letting yourself get exploited, or if you only know how to be the exploiter, love can feel forever out of reach. This can make survivors of relational trauma feel broken, defective, and unlovable. Especially when society tends to demonize or pathologize trauma survivors for the adaptative strategies we develop as workarounds to compensate for a lack of relational skills, even talking about this issue can elicit a flood of emotions.

We have to start thinking of relational skills as no different from tennis skills. If we didn't learn them—and how could we, if our caregivers sucked at it and nobody ever gave us lessons—we can't be expected to know how to be in an equal relationship. It's not our fault if we don't know how to have healthy relationships. But it is absolutely our responsibility to hold ourselves and others accountable, if relationship lessons are what's needed now.

The good news is that this is something within your power to do, something you might not have tried yet—and something that could potentially have remarkable effects on your health.

THE BODY IS A TRAILHEAD

In her essay "The Body Is a Doorway" (later expanded into a memoir by the same name), Sophie Strand, who waxes eloquently about her struggle with Ehlers-Danlos syndrome, writes, "The body is a doorway. And for survivors of early trauma and abuse that doorway is always open. Wide open."

We love imagining the body as a doorway, an aperture opening us to relational connections and disconnections. We can also imagine our bodily illnesses or physical symptoms as trailheads into our inner world. Just as we might park our car at the trailhead and go walking down a hiking trail to explore a national park, we can use our illnesses or symptoms as a starting point to walk down a path of self-inquiry, to discover what our body might be trying to communicate. We can use them to get curious about what might be causing nervous system dysregulation and the accompanying immune system dysfunction and chronic inflammation.

As has been popularized by the work of physicians like Gabor Maté (*When the Body Says No*) and Bessel van der Kolk (*The Body Keeps the Score*), the body can be seen as a repository for trauma, its symptoms betraying the secrets we try to keep or the memories we bury deep. But what if we see the body less as keeping the score or carrying the weight of our stories, and more like a trailhead that might point the way toward not just symptom relief but also unexpected healing of past or current trauma? What if the body can open us to deeper self-compassion, behavioral change, relational repair, and, dare we say, unconditional love?

When we approach the body as a trailhead, we can use physical symptoms, diagnoses, or disabilities as an opportunity to get curious about what brokenheartedness we might discover were we to explore the path that lies beyond with compassionate inquiry. Sometimes we walk down those trails and discover traumas unrelated to relationships, or nothing of relevance to our current disease processes. Other times, we discover the holy grail, the lynchpin of our therapeutic journey, the wounds we may have been trying to escape that, when healed, can finally make us whole—not just our inner world, but our physical bodies too.

As we now know, relational trauma can underlie or at least exacerbate disease, especially the common stress-related diseases that fill most doctors' offices. When we approach the body as a trailhead, many of us find that it gives us clues about unhealed trauma that's making it hard for the body to self-repair. And if we know how to use the symptoms and diseases afflicting our body as a portal to healing relational trauma, sometimes those symptoms and diseases really do get better. They even, on rare occasions, disappear altogether.

Diving in will require sacred courage. It takes courage to name the ways you've given too much, received too little, felt hurt or exploited, been manipulated or diminished, or even tolerated outright abuse, either now or in the past—or both. It's not easy to see clearly what we once needed to blur, deny, numb, or suppress in order to survive. It's a struggle to reckon with the ways we've self-abandoned to avoid abandonment by others. But look at you, dear reader! Here you are—still reading. Still listening. Still open.

If you're already dealing with a health crisis, it can feel overwhelming to add relational recovery to your physical recovery efforts. We understand if you decide this is not a path you wish to journey upon further. There's no shame in saying no. In fact, saying no is part of recovery. You have a right to your own autonomy, agency, and decision-making. Even if someone else has given you this book and is pressuring you to say yes, this has to be solely your decision. Nobody can choose to embark upon a relational recovery path but you. But . . . if you're curious, if you're at least interested in entertaining the idea of what this might involve, we invite you to continue on.

Maybe you're grieving or angry or confused or scared or wanting to slam this book shut and pretend you never saw what you now can't unsee. That's okay. All reactions are welcome. We want you to know that you weren't "too sensitive." You weren't imagining it. You were adapting to survive. Because you never should have been asked to overgive; tolerate what felt hurtful; or shrink, contort, or disappear yourself in the first place.

Now, as you turn the page, the tide is turning. Part two of this book is an invitation—not into blame or retaliation, or going one up after being one down—but into liberation, authenticity, courage, consent, and choice. It's an invitation to break fawning patterns without losing your tenderness or your care for others, into reclaiming your voice, your truth, your body, and your clarity. It's an invitation into learning how to stand up for yourself—not with fire and fury (unless that's needed), but with rootedness, grace, and self-respect.

We'll explore how to heal your trauma by getting to know the parts of you that participate in one-up or one-down relational dynamics. You'll learn how to make your fawning less reflexive, so you can choose more authentically when you're a "yes" and when you need to let someone down by saying no. You'll learn relational skills, like how to set and uphold boundaries, negotiate healthier agreements, and hold others accountable if they cross your boundaries or break agreements, without becoming cruel or passive-aggressive. You'll learn how to discern when repair is possible—and when the bravest, kindest thing you can do is to walk away, even if your knees are shaking.

You deserve love that doesn't cost you your health, your safety, and your vitality. So take a breath. Gather up your courage, without bullying yourself but also without backing away from what you might sense is coming. Be gentle with yourself. You don't have to do this perfectly. You just have to keep showing up—curious, compassionate, clear, confident—even when you're quaking in your boots. You don't have to be healed to take the next step.

As Alice Walker says, "The way forward is with a broken heart."

PART II

Healing Relationsickness

CHAPTER 8

The Medicine of Putting Yourself First

There comes a time when you have to stop crossing oceans for people who wouldn't jump puddles for you.

—Dr. Laura Schlessinger

Remember Ginger and Aaron from chapter five—how, instead of canceling his tour and staying home to caretake Ginger after her heart attack, Aaron found someone else to be his roadie and headed off on his next gig, leaving Ginger devastated and wondering if she'd just thrown years of her life away for someone who couldn't be bothered to care for her, now that she really needed it?

Once Ginger recovered from the shock of realizing she'd been wrong to assume that, in her hour of need, Aaron would be there for her as she'd been there for him all those years, and once the doctors gave her the green light to do so, she signed up for a workshop Lissa was coteaching with Dick Schwartz, the founder of Internal Family Systems (IFS), about trauma, medical illness, and how to heal. A person working with Aaron, with whom Ginger had become friendly, had suggested it might help her recover from her heart disease and prevent future issues.

Ginger learned that IFS is a compassionate, non-pathologizing, evidence-based way of healing trauma that views all humans as a constellation of "parts." Just as we might have the angel on one shoulder that wants us to make New Year's resolutions and the devil on the other that causes us to break them, we all have parts that polarize inside of us, including parts that want us to fawn and parts that want to push back and say no sometimes. We also have wounded inner-child parts—like those that feel scared to say no or exercise our autonomy because it wasn't safe to do so in the past—that can exacerbate those inner conflicts.

Lissa and Dick explained that medical illnesses can sometimes be related to these parts, especially caregiving parts or those that fawn instead of protecting us. If we see the body as a trailhead and walk down those paths into our inner world to get to know parts that may be using the body to get our attention, sometimes medical illnesses that were hard to treat can improve or even resolve altogether. Lissa and Dick were especially focused on people who give too much, who caretake everyone but themselves, who throw their parts under the bus for everyone else—and wind up sick.

They shared a story about a physician named Avery, whose experience Lissa had related in her book *Sacred Medicine.* Avery had breast cancer in her thirties but never told anyone—not her staff, not her patients, not her own kids. She endured the grueling treatment while keeping it all a secret. And then, a few years later, the cancer came back. When she worked with Dick and Lissa to use the cancer as a trailhead worthy of exploration, the cancer told her it had to come back, because Avery hadn't learned her lesson. She hadn't stopped throwing her parts under the bus the first time, and now the cancer was back to force her to prioritize her own needs, no matter what.

For this second cancer journey, she rallied the troops, telling everyone close to her what was happening. She took time off work, and started doing IFS therapy to heal the parts of her that her over-caretaking parts had been trying to avoid feeling. And at the time of the workshop Ginger attended, she'd been in remission for several years.

Ginger felt a little wobbly hearing this story, but she was also intrigued. Did she have hurt parts inside that might be related to her heart disease, and if she healed them, was it possible she'd have a better long-term health outcome?

During the workshop, Dick led everyone through a guided IFS practice, so the sick people in the room could get curious about whether there might be any parts involved in their illnesses. When Ginger went inside, she initially felt her heart contract, like it was in labor. She panicked, wondering whether she was having another heart attack. But as she followed Dick's instructions and tried to love her heart the way she would love an innocent little child, she felt it open. She'd thought she had a broken heart, but when she went inside, her heart told her it was a healing heart. It just needed her to tend to it more gently and more frequently, to protect it from being mistreated the way Aaron—and others—had.

After the workshop with Lissa and Dick, Ginger heard that Lissa and Jeff were teaching a workshop specifically for people who were in recovery from medical illnesses related to unbalanced or narcissistic relationships, and had a lightbulb moment. Narcissistic relationships? Was that what she'd been dealing with for over a decade? Was her husband a narcissist? Was it possible that her heart attack was related to her unbalanced relationship with Aaron?

From what she learned in that workshop and from the reading and therapy she did afterward, Ginger realized she had fawning and enabling parts that had been giving in to Aaron's demanding tantrums. Putting up with Aaron's entitled, overbearing one-up parts without pushing back against all the over-the-top demands wasn't helping either of them grow, heal, or thrive. It certainly wasn't doing her any favors physically. She realized she'd have to heal young, wounded parts that got too scared and intimidated to speak up, be assertive, say no, or set boundaries. These conflict-avoidant, fawning parts had been cooperating with other parts of her that had spiritualized the way she let Aaron exploit her without protest. She'd been telling herself that her ability to love and tolerate even her antagonistic, difficult husband reflected her spiritual growth, and how good she had become at unconditional love.

Now she was questioning all that, wondering whether, as Jeff and Lissa suggested, she might have been spiritually bypassing because parts of her were terrified of confrontation, saying no, or letting down not just Aaron, but anyone. All of this felt very confusing for Ginger. She thought of herself as a spiritual person, long priding herself on her generous parts and viewing herself as a giver. It felt uncomfortable when Lissa and Jeff explained that, while her giving parts had done a wonderful job helping her survive, in order to optimize her health outcome she might need to be as generous with *herself* as she'd been with Aaron, at least for a little while, experimenting with giving herself the medicine of "me first."

Ginger got to know her giving-tree parts and understood how she was making it easy for Aaron to expect her to handle all sorts of things that were not her responsibility. She realized she had taken on a variety of burdens that were not really hers to carry, such as bailing out Aaron whenever he did something stupid and reckless. She learned about dual relationships, like when you work with your romantic partner, become friends with a client, or date someone in your workplace, and how they can make boundaries confusing. She realized that it wasn't healthy to be both Aaron's wife and his personal assistant, and that Aaron should hire someone who could be "just business" with him, and therefore have an easier time setting clear boundaries. And she learned about "enmeshment"—how two people can get all tied up in each other's shoelaces when there aren't good boundaries to keep them separate enough.

Ginger also did the healing work of going deep inside her own heart to attend to the sad little girl from childhood who was neglected and abandoned. That little girl dominated a lot of her life. This little one felt so unworthy, so unlovable, and so much less valuable than powerful, smart, confident people like Aaron, that Ginger didn't feel deserving of having her needs met. With IFS, she learned how focusing on other people's needs served as a valuable "protector part," preventing her from sensing the painful emotions of that "unlovable" little girl, by feeling useful and needed. Winning the approval of other people by being helpful and serving everyone was a cheap substitute for the unconditional love she didn't think she'd ever get, but it had been better than nothing. Until it wasn't. Until her heart gave out.

Ginger sobbed when she closed her eyes and held that little girl in her own arms, mothering her the way she'd never had a mother's nurturing maternal love or a father's strong protection. She vowed to protect that little girl inside of her, by saying no more often. She promised her that she'd start standing up to Aaron, insisting on a better balance between giving and receiving.

Ginger wasn't sure how her healing journey would unfold or what the outcome would be for her physical health. But it was clear to her that this healing work was necessary and would lead to a happier, more fulfilled life, regardless of whether it resulted in better health.

INTRODUCING IFS

Internal Family Systems, founded by family therapist Dick Schwartz, PhD, is a trauma-healing psychotherapy developed in the 1980s, which over the decades has evolved from a psychotherapy model into a spiritual path, trauma-healing framework, and way of life embraced by therapists, doctors, coaches, and seekers alike. It bridges psychology and soul, offering a map for inner reconciliation that allows us not only to heal our wounds but to live a more integrated life, one that doesn't require us to cut off vital parts of ourselves in order to fit certain molds or please other people.

Dr. Schwartz developed the IFS model while working with adolescent clients with eating disorders like restrictive anorexia, who were often raised in high-achieving, perfectionistic environments and enmeshed with caregivers with high expectations. When working with these clients, Dr. Schwartz noticed that the inner world of the mind often mirrored the external family systems he was trained to study as a family therapist. His clients spoke of "parts" of themselves that had distinct feelings, beliefs, and roles, like anxious inner children, perfectionistic inner-critic parts, or parts that tried to numb them out and make them not feel.

Dr. Schwartz became curious about these parts' origins and intentions. He discovered that even the most destructive behaviors came from parts trying, in their own distorted ways, to protect more vulnerable, wounded inner children who were carrying pain from the past, like parts that craved unconditional love and felt unlovable unless they pleased their hard-to-please caregivers and won their approval through overachieving. What emerged was a radical new framework for healing based on the idea that we're all made up of a multitude of these parts, like an internal family composed of little autonomous beings.

While some of these parts might cause us to act out in ways that harm ourselves or others, at the root of the IFS model is the idea of "no bad parts." It's not that parts don't sometimes lead to harmful action; it's that they have good intentions and think they're helping us, even if they're also hurting ourselves or others. Their main goal is to prevent us from getting overwhelmed by a flood of painful emotions that they've sworn to protect us from feeling. Through the IFS lens, even our most seemingly scary and destructive parts—not just anorexic or bulimic parts, but also angry parts that lash out, addicted parts that try to numb the pain through drugs and alcohol, and even suicidal parts that try to escape it—are held with compassion and appreciation for their good intentions, even as we strive to contain them and help them relax so they don't have to act out so much.

Also at the heart of IFS is the concept of the Self—a calm, curious, connected consciousness that exists alongside all our inner chaos and that can become the ideal healer for our parts. When we access Self energy, we can become intimate with our parts and open our hearts to them, listening to them with love instead of judgment, unburdening them of the pain they carry, reparenting those that didn't get adequate parenting, and restoring harmony inside our inner family. Doing so can transform our behaviors, help our nervous systems relax, bolster our immune systems, dial down chronic inflammation, and generally feel better—emotionally, physically, mentally, and spiritually.

Lissa was first exposed to IFS in 2014, and she introduced it to Jeff in 2020. We view IFS as an unusually clear map of our inner worlds, a good reflection of how our psyches are actually built—and what it takes to actually heal, not just psychologically, but also physically. What makes IFS unique is that it helps us understand why our parts behave the way they do, providing a path for healing that is not completely dependent on the fifty-minute meetings you might have with your psychotherapist, while offering ways to make sense of our sometimes-nonsensical behaviors (say, why we might give until we're depleted).

IFS is a helpful tool for overcoming overgiving. It offers us a map for figuring out not just *why* we fawn, overfunction, and prioritize others too much (as a wise, necessary survival strategy that kept us alive when we were young). It also offers the "how" of stopping those behaviors: not by bullying or hating on our parts, which only makes things worse, but by getting to know the brokenhearted inner-child parts those outer parts protect (such as those who couldn't comprehend why caregivers might not have loved us just as we are).

By turning our attention away from everyone we're giving to and instead turning inward—doing what IFS calls the "YOU-Turn"—we can stop the compulsive tendency to focus on others and begin giving ourselves the love, care, attention, validation, and support we didn't get as children. The YOU-Turn describes what happens when you stop putting all your energy, attention, emotions, or focus outside of yourself and go inside to check on what's happening with your own protective parts or exiles. The YOU-Turn is also a way to gain consent from your parts before saying "Yes," "No," or "Maybe," allowing you to take an inner inventory to assist in decision-making. When you point that finger of care and compassion back toward yourself instead of at others for a change, you're doing a YOU-Turn. That's how you avoid reflexive fawning.

We can't control what someone else does. The only person we have the power to change is *ourselves.* Doing that YOU-Turn can be a game changer when it comes to healing relationsickness.

The practice of IFS involves three essential healing tasks:

1. **Cultivating Self energy**—the calm, compassionate, curious presence that serves as the inner healer and parent to all your parts.
2. **Building intimate relationships with your protector parts,** the ones who have worked tirelessly to help you survive what once felt unbearable. As we learn to use the YOU-Turn to separate from these protector parts and approach them with compassion, Self can begin to lead the whole inner family with wisdom and care, helping the more unruly parts relax.
3. **Unburdening the exiles.** Our protector parts often guard tender, wounded inner children IFS calls "exiles": the parts of us that we banish from conscious awareness and store in the deep recesses of our psyche and nervous system. We earn "protector permission" so Self can approach these wounded inner children, who can be safely witnessed, retrieved from the scenes of the trauma, released from their burdens, and lovingly reintegrated into the system. When you're first beginning, this step might require the intervention of someone who can facilitate IFS, like a therapist, doctor, or other trained practitioner.

These three tasks are how we move toward true Self-leadership—a state where our inner world is guided not by fears or defenses, but by love, clarity, integrity, courage, and connection.

THE PART THAT'S NOT A PART: SELF

As Dr. Schwartz reinforces in his book *No Bad Parts,* all parts are valuable and full of gifts, even if they make some trouble for us or cause harm to other people. We all have parts we like and parts we don't like, and those polarized parts tend to make us feel confused or lead to behaviors that seem to interfere with the goals of more well-intentioned parts. When he was working with young women with eating disorders, Dr. Schwartz found that they often had one part that wanted them to eat, be healthy, and stop disordered eating behaviors, but they'd have another part that drove them to binge or purge or restrict to feel some sense of control, often because they felt out of control in other aspects of their lives.

Initially, Dr. Schwartz tried bullying the eating disorder parts, making the girls promise they'd eat and avoid binging. But bullying parts only made things worse. He tells a story in *No Bad Parts* about one girl who tended to superficially cut her arms when the pressure to adjust her eating habits increased. By the end of a particularly contentious session, she had agreed to not cut herself anymore. But when he opened the door at their next session, she had a big gash across her face. In his telling in *No Bad Parts*:

> I collapsed emotionally at that point and spontaneously said, "I give up, I can't beat you at this," and the part shifted, too, and said, "I don't really want to beat you." That was a turning point in the history of this work, because I moved out of that controlling place and took on a more curious approach: "Why do you do this to her?" The part proceeded to talk about how it had needed to get my client out of her body when she was being abused and control the rage that would only result in more abuse. I shifted again and conveyed an appreciation for the heroic role it played in her life. The part broke into tears. Everyone had demonized it and tried to get rid of it. This was the first time it had the chance to tell its story.[36]

When he finally gave up trying to fight or bully these young, hard-working parts, asking them if they would consent to "stepping back" instead and giving him a chance to get to know other parts in the system, he found that the destructive parts would relax, and a wise, loving, courageous, compassionate presence would emerge and know what needed to be done.

Dick would ask, "What part is that?" And the teens would say, "That's not a part. That's my *self*."

The Self is the incorruptible, beautiful place in all of us that can't be touched or hurt by trauma or pain. For a decade before discovering IFS, Lissa called this aspect our "Inner Pilot Light" and spent ten years publishing *The Daily Flame,* love letters from your Inner Pilot Light to your wounded parts. Jeff also discovered something akin to the Self, which in *Cured* he called PII: Perfect, Immortal, Indestructible.

In IFS, Self is that noble goodness at the center of every human being—the essence that Trappist monk Thomas Merton glimpsed when he wrote of seeing "the secret beauty of their hearts . . . the core of their reality . . . the person that each one is in God's eyes." Self is the part of us untouched by trauma, shame, or conditioning—the radiant awareness beneath all our defenses and wounds. When we're led by Self, we see ourselves and others through that holy lens: not as our strategies or our pain, but as who we truly are at our deepest core.

We think poet Marc Nepo describes it best. He writes, "Each person is born with an unencumbered spot, free of expectation and regret, free of ambition and embarrassment, free of fear and worry; an umbilical spot of grace where we were each first touched by God . . . Regardless of subject matter, this is the only thing worth teaching: how to uncover that original center and how to live there once it is restored. We call the filming over a deadening of heart, and the process of return, whether brought about through suffering or love, is how we unlearn our way back to God."

IFS gives us the "how" for this monumental task. This Self inside can help even our most destructive parts stop engaging in their harmful behaviors, not through strict, rigid discipline but through lovingly helping those parts feel appreciated and understood, so they can relax and act out less. When the wise, compassionate Self can witness the pain and burdened beliefs of our inner-child parts, and hold and reparent them, the parts that typically engage in harmful behaviors sometimes just stop, because they are no longer needed to push down, distract from, and bury unbearable pain. And when Self develops this kind of compassionate relationship with our protector and exile parts, something mysterious occurs. Both psychiatric and medical conditions can sometimes get much better, in seemingly miraculous ways.

In his work with clients, Dick saw that the healing that happens when Self reunites with parts isn't limited to a select few. While the process can take longer for people with complex trauma or strong dissociative defenses, with the right pacing, sequencing, and relational safety many people can experience meaningful access to Self. IFS holds that the essence of Self is unbroken in all of us, regardless of what we've survived. We don't have to develop it or earn it through spiritual discipline. Instead, we gently get to know the protective parts that block Self out of fear, helping them relax so that Self energy can emerge more reliably. When that happens, it often feels like grace.

GETTING TO KNOW YOUR PARTS

As we've discussed, IFS is based on the idea that we're all made up of a multitude of parts, little autonomous beings inside that make up our internal family. These parts compete for our attention and influence our choices, similar to the conflicting parts of you that might make a New Year's resolution and then struggle with it a few weeks later. Sometimes our parts gang up together to cooperate with an agenda, but there are often other parts that want just the opposite. Our struggle to resolve these inner polarizations is why we sometimes have trouble making decisions.

IFS teaches that we are born with all of our parts. They are innate aspects of the mind's natural multiplicity, not just products of trauma. Multiplicity, Dr. Schwartz teaches us, is normal and healthy. Every person, even those who grow up in ideal circumstances, have parts with different roles, desires, and perspectives. That said, what *does* happen as a result of trauma is that parts take on extreme roles. For example, a part that naturally protests being mistreated might go underground if you were beaten when you stood up for yourself. A playful or spontaneous part might be dampened after being humiliated for your exuberance. Or a part that naturally wants you to excel in learning might become rigid, controlling, perfectionistic, and self-critical after being shamed for making a mistake in school.

As Dr. Schwartz puts it in *No Bad Parts*, "We are born with all our parts, and they are all good. Trauma and attachment injuries force them out of their naturally valuable states and into roles that can become destructive. Healing is about helping them unburden and return to their original, valuable functions."

Understanding Your "Exiles"

All of us are born with vulnerable, vital, childlike parts, but many of us grew up with caregivers who violated the contract for care and made it unsafe to be vulnerable, needy, or exuberant. Many of us learned early that our natural states of being—our tenderness, our bright life force—were too much or not enough for the people around us. If our vulnerability made our caretakers uncomfortable or threatened them, if we got overwhelmed by our emotions and stuffed them down because nobody helped us learn to handle them, or if our innocent expressions of emotions like fear, anger, frustration, or sadness led to punishment or shame, we learned to hide those qualities and feelings away. These became our exiles.

In some families, a child's neediness clashed with a parent's depression or self-absorption; in others, a child's vitality bumped up against fear, trauma, or rigid religious beliefs about exuberance being sinful. And sometimes, what got these parts of us exiled wasn't the original wound but our reaction to it—the anger, grief, or fear that spilled out after we were hurt, only to be met with more rejection. Over time, these precious aspects of our being retreated underground, carrying both the pain of the original injury and the added shame of being deemed unlovable. In this way, our most beautiful qualities—our innocence, our joy, our sensitivity, our vulnerability—became the very parts we learned to banish.

Our exiles aren't the problem; they're the hidden gold we buried when the world told us our tenderness was too much. Because their pain feels radioactive, we mistake these parts for the toxin, when really, it's the shame, fear, and false beliefs they have been burdened with that are poisonous. So we lock them away, convinced we're safer without them. But what we've imprisoned in the dark are the very qualities that make us most beautifully human.

While we all have exiles, people who had "good enough" caregivers don't have as many. Because it was safer to be vulnerable, we learned to relate to those parts sensitively, with unconditional positive regard for our tender feelings. But if these parts were met with abandonment, neglect, shame, humiliation, or rejection, we learned instead to take on our caregivers' stances toward these parts and start rejecting, abandoning, shaming, ignoring, and feeling disgust toward them. We no longer need our caregivers to push those parts away; we do it ourselves.

Meet Your "Protectors"

Other parts, which IFS calls "protectors," take on extreme roles to make sure we don't get overwhelmed by all the unbearable emotions of those burdened exiles. These protector parts shape our personality and character structure, and together make up our identity. But they're not all of who we really are, which can be very healing to realize. We are neither as worthless nor as grandiose as parts of us might imagine we are.

At the 2019 IFS conference in Denver, Lissa saw a video about a fourteen-year-old boy in China who had murdered two fifteen-year-old boys, and who had been mute since the murder. The district attorney of his small village had been trained in IFS, and when she approached the boy in jail, she asked if she could speak to his mute part. She acknowledged that his murderer part was only a part of him, not all of him—and given just this tiny bit of space, he found a voice for his mute part.

The DA invited the boy's family, as well as the families of the two boys who had been murdered, to witness her working with the boy's murderer part. It was an extreme protector part, looking after a young, vulnerable, wounded exile that had been overpowered and devastated. Witnessing his tears and vulnerability opened the hearts of everyone watching, including the parents of the victims. And in an impulse of restorative justice, the boy's parents sold their home to give the money to the families of the victims, which helped bring healing to the village after such a terrible tragedy.

Protector parts develop to shield you from being overwhelmed by feelings of helplessness, hopelessness, powerlessness, confusion, unlovability, worthlessness, loneliness, sadness, terror, and/or disorientation from your exiles. One way to think of protector parts is as what in meditation classes they call "the monkey mind." These parts chatter away inside like little monkeys with endless commentary, worries, plans, and fantasies, distracting us from the painful emotions, burdened beliefs, somatic sensations, and memories of what our exiles went through. Those monkeys are voices we often grow to hate, like the inner critic, impostor syndrome, self-sabotaging parts, obsessive to-do list parts, and perfectionist parts, which tear us up or shame us when we make mistakes.

All of these parts *think* they're helping us, even though they might be hurting other parts and even making us sick. How could something like an inner-critic part be helping us? Often, if you get to know your inner critic, it will point you to a time, usually when you were quite young, when you were humiliated for not being good enough at something, leading the inner critic to come in and try to prevent you from ever making mistakes or being humiliated again.

Let's look at how some parts related to fawning and enabling might have come into being. Perhaps your mother ordered you to clean your room, but you were so engrossed in a book that you didn't hear her, and didn't comply. So she pulled you up by the scruff of your neck and took a switch to you as a way to exercise control over you. Or maybe she didn't even have to hit you. Maybe she just gave you "the look," which was so terrifying and humiliating to your vulnerable young self that you developed a hypervigilant part whose job it was to make sure you heard any order your mother made, so you could jump to attention whenever she demanded. While every parent messes up every now and then, if this happened repeatedly throughout your childhood, over time your reliance on that hypervigilant part might have meant losing the ability to slow down, listen to a request, filter it through your discernment and moral compass, and decide autonomously how to respond.

Similarly—and especially if there was violence in the home—if confronting your caregivers when they mistreated you didn't go well, a conflict-avoidant part might come into existence, protecting you by silencing your natural inclination to protest being abused, overpowered, or controlled. To suppress your natural anger, disappointment, frustration, and hurt, you might have developed a dissociative part that took you out of your body, either guiding you to a fantasy world or causing you to space out. Then, because you might have amnesia from when your consciousness was somewhere else, you might have developed a paranoid part, because it's scary when time passes and you're not exactly sure what might have happened to you. If things got bad enough, you might even end up with an addict part that attempts to anesthetize the pain, or a suicidal part that promises you that if the pain gets extreme enough, it's got a plan to get you out of there.

Even the parts that make up narcissism, like attention-seeking parts, love-bombing parts, manipulative parts, grandiose parts, entitled parts, defensive parts, parts that lack empathy, and perpetrating parts, have good intentions and think they're helping. Often, these parts develop because someone was the victim of abuse, and a part of them decided, *Never again will I be the least powerful person in the room*. Underneath all that bluster usually lives a scared, sad little child who feels like they're never good enough and who wasn't nurtured, loved unconditionally, and permitted agency and consent the way they should have been.

THE "HOW" OF SELF-COMPASSION

The goal of IFS practice is to do the YOU-Turn, becoming intimate with all of our parts, developing an understanding about their roles and the burdens they are holding. We need to make sense of what they are trying to protect us from, and eventually gain at least some degree of "Self-leadership" over them, so they don't just act out, with no boundaries or containment. In the process of developing this much deeper understanding about why and how our parts are acting the way they do, we learn how to negotiate the differences between our parts the way a good mediator might negotiate between two people in conflict. This helps us determine whether our parts are really in consent when other people want us to do something or whether we're "blending" with a part that reflexively fawns, as a kind of trauma response.

In IFS, *blending* happens when a part of us takes over the inner stage so completely that we lose access to our centered, witnessing Self. Instead of making decisions from the spacious, compassionate awareness that can hold a part with curiosity, we *become* the part—flooded with its emotions, hijacked by its beliefs, and convinced that its story is the whole truth. When we're blended, we might think "I'm furious" rather than "a part of me is furious at this person and another part of me loves this person." Rather than being present with our pain, we are possessed by it. The practice of IFS invites us to gently *unblend*—to create enough inner distance that the Self can re-emerge, hold the part with loving attention, and begin the sacred work of healing it.

This process requires first approaching our parts with compassion and curiosity rather than judgment, so we can be *with* our parts without denying that they are a part of us. If we deny that we have a compulsive people-pleasing part, we can't heal it. But if we can hold that part with love and compassion, we can unblend from it and help it heal so it doesn't have to compulsively fawn.

When we acknowledge the good intentions of our protector parts and let them know their impulses make sense from a survival perspective, these parts—exhausted from doing what they felt they had to do to protect us, and from being hated by other parts of us—start to soften and relax their extreme self-destructive and/or abusive behaviors. This allows us to stop compulsive behaviors we might have struggled to get under control, like fawning or freezing and dissociating when someone else gets angry. It also gives us the capacity to pause, regroup, and choose healthier behaviors, like saying no, standing up for ourselves if we're getting exploited, and taking better care of our nervous systems and our health.

Like exiles, protector parts also stem from good qualities, but they may have been forced into unnatural roles that hinder their ability to express their natural gifts. When we unburden the exiles they protect, those protectors can transform and take on healthier roles. For example, an inner-critic protector, once unburdened and no longer needing to shield an exile from messing up and getting attacked, might instead take on the role of a loving cheerleader who cares about excellence. Or a bankruptcy-inducing shopaholic part that needed to numb and distract us from the painful feeling an exile carries deep down can become the fashion consultant who creates creative style while thrifting.

When engaging with the IFS model, we must seek understanding rather than judging, condemning, bullying, or otherwise pushing away your parts. Prolonged or permanent behavior change almost never happens through bullying or demonizing our parts. If it did, our inner critics and self-help parts would be successful in making sure we kept those New Year's resolutions!

Still, it can be challenging to try to love the parts of us that get us in trouble, hurt other people, or otherwise prevent us from finally getting the inner peace, secure relationships, and good health we crave. How can we love and heal the parts of us that repeatedly give away all of our apples? Or even more challenging, how can we love parts that get us addicted, sabotage our dreams, hurt our kids, or impair our health?

IFS shows us how. It doesn't just blithely tell us to "be kind to ourselves." It shows us what that actually looks like in the moment, especially when we're face to face with a part whose behavior other parts resent or fear. Instead of trying to override, banish, or shame these parts into submission, IFS teaches us to turn toward them with curiosity and care. When we pause long enough to ask a sabotaging protector what it's afraid would happen if it stopped doing what it's doing, we make space for understanding. We begin to see that even our most destructive impulses were originally attempts to help us survive something overwhelming, opening our hearts to ourselves.

When these protectors feel understood rather than attacked, something profound shifts. The behaviors we hate—overdrinking, snapping at our kids, zoning out, procrastinating, or fawning—no longer have to act out or give away all our apples in order to get our attention, so we can help them heal. Because compassion is regulating, it brings safety online in our internal system, which paradoxically calms the very impulses that have caused us and others harm.

This is why self-compassion doesn't make our behavior worse—it helps improve it. When our parts trust that Self is leading with steadiness and warmth, we naturally have more access to impulse control, containment, clarity, integrity, and empathy. We don't have to white-knuckle our way into being "good." Our goodness emerges spontaneously once our system is no longer at war with itself. In this way, IFS doesn't let us off the hook. It puts us gently, lovingly back on it, supported by a wiser inner leader who can help us repair the harm we've caused, stop compulsive behaviors, deepen our relationships, and make choices that reflect our better selves.

BECOMING INTIMATE WITH OUR PROTECTORS

In the IFS model, two kinds of protector parts are trying to make sure we don't feel the suppressed pain of our wounded exiles. The first, "managers," try to protect you by preemptively warding off danger. Think inner-critic part, anxious part, financial manager part, worst-case-scenario catastrophizing part, people-pleasing compliant part, self-neglecting caregiving part, control freak part, and the like. Most fawning or enabling parts that may lead to chronic illness are proactive manager parts.

The main job of proactive manager parts is to ward off danger. They're the first line of defense, protecting the vulnerable, traumatized exiles from getting activated and thus evoking intensely painful emotions that feel like too much to handle. The biggest fear of most protectors is that these exiles will escape from their inner dungeons and flood you with intolerable feelings, and then you'll get overwhelmed and fail to function the way you need to.

The second kind of protector part is the "firefighters." While the managers are proactive in warding off danger, firefighters are reactive, showing up when the alarm bells go off, hoses squirting and sirens blaring, to put out the flames of overwhelming emotion that flare up from those burdened exiles. These firefighters are emergency backup, coming online if the managers fail to keep the painful emotions of the exiles buried. If anyone (including you) gets too close to the pain the exiles are feeling, they grab their firefighting tools.

These reactive firefighters tend to be more extreme parts, saddled with intense roles that often don't look like protection and are more likely to be pathologized by the medical and psychological world. These are the parts we tend to hospitalize, medicate, imprison, and demonize. Parts that create symptoms or diseases in the body are usually extreme firefighters. Think addict part, eating disorder part, bipolar part, perpetrator part, dissociative part, suicidal part, narcoleptic part, and so forth. In other words, pretty much everything in the psychiatric *DSM-5*.

Extreme firefighters can also show up as physical illnesses—or use some physical vulnerability in your body—to distract you from emotional pain or try to get your attention because you're self-abandoning or failing to set appropriate boundaries. Think migraine part, back pain part, chronic fatigue part, asthma part, or even cancer part. Parts that use the body may give you digestive problems, allergies, chest tightness, chronic joint or muscle pain, fatigue, and clusters of symptoms that, together, make up a diagnosable disease.

The IFS model does not suggest that these are purely psychosomatic illnesses. They are clearly real pathology in the body, and some illnesses may not be related to parts at all. Some diseases are multifactorial, caused not by our parts but by toxins like black mold, the ravages of inflammatory foods on our bodies, or a genetic predisposition to a certain illness. But our parts can also exacerbate even those kinds of illnesses.

As we know from part one, many illnesses derive from years spent with a dysregulated nervous system, where your brilliant immune cells and body parts have marinated in a toxic brew of chronic stress hormones instead of the healing ventral vagal neurochemistry of the parasympathetic nervous system.

However, from a different perspective, we can view nervous system dysregulation itself as an effort to protect you—as a firefighter part using the body to get your attention or to get the needs of other parts met. Your parts may know that the only way you're going to stop overfunctioning or let other people take care of you, instead of you taking care of them, is if illness knocks you flat.

PRACTICE

THE "GET TO KNOW YOUR PROTECTORS" PROTOCOL

After we turn our attention away from others and toward ourselves by doing the YOU-Turn, we become intimate with our protectors by practicing the "6 F's": Find, Focus, Flesh out, Feel Toward, beFriend, and Fears. Doing so also helps us unblend from our protector parts, so there's more space inside and more Self energy present.

To practice the 6 F's, first identify a protector part you wish to get to know, like a fawning part or maybe one that's related to an illness. Then:

Find the part in your body. Is it in your belly? Your heart? Your throat? Your pelvis? The top of your head?

Focus your attention on it. See what arises or happens in your body.

Flesh out: Get to know the part and how it thinks it's helping you. Does it have an image? A name? A color? A sound or smell? How close are you to this part? How old is it? Is it linked to a memory? Is it evoking feelings?

Feel toward: Assess how you feel toward the part. Do you like it? Not like it? Are you afraid of it? Are you grateful for it? If you feel open, kind, loving, or any of the 8 C's of Self energy—Curious, Calm, Compassionate, Creative, Courageous, Clear, Confident, or Connected—there's probably enough "Self" there to proceed.

If you're judging the part, don't like the part, or are scared of the part, then you've just identified another part—a judging part, a critical part, or a frightened part. The goal is to be in Self when you're getting to know your protectors. If the parts that don't like another part won't stop judging or being afraid, you might need to get to know the part that doesn't like the target part first. Especially when dealing with fawning parts or parts that use the body, other parts may fear those parts, be angry at them, hate them, or feel embarrassed or ashamed of them. If that's the case, you can get to know those parts too, understanding how they relate to the target part and seeing if they'll relax enough to let you keep going.

Sometimes, during this step, a protector will imitate the voice or qualities of Self, appearing calm, wise, or spiritually evolved, yet something about the interaction feels flat or slightly performative. These are what IFS calls "Self-like" parts—well-intentioned managers who've learned to mimic

Self in order to keep you safe from feeling what's underneath. They might say all the right things—"I'm curious about this part," "I'm sending it love"—but if you sense numbness, mental chatter, or an urge to rush through the process, you may be blended with one of these Self-like protectors rather than resting in true Self energy. When this happens, there's no need to force yourself back into "real" Self. Simply shift your attention toward the Self-like part with the same curiosity and compassion. Once that part feels seen and no longer has to perform, genuine Self energy—warm, grounded, and embodied—naturally reemerges.

Assuming Self is present, it's safe to move to the next step: befriending the protector part.

beFriend: You can befriend the part by asking the following questions:

- How did this part get this job?
- How effective is it at doing the job?
- How does it feel about the job it has?
- If it didn't have to do this job, what would it do instead?
- How old is this part?
- How old does this part think you are?
- What else does this part want you to know about itself?
- Assuming it has good intentions, what does this part want for you?
- What does it need from you?

Fears: Ask what this part is afraid would happen if it didn't do its job. Often the answer will lead you to a wounded, vulnerable part. For example, if you're working with a fawning part, it may be protecting a part that doesn't feel lovable, worthy, or valuable unless you're serving others or martyring yourself. The fawning part may have shown up to protect you from those unbearable feelings by convincing you that by letting yourself get exploited, you'll earn love.

Common fears protectors carry include the fear that you'll be overwhelmed with pain and won't be able to function, that Self isn't competent to do its job, that another part will take over and cause damage, or that the part will be kicked out of the internal family system and be annihilated.

For a guided IFS meditation leading you through the 6 F's of Getting to Know Your Protectors and preparing you to let your protectors take the pen and write, visit Relationsick.com.

THE RELATIONSHIP BETWEEN PARTS AND HEALTH CONDITIONS

Some illnesses are linked to protector parts in obvious ways. If you have alcoholic parts that help you not feel, you might wind up with cirrhosis. If you have parts that make you smoke, you might get lung disease. If you have sugar addict parts, you might get type 2 diabetes. If you have parts that won't let you exercise or cause you to binge-eat, you might wind up overweight, with obesity-related medical conditions. But even if you eat a perfect diet; work out regularly; avoid smoking, drinking, illicit drugs, and other health-eroding habits; and keep your weight within normal limits, a history of trauma and what it does to your nervous system can still increase your risk of illness. These are the patients we've studied in depth, the ones who do everything "right" and still get sick way too young.

Some of them report that their illnesses helped them finally have a legitimate excuse to not spend time with people who'd mistreated them. Others said their illnesses helped parts that were previously scared to set boundaries say no. Some said they'd been working in jobs that were sucking their souls, and getting sick gave them a much-needed reprieve or a disability check and a reason not to go back. Others were so exhausted from burning the candle at both ends, trying to fix everyone else's messes, that getting sick finally forced them to rest. Getting sick got them much-needed attention and help from others.

If their illnesses caused pain and suffering, that physical pain also worked to distract them from feeling overwhelming emotional pain. When your back is killing you, your focus on tolerating or relieving the physical pain can be so consuming that you barely notice the young, wounded exiles crying inside.

You never know what you're going to find when you go inside to get curious about parts that might be related to physical illness or injury. When Avery, the young doctor we met earlier in this chapter, approached her cancer as if it had benevolent intentions for her, asking it why it was there and how it meant to help her, it told her that when the cancer came the first time, it helped her prioritize her own self-care. But once she went into remission, she went right back to her old self-neglecting ways. Now, the cancer was back to try to get through to her again, to help her remember she deserves to let others take care of her too. But underneath that part was a very vulnerable young part that didn't get to be a child because Avery's mother was sick when Avery was young. Very early on, Avery developed a parentified child part that became the caregiver of her mother and brother, falsely empowering abuse that robbed her of the chance to be a little girl receiving care, instead of giving it.

That young "parentified child" protected an exile that carried burdens of worthlessness, fear, sadness, and shame. When Avery was able to go to that little girl, in Self, the girl cried and cried for the mothering she never got. Avery was able to promise that little girl that Avery would mother her now, the way Avery was mothering her own young kids. With the intense emotions and burdened energy of that little girl brought to the surface for healing, and the help of conventional medical treatment and more IFS treatment, Avery's cancer went into remission again. She came away from the whole thing grateful that her cancer journey kept her accountable to the deeper work she was committed to doing—caring for her own parts with the same devotion she'd been caring for everyone else all those decades.

In working with sick people who attended our trainings and workshops, we've heard the deeper stories of many others who struggled from medical illnesses. Yael, the descendant of a Holocaust survivor, suffered from gastrointestinal problems her doctors couldn't seem to diagnose, much less cure. With the help of an IFS therapist, she went inside her belly and found what IFS calls a "legacy burden." The horror of the Holocaust had taken up residence in her belly, even though she hadn't been part of that tragedy directly. When that legacy burden was healed and released using the IFS model, her physical symptoms improved.

When Harry put his attention on his chronic neck pain, he met a part that thought Harry needed to carry the weight of the world on his shoulders. He liked some things about that over-responsible part, because the altruistic acts of service it did for other people got him a lot of praise and approval. But it meant he was burdened with worries that shouldn't have been his. When he was a young boy, his father had been very violent with his mother, and he had felt helpless to prevent her from suffering. He wound up standing up to his father as he got bigger and stronger, and parts of him liked feeling like the hero. But it was just too much pressure, trying to be the hero to so many people with such enormous problems. When Harry started getting better with his boundaries, improved his capacity to say no, and stopped taking on so many of other people's problems, he was shocked to find his neck pain improving.

What Avery, Yael, Harry, and many, many more finally understood, not in a self-blaming way but in a self-compassionate way, was how their parts were really trying to protect them, by using their bodies to help them get core needs met, while other parts that hated the illness or were angry at the parts that were using the body began to relax. After doing the IFS work, they often found they could even feel grateful for their back pain or their cancer or their headaches, and for the parts that did what they felt they needed to in order to get core needs met or avoid being overwhelmed by painful emotions.

People in healthcare often get this completely wrong. They'll say someone is "somatizing" or the symptoms are "psychosomatic," which patients hear as "not real." They say it's "all in their head." Or they're "malingering," or getting "secondary gain." This shows an utter lack of understanding of how the relationship between trauma and disease works. These physical illnesses are physiologically real. Trauma lives in your nervous system, your immune system, your hormonal system. It's *in your body.* It's not just in your head.

As neurologist and traumatologist Robert Scaer says, "The body bears the burden."[37]

Sometimes, of course, diseases are not related to parts at all. Congenital diseases like cystic fibrosis, sickle cell anemia, Huntington's disease, or Tay-Sachs disease are pure Mendelian genetics. Other times, health issues are related to chromosomal abnormalities, as with Down's syndrome or Turner syndrome. Some kids are diagnosed with type 1 diabetes as infants or develop seizure disorders or cancers related to living next to a toxic waste dump. Epigenetic influences related to trauma can still affect disease outcomes in these cases, but these illnesses are not fundamentally about traumas held in your body or nervous system. Not all diseases are related to parts.*

---

* Epigenetics is the study of how behaviors and environmental factors (such as diet, stress, and toxins) cause changes that affect how genes work, without altering the underlying DNA sequence. These modifications, which act like switches to turn genes on or off, are often reversible and influence disease risk, development, and, in some cases, can be inherited.

However, when they are, that can actually be a promising sign. Because if a disease is related to parts, it means healing our parts could potentially change the course of the disease.

We have to be realistic. Sometimes we catch disease too late in the process, and there's not enough time for the long, slow journey of trauma healing to turn things around, or there's too much damage already done for medical treatment or our body's natural healing systems to repair what was damaged. But you might be surprised how quickly symptoms begin to improve once you identify the protector parts underlying an illness and become intimate with both those parts and the exiles they're tasked with protecting.

PRACTICE

GET TO KNOW PROTECTORS RELATED TO ILLNESS

If you're struggling with physical symptoms, get curious about whether there might be protector parts using your body to get your attention so other parts can get the healing they need. What might those parts want from you? Are there any core needs your illness is helping you get met, that you were otherwise ignoring?

Try not to let parts that might judge any answers that come up get too activated. Just stay open and curious and see if parts that are scared or don't like physical-health-related parts can step back and relax.

WRITING PROMPT: If my physical health issues were trying to help me get core needs met or distract me from feeling unbearable feelings because of past trauma, how might my symptoms be trying to help or protect me?

THE IMPORTANCE OF GETTING "PROTECTOR PERMISSION" SO SELF CAN UNBURDEN EXILES

In IFS, we say IFS practitioners are "hope merchants for hopeless parts." We are selling hope to both our exiles and our protectors, but mostly to our protectors. Our protector parts are the reason we struggle to get close enough to our exiles to heal them. And that's fair enough. Our protector parts helped us survive and got us here, even though they may be creating carnage in our lives today.

One cardinal rule of IFS, which differentiates it from a lot of other healing methods, is that we never override protectors or go to the exiles without their permission. Instead, we work hard to recognize and understand these protectors, to credit them for the guardian roles they play, and to unblend from them, earn their trust, and Self-lead them, so they no longer have to act out their extreme roles. Sometimes our exiles are so desperate to get out of their inner prisons that they'll storm the gates if you go to a workshop, see a therapist, or try to write the story of what happened to you. They'll overshare to a total stranger just so they can get a voice. But afterward, other parts can cause backlash—by leaving you with a vulnerability hangover, causing you to go on a bender, or maybe even making you sick.

That's what often happens in Large Group Awareness trainings and other personal growth workshops where some culty group leader plucks you out of the crowd, puts you on the spot, "intuitively" reads you, and needles your core wound in front of hundreds of other people, all in the name of personal growth. It may feel great in the moment, leading to catharsis and positive attention from the group. But afterward, when you go home, you crash and start binge-drinking, feel suicidal, or can't get out of bed because of pain all over. This can also happen in spiritual communities, actual cults, bad therapy, poorly run psychiatric hospitals, unsafe self-help workshops, twelve-step or other recovery programs that are not adequately trauma informed, dangerously facilitated psychedelic journeys, doctor's offices, and countless other ultimately harmful interventions that are intended to help (or pretend to).

Backlash is the natural consequence of going to exiles before your protectors are ready. It can look like a coincidence or even an accident, but it rarely is. It can look like tripping and falling, a psychotic episode, a migraine, dissociating, or falling asleep with no warning. Your protectors will sometimes do anything to make sure you don't feel what your exiles feel, and if you or someone else tries to go to them without the express permission of all your protectors, they may punish you.

When we've taught or attended IFS workshops, we've been shocked at how creative our parts get to prevent us from doing our inner work! When Dick Schwartz invited Jeff to attend his first IFS workshop, Jeff lost his keys, for the first time in his life, just as he was supposed to get in his car and drive to the workshop. He wound up missing the whole thing, and Dick said that wasn't the first time he'd heard that. When Lissa brought a friend to an IFS workshop for the first time, he totaled his car at the end of the first day and missed the rest of the five-day workshop, never making it to the part where we heal the exiles. Mission accomplished. Good job, protectors!

Protectors know what they're doing. They will pull out all the stops to ensure that you never let those exiles out of prison . . . *unless* you offer them hope that they can stop working so hard, let Self care for the exiles instead, and allow the protectors to take on lighter roles within your system. That's why we say we're hope merchants for hopeless parts. We offer protectors hope that, under the right conditions, it will be safe to get those exiles out of the prison of the past, unburden them, and integrate them back into present time.

Most of our exiles have given up hope that we will ever come and rescue them from their inner prisons. Most of our protectors have given up hope that we will ever free them from their exhausting responsibilities as jailers for our exiles. Our protectors typically don't want to keep doing what they're doing. When given the choice to choose other jobs inside the internal family system, every protector I've met chose to do something much easier and more fun! Our parts do not want to have to pull the cancer card or take us out with a car crash. They just don't realize there's any other safe way to live.

PRACTICE

UNBURDENING YOUR EXILES

Once we've used the 6 F's to Get to Know the Protectors to unblend, we can finally go to the wounded inner children (exiles), one by one, and safely do the real healing work.

1. Get protector permission. Start by checking with any protectors responsible for protecting the exile, and ask if it's okay to proceed. Sometimes when we begin to approach an exile, protectors will kick in. You'll suddenly feel sleepy or get a migraine or start thinking about your to-do list or convince yourself that washing the dishes can't possibly wait. These are all the work of our protectors, who will do anything to distract us from feeling emotional pain. We can't skip over or override these parts, because if we go to our exiles too soon, without first getting protector permission, we might get what therapists call "backlash"—adverse reactions that hit us later.

If a protector keeps stepping in, even after working through the 6 F's on your own, you might need a professional IFS-trained therapist to facilitate the next parts of this work, in order to work with those protectors, earn their trust, and help them step back and relax.

2. Connect the exile with Self. An exile carrying the pain of the past often feels abandoned and alone. Because it split off long ago, this part doesn't realize that within you now lives a wise, grounded, compassionate Self—an inner presence capable of caring for it in ways no one could before. One of the goals of IFS is to bond your exiles with Self. As Dr. Schwartz titled one of his books, you are the one you've been waiting for. Self becomes the primary attachment figure for the secure attachment you may not have gotten as a child, allowing you to care for your vulnerable exiles with less clinginess, neediness, and dependence on others.

Once the protectors have softened and allowed access, you can invite your Self to gently approach the exile in your inner world. It helps to close your eyes and imagine this meeting as a reunion between the "you of today" and the "you of then." The goal isn't to regress into the exile's pain or relive the old story, but to bring the strength, love, and steadiness of Self into connection with the exile, who has been carrying its burden on its own.

Sometimes the exile lights up with relief at finally being seen and loved. Other times, it may be wary, distrustful, or even angry that you've been gone so long. All of these reactions are natural. Like a rescue animal or foster child learning to trust again, the exile needs to feel your patience, consistency, and genuine care. Over time, this relationship between Self and exile becomes the foundation for deep inner healing—because the exile finally knows it is no longer alone.

3. Self bears witness to what the exile went through. Once the connection is made, the exile is invited to show your wise Self everything it feels, remembers, senses, and believes. There might be flashbacks, images, sensations, sounds, and intense emotions. Self simply holds space and witnesses the exiled part's pain, helping to coregulate the part and letting it feel seen, heard, validated, believed, and safe.

WRITING PROMPT: Let the exile write what it wants your Self to know about what it experienced.

4. Redo what should have happened. When the exile has shown Self everything it wants you to see, feel, and know, go back in time and enter the scene where it's stuck to do a "redo" of what should have happened. Don't think too much about this. The exile will instruct you on how it should have gone. With your inner vision, you can imagine redoing the scene, following orders from the exile to give it what it needed and didn't get back then. Even though it didn't really happen that way, neurologically your exile doesn't know this! This is how neuroplasticity works. You lay down new pavement on old superhighways of pain for a healthier, healing, disconfirming experience.

WRITING PROMPT: Let the exile write what should have happened in as beautiful a way as it can possibly imagine.

5. Retrieve the exile from the scene. When the redo is complete, rescue the exile from that stuck place back in time and, in your imagination, take it someplace peaceful and relaxing, someplace it feels safe and happy. The exile will tell your wise Self where it wants to go—a favorite beach, Grandma's house, a cloud in the sky tended by angels, or somewhere in your home now. Let it pick and then take it there.

6. Unburden the exile. Invite the exile to let go of all toxic beliefs, feeling states, and sensations that it has carried since the original traumatic event. Your exile will usually be happy to give these up to the elements—wind, water, fire, earth, or sometimes light. Real-world rituals can help memorialize this step. You might burn things representing the beliefs and feelings the exile wishes to let go of in an actual fire or throw stones imbued with those things into a body of water.

7. Invite in positive qualities. Call in positive qualities that might have failed to develop because of the trauma, like assertiveness, empathy, or the ability to protect yourself, to fill the space created by the unburdening.

8. Check in with protectors. Once the unburdened exile is safely in its new place with these newly installed qualities, invite the protectors who gave permission and stepped aside to let Self do the healing to come see how the exile is doing. Usually, the exile is relaxed or even blissed out, and the protectors feel happy and relieved. This also helps the protectors learn over time that Self does a better job of protecting and healing exiles than the (usually also young) protectors do.

9. Visit the exile every day for at least thirty days. The exile will tell you how often it wants to be visited by Self in your inner world in order for the unburdening to stick. Usually, it takes thirty days of daily check-ins to repattern neural pathways, hardwire them, and make the healing permanent. But if the exile gets stuck in the past again, it might need more witnessing. There may be more layers to reveal and heal, so go back to step 3, Self bearing witness.

WRITING PROMPT: Let Self write a love letter to the exile every day for thirty days. Let the exile write back and let Self know if it needs anything in the inner or outer world.

To listen to Lissa guiding you through an IFS meditation, facilitating you gently through some of the steps of an exile unburdening process, visit Relationsick.com

IFS PRACTICES TO HELP YOU HEAL AND RELAX YOUR NERVOUS SYSTEM

The more we unblend from our protectors and unburden our exiles, the more Self we tend to bring to our relationships and our lives. In this way, IFS becomes a non-bypassing spiritual path that helps us get closer to the best parts of ourselves, others, the natural world, and whatever we might call God, including the divine spark in us all, Self. The difference between IFS practices for cultivating Self energy and many other spiritual practices is that we never bypass our parts, nor do we negate our responsibility to work with our protectors and heal our exiles.

PRACTICE

IFS DAILY PARTS "CHECK-IN" MEDITATION

Some forms of mindfulness meditation might instruct you to see your thoughts like clouds in the sky and just let them pass without paying much attention, dismissing them as products of the ego that are not worthy of attention. In IFS meditation, by contrast, we don't bypass our parts or their concerns. We listen to our parts and let them know we're here to help them get their needs met. We don't demonize any part or stigmatize it as "just your ego." Instead, we become intimate with what they're thinking, what they're scared of, what their dreams are, and what's in need of healing.

> *Close your eyes and go inside. Take a few deep breaths to relax into your body and begin to bring your nervous system into an open, loving, ventral vagal parasympathetic state. Try to bring in qualities of Self, like the 8 C's: curiosity, compassion, calmness, clarity, confidence, courage, creativity, and connectedness. If it helps, call in any spiritual energies that align with your "baby in the bathwater" spirituality, like God/Goddess or other deities, spirit guides, angels, nature spirits, saints, mystics, or ancestors who might help you feel more connected to Self energy.*

Then, staying in your body and Self-leading any parts that might be tempted to dissociate, be present with any parts that need you. Check inside and see if any parts are front and center, needing you to be with them. Notice and extend kindness to any pain, tightness, or other physical symptoms in the body. If any emotions arise, be with them compassionately and with curiosity. Pay attention to whether you get any imagery—a symbol, a color, a song, a poem, or a flashback memory.

Try practicing the 6 F's of Getting to Know Your Protectors with these physical sensations, emotions, images, or memories. See if you can get a sense for how your protectors are trying to help you or protect you from difficult emotions. See if you can help them unblend, so you can get to know them and help them learn to trust that, in Self, you can do a better job caring for your wounded inner children than your protectors can.

While you're there, do your best to extend loving kindness to your parts. Ask them if they need anything from you or if they need you to ask for something from someone else, or speak up on their behalf to keep them safe. Make sure they know you've got their back.

When you're ready, thank any parts that came to the surface for giving you a chance to get to know them. Let them know you'll be back to keep getting to know them better.

To listen to a guided meditation recording of this meditation, go to Relationsick.com.

In the beginning, when parts first realize you're in Self and curious about listening to them, they may storm the gates. They tend to be so excited and relieved that you're finally present, listening, and interested in helping them that they can be little chatterboxes when you go inside. You can ask them to line up and take turns, and usually, they'll cooperate, once they know you're coming for them.

But once the initial rush is over—once you've been doing the daily check-in for a while, and things are reasonably calm inside—you can move toward a more advanced IFS meditation we call the "The Path."

PRACTICE

THE PATH MEDITATION

This meditation is closer to what mindfulness or Buddhist meditation would be like, only you'll be meditating with permission from your parts and care for how they're doing.

> *Close your eyes, and in your mind's eye, imagine yourself at a trailhead, preparing to go for a hike somewhere beautiful. Because you're working on earning the trust of your parts and helping them securely attach to Self, they might have some separation anxiety if you go on this path without them. So, first, check in with them, reassuring them that you'll come back for them, that nothing bad will happen while you go down this path. Let them know that if they let you do this, over time, it'll help you take better care of them. You can invite some of the older parts to look after and comfort the younger parts if they're worried.*
>
> *Then, only if they say it's okay, start to walk down the path, leaving your parts at the trailhead. If one of*

them starts following, chattering away, just remind it to go back with the others. See if you can quiet your mind and feel the space between your thoughts. You might even feel a vibrating energy moving through you as you unblend from your parts and take more space.

Walk on the imaginary path, separate from your parts, while you sit in silence for as long as you like. If you start noticing a lot of thinking, you can walk back up the path, check in with your parts, and try again if they'll let you. If not, thank your parts for granting you some time to rest in the space between their thoughts, feelings, and busyness.

To listen to a guided recording of this meditation, go to Relationsick.com.

WELCOMING PARTS RELATED TO RELATIONSICKNESS

Once you begin to know your parts through the IFS lens, you may start to understand more deeply what we explored in part one about how unbalanced relationships can make us relationsick. You might recognize in yourself giving-tree parts, or parts that overextend until your body rebels and your nervous system burns out. Perhaps you have fawning and enabling parts; Self-like spiritual bypassing parts; conflict-avoidant or passive parts; overfunctioning "busy-aholic" parts; distracting or disoriented parts; empathic parts; justice-denying parts; or dissociative, anxious, or depressed parts.

All of these parts are trying to help in the only ways they know how. They may be protecting exiled parts that feel worthless, hopeless, defective, or unlovable unless you're endlessly generous or self-sacrificing. The beauty of IFS is that, from this perspective, there are no bad parts.

Even the self-sabotaging parts that hurt you—or the perpetrating parts that hurt others—carry benevolent intentions once you take the time to understand them.

So what can you do, now that you recognize these parts? In the next chapter, we'll introduce you to the Six Steps from Fawning to Freedom, a process designed to help you break the habit of compulsive fawning and begin standing up for yourself with courage and compassion.

If you've spent a lifetime avoiding conflict, this won't be easy—but then again, real transformation rarely is. If the practices we suggest feel frightening, please know our hearts go out to you and your scared parts. We invite you to wrap them in the warmth of your own loving, nurturing Self energy. From that place, you may find the courage to show up differently in your relationships—and that just might save your life.

CHAPTER 9

The Six Steps from Fawning to Freedom

To love another is to cradle their storms and celebrate their light, while never forgetting that you are the keeper of your own flame.

—Lissa Rankin, MD

When someone is in an unbalanced relationship, there are typically many traumas to heal, a lot of psychoeducation to learn, and quite a few behavior patterns to change. Doing the IFS work can help with healing the trauma and learning to communicate with your many parts, so you don't defer only to your fawning parts. But healing relational trauma also requires developing new relational skills, like negotiating fair agreements, setting and enforcing boundaries, holding people accountable, repairing ruptures, and discerning when you need to end a relationship.

Relational recovery is two pronged. First, we must heal our relationships with our own parts. Because giving-tree types tend to abandon and betray our own parts in order to please other people, our internal family systems often hold a lot of mistrust. Committing to doing this deep internal trauma-healing work is a necessary pattern interruption, and learning to break the pattern of reflexive fawning so you can buy yourself time to do the YOU-Turn can be a game changer here.

But you can't stop there. Once you understand what your parts need from you, you'll discover that this requires you to confront, challenge, and negotiate with other people. This can be uncomfortable for them, because they may be accustomed to your compliance, and for you, because it's easier to avoid conflict if you reflexively do what others want and give people hall passes when they do hurtful things. Relational recovery requires *sharing power*, which means learning to advocate for the needs of your parts without bullying yourself or others and without unfairly neglecting the needs of other people's parts. The goal is not to flip into the opposite role in unbalanced relationships; it's to create real reciprocal relationships that benefit everyone involved.

Some relationships will be easier to rebalance than others. As we saw in chapter five, unbalanced relationships fall on a spectrum, from Level 1, where one partner overfunctions due to circumstances outside either partner's control, to Level 4, in which both coercive control and criminal behaviors are involved. Imbalances in Level 1 and 2 relationships have the potential to be rebalanced, as long as both parties in the relationship are game for a journey of relational recovery. But if your relationship is at Level 3 or 4, or if you're in a Level 2 relationship with someone who has no interest in healing and relational recovery, the steps we're recommending in this chapter most likely will not be helpful. You might have to extricate yourself from those relationships if you want to optimize your chances for a full health recovery.

If you're relationsick in a Level 1 relationship, caused solely by one relational partner's physical or mental health disability, disparities in trauma burdens, or neurodivergence, and if there's no evidence of narcissistic abuse, coercive control, violence, or other types of criminality in the relationship, treatment is relatively simple. Burned-out caregivers who themselves get sick as a result of over-caregiving sometimes need the relationship-rebalancing tools in this chapter less than they do more and better support. Certainly, we don't intend to oversimplify or minimize the difficulty of making this happen. And often, caregiving types have parts that aren't good at asking for help or receiving it when it's offered, which IFS work can help with. But dealing with caregiving a disabled loved one without throwing your own parts under the bus is beyond the scope of this book.

Accordingly, most of what we'll focus on in this chapter is rebalancing Level 2 relationships, wherein one party is more like the fawning giving tree and the other is more like the entitled boy. Some of these relationships might be romantic ones, but Level 2 relationships can also happen between parents and their kids, siblings, close friends, employees and their bosses, twelve-steppers and their sponsors, priests and their parishioners, and anywhere else power can be leveraged to unduly influence someone else.

The primary pattern we want to address is the tendency to say yes when you mean no and to avoid conflict or confrontation when pushing back would be appropriate. You'll learn to set boundaries, hold someone accountable if they can't or won't respect those boundaries, and participate in repair when relational connections inevitably get ruptured—because we're all flawed humans who make mistakes. We'll also help you determine when you may need to get more distance in your relationship or end it altogether for the sake of your health and well-being.

If you've been conditioned to believe that always doing what others expect of you is what good, moral, or spiritual people do, the tools we'll be teaching you in this chapter will help you deconstruct that belief so you realize that wise, mature, relationally healthy people do what they must to get their needs met, protect themselves from anyone who does not wish them well, and hold people who mistreat them accountable. We'll help you discern the difference between reflexive compliance and real consent, meaning that you've checked with all your parts, not just the fawning ones, to ensure they're actually on board.

People who get relationsick often say yes when they're not really a yes. This makes it sound like they're consenting when they're only complying. Many people struggle to tell the difference between compliance and consent, between an automatic trauma response and legitimate agreement. The good news is that understanding and working with the IFS model can help you do just that. Once you understand and can practice IFS, you'll know how to check in with all relevant parts and discern the difference between compliance from fawning parts that override the consent of other parts, and true Self-led consent, obtained by negotiating with all of your parts.

If the giving tree had known the difference between compliance and consent, she could have slowed things *waaaay* down each time the boy asked her to give something away. Instead of reflexively complying with his entitled requests, she could have checked in with all relevant parts of herself to see whether what the boy was requesting was good for them both. Maybe a part of her liked to feel useful and appreciated the opportunity to fulfill a purpose. Maybe another part really loved making the boy happy and enjoyed seeing his joy when she met his need. But maybe she had another part that was worried about her health as she gave more and more of herself away. Maybe she had a resentful part that started feeling used and unappreciated. Maybe she had a part that didn't feel worth much unless she was giving the boy whatever he wanted. Maybe she had a part that felt ugly, stripped bare the way she was.

If she'd known and considered all relevant parts, and worked out a plan taking these varied parts into account, she could have granted true consent, rather than just complying with what she thought the boy wanted. She could have negotiated to make sure the relationship was mutually beneficial and reasonably equal in give and take. She could have gotten useful information about whether the boy was still interested in her if she wasn't just giving unilaterally. And most importantly, she might have survived to live a long, lovely tree life.

Similarly, let's go back to Ginger and Aaron. If Ginger had the tools we'll be sharing with you, whenever Aaron approached her with a lot of entitled expectations, Ginger could have taken a pause, slowed things down, checked in with her parts, and really figured out whether she was a yes or a no. Aaron might not have liked that at first, but then he'd have had the chance to manage his expectations and learn to hear and respect Ginger's no. This would have been good for both of them, raising Ginger from her one-down position and bringing Aaron down from his one-up one, pulling them both into the healthier range, so they could be more intentional about making sure both of their needs were getting met. And if Aaron didn't allow Ginger to pause and check in with her parts, if he refused to tolerate Ginger's no, if he wasn't willing to negotiate to make sure her needs were considered equal to his, that would be important discernment information for her about whether their relationship was safe enough to continue.

WHAT LEVEL IS MY RELATIONSHIP?

Before we get into the relationship road map intended to help you figure out the "how" of rebalancing your relationships, we want to make sure that if you're dealing with an unbalanced relationship, you're crystal clear about which levels your various relationships might be. This will help you figure out whether the six-step process we'll be guiding you through is likely to be safe and effective—or not. Just remember: We don't know what's going to happen to our relationships until we start practicing the exercises in this book, begin breaking our fawning habits, and see how people react.

If, for example, you're the overfunctioning neurotypical partner of a person with ADHD, going through this process will help you understand whether your partner is someone who is simply neurodivergent (Level 1) or someone neurodivergent who also feels entitled to take more than they give and ambushes you or gets defensive if you try to have a conversation about rebalancing the relationship (Level 2). If you're the neurodivergent one, and in a relationship with someone neurotypical who understands and is sensitive to your challenges with keeping up equally with division of labor and responsibility, then your relationship is most likely Level 1. If you're neurodivergent and partnered with someone who doesn't make any effort to understand your differences, and shames and blames you for not helping out enough, then your relationship might fit more in Level 2, with your partner as the one up and you as the one down.

If you're being controlled in any of your relationships, and any pushback on your part activates even more attempts to control you; if standing up for your rights and fighting for more relational balance gets you verbally attacked, threatened, or blamed for expecting more—you're looking at something more than a Level 1 relationship.

How can you tell the difference between Level 2, which is sometimes treatable, and Level 3, which usually is not? Some of the one-up behaviors in Level 2 and 3 relationships may overlap. In Level 2, the one-up person may make everything about themselves, lack empathy, be attention seeking, need lots of validation, get defensive when asked to help out more, struggle with accountability when feeling ashamed, and, generally lack the skills to share power. However, a Level 2 one-up partner typically doesn't engage in a sustained campaign of power, fear, and isolation. Their behavior may be frustrating, immature, entitled, narcissistic, and self-centered—but it's not usually intentionally strategic domination.

In Level 3 relationships, however, the need to overpower and control you is intentional, strategic, and abusive. It's coercive control, which is illegal in some parts of the world (and should be illegal everywhere, we believe). Coercive control is a violation of your human rights. It's not a single event; it's a system of power designed to instill fear, confusion, dependency, and self-doubt, a *pattern* of domination that seeks to strip someone of their autonomy, undermine their sense of reality, and keep them trapped through manipulation, isolation, threats, and micromanagement. Coercive control doesn't just harm a victim's self-esteem; it erodes their sense of self, decision-making capacity, autonomy, and perception of reality and safety. Over time, it may leave the victim confused about whether they're even being abused. When coercive control also involves physical violence or other criminal behavior, we're calling those relationships Level 4.

We don't believe a book can help rebalance Level 3 or 4 relationships. We also don't believe it would be safe to practice the steps in this chapter that we recommend for Level 1 and 2 relationships. If you think you might be relationsick because of coercive control, with or without violence, we recommend you seek out the experts—therapists who specialize in coercive control and narcissistic abuse. You may also need social services, lawyers, and law enforcement, if you need help getting out of a severely abusive situation safely.

But if you're in a Level 1 or 2 relationship, the relational recovery tools in this chapter may help heal your relationsickness, improving both your health outcome and the quality of your relationships.

THE SIX STEPS FROM FAWNING TO FREEDOM

In Lissa's book *Mind over Medicine*, she taught patients the Six Steps to Healing Yourself as a way to navigate creating a self-guided, trauma-informed, holistic treatment plan for those managing a medical condition. In this chapter, we're going to riff off that six-step format and teach you the Six Steps from Fawning to Freedom, a tool designed to help you interrupt the fawning and enabling pattern that might be predisposing you to illness. We don't mean to oversimplify a complicated trauma recovery process. But we do want you to understand at least the basics of what you can do, now that you see how your relationships can be either medicine or poison, to bring greater balance to those relationships and help support your healing.

Remember, you can use these steps with any type of unbalanced relationships, not just a romantic partner but also an overbearing parent, a toxic friend, a controlling sibling, an adult child who bullies you, or an unethical caregiver (therapist, priest, guru, healer, etc.). Once you've interrupted this pattern and taken responsibility for changing the one thing you *can* control—yourself and your behaviors—your nervous system might finally be able to rest, and your body begin to self-repair.

First we'll review the Six Steps, then we'll break down each step into a series of self-help recovery exercises you can practice at home or with the aid of a couples therapist or trauma therapist. As you read each step, notice whether a part of you is saying, "Oh, no, the other person I'm in a relationship with is not going to let me do this." Maybe that's true. But changing that other person is not your job. Your job is to observe how the other person responds to the changes you initiate, and reality-check your relationship based on what you learn. You won't know how this is going to go until you try it.

The Six Steps are a sort of decision-tree action quiz. If your relationship is a Level 2 relationship, and the person you're in an unbalanced relationship with is an 8/10 on the narcissism spectrum and not a 10/10, you might be able to heal *with* this person, if they're willing to journey with you. If someone truly won't let you engage in these healthy, mature relational behaviors, it's possible you'll have to create more space or even go "no contact" with this person if you want a shot at healing. You won't truly know what someone else will tolerate until you try out these practices and see how they respond. People might surprise you when you show up feisty and "unf*ckwithable" and they realize you mean business and aren't going to be giving away those apples anymore without a fair negotiation.

Keep in mind that the Six Steps from Fawning to Freedom are intended for people who play more of the giving-tree role in your relationships, not for those who are more like the boy. A different kind of medicine is needed for those who have overactive exploitative parts and need to learn to manage high levels of entitlement or grandiosity.*

If you're in a relationship with someone who is more like the boy but is interested in growth, healing, and rebalancing your relationship, they may wish to read this with you, so they can support your growth and cooperate with your recovery journey. But you don't have to get buy-in from the other person to do this for yourself.

The Six Steps from Fawning to Freedom

Step One: Pause

If someone makes a request and you're tempted to reflexively fawn, or if you're triggered or being mistreated, remind yourself of your rights and your inherent value, take a pause, and, if need be, take some physical space.

Step Two: Do the YOU-Turn

Turn your attention inward and check in with your "parts." Get to know your protectors and unburden your exiles if you can do so yourself, or get help from a therapist. Notice any indoctrinated thought patterns. If need be, get a neutral third party to give you some feedback.

Step Three: Negotiate

In conversation with the person who has made a request or triggered your fawning part, speak on behalf of your parts, making self-advocating requests for what your parts need. Take turns with the other person, listening to what

---

* We recommend Terry Real's books and audio programs, and finding a therapist trained in Real's Relational Life Therapy (RLT) method, designed for grandiose people who want to heal relationally.

they need and want, sharing power, and negotiating appropriate boundaries and agreements. If helpful, document what you both agree upon.

Step Four: Troubleshooting

If you've been successful in coming to a negotiated boundary agreement, the next step is to troubleshoot whether both of you are able to follow through on what you've agreed upon.

Step Five: Repair the Rupture

If trust has been breached, work together to heal the breach and agree on a change in behavior for the future.

Step Six: Reward or Create Space

Depending on whether or not repair was successful, reinforce positive behavior or be proactive about creating more distance in the relationship.

Each of the Six Steps is a new node in a decision tree. If you can pause and take a break in Step One and the other person tolerates your pause, proceed to Step Two. If you can access Self energy and do the YOU-Turn in Step Two and then negotiate an agreement with the other person in Step Three, great! Proceed to Step Four. If you can both adhere to the agreement, or renegotiate a new one if you had a misunderstanding in Step Three, you're doing well. If one or both of you broke the agreement, but you're able to renegotiate the terms and then repair in Step Five, this is good news. There's hope for improving the health of your relationship, and in Step Six, you can celebrate your relational success.

If, however, the other person refuses to cooperate with any of these steps, well, to quote Mel Robbins, "Let them." That's information about their character that's worth knowing. Based on what you learn, Step Six may be creating more space from this person for you to be safe enough to let your nervous system and body heal.

Remember, you can't control how someone else will behave when you start prioritizing your recovery and getting healthier. But you can control how *you* respond. You have the right to push back against relationship imbalance in ethical, safe ways that respect both you and them. You are entitled to change how you show up, stop silently tolerating what is not okay with you, set boundaries, establish consequences if those boundaries are not respected, expect repair when relationship ruptures occur, and create more closeness or distance, depending on how someone else reacts when you show up differently. If you get stuck in any step of this process because the other person is not cooperating in a relational way, you always have the option to skip straight to Step Six and create space. But don't assume someone else will not let you practice these steps, because you might be wrong. It's possible that you're making assumptions about what they will or will not tolerate because of your past conditioning. Again, you won't know for sure until you try.

If you find that you can't do even Step One without a therapist, please don't beat yourself up. Depending on your trauma burden, some of these steps might simply be too scary to do without support. We don't want you to feel like there's something wrong with you if you can't practice these self-help steps without therapeutic aid. And even if you can't practice the steps yet, just having this map for where you'll be going can hasten the process and save you time and money in therapy.

Now let's dive into the "how" of putting these healing steps into practice. Before you get started, you might want to check which parts are active as you read through each step's practices. When a survival strategy like fawning is ingrained over a lifetime, breaking that pattern can feel absolutely terrifying to some parts, so you might notice a great deal of resistance. Typically, if an illness is related to a part that's trying to get your attention so you'll stop fawning and start giving more space to other parts, it's helpful to start by bringing into awareness what the fawning part is afraid will happen if it stops doing its job. Fawning parts are typically afraid of angry parts in other people, as well as angry parts within your own internal family system.

It can also help to connect with your wise, loving Self before you proceed. Take a few deep breaths to connect with whatever spiritual Source of love, safety, compassion, or connection you can access inside. Let this aspect of your being, your Self, give you a little pep talk. You've got this!

STEP ONE: PAUSE

If someone makes a request and you're tempted to reflexively fawn, or if you're triggered or being mistreated, remind yourself of your rights and your inherent value, take a pause, and, if need be, take some physical space.

Fawning stems from very low self-worth, so if someone makes a request and you're tempted to fawn, or if someone mistreats you and you're inclined to just ignore it, start by reminding yourself that you have rights, that you have as much value as anyone else, and that this is separate from anything you do or don't do. It's okay to pause before you react. In IFS, our goal, if there is one, is to get Self to lead our parts. As Lissa's therapist Nancy Morgan, PhD, once told her, "Self is in the pause."

Protector parts, like those that fawn or avoid conflict, tend to be reflexive. They can jump in so fast you may not even remember afterward what happened, because you might dissociate. But if you can take a breath and get some physical distance from the other person, you might be capable of unblending from those reflexive parts long enough to buy yourself a little time in Self.

Fawning is such a key survival strategy for some trauma survivors—so deeply ingrained, so terrifying to break from, and so somatic in its instantaneousness—that it's practically what Terry Real calls a "whoosh": a full-body rush of submission, the nervous system's reflexive flood of appeasement energy when conflict, disapproval, or threat is sensed or even imagined. Before the mind can even register what's happening, the body has already leaped in to smooth things over and keep the peace at any cost. Now that you know that fawning is a severe trauma symptom, and also the dire consequences fawning can cause, you can hopefully bring in just a little bit of Self energy to slow down that reactivity. The pause can help you assert and advocate for yourself.

Let's say your partner, boss, or best friend makes a request. Maybe it's a totally reasonable request, or maybe it's an outrageously entitled demand. It doesn't matter. You start with a pause, so you can bring in a little Self energy and consult with any relevant parts before you make an automatic decision.

PUSH THE PAUSE BUTTON

When we blend with fawning parts or reactive parts, we bypass our wise Self, leading to automatic, compulsive compliance or exaggerated reactivity. And any decision we make urgently is likely to be one that doesn't account for all of your parts and is most likely parts-led, not Self-led. You can learn to do this differently by pushing the pause button.

When someone makes a request, expects you to do something, or does something that triggers you, see if you can interrupt the automatic pattern of fawning and just pause. It can help to say "Pause" inside, just to create a little more space from the fawning part. Pausing allows you to move from your limbic lizard brain to your prefrontal cortex and your somatic awareness, where you can access more Self energy and have a better chance of making mature, healthy decisions.

If you're out in public, you might be able to do this by asking for a time out or closing your eyes to take a moment to yourself. If that's too awkward, you can always excuse yourself to the restroom. If you're a passenger in a car, you can ask the driver to stop, then get out of the car. If you're home, you can just step into another room. It's often helpful to get out of the other person's physical energy field, so you can feel yourself better and remind yourself that you're safe now (assuming that you are). Even if it wasn't safe in the past to disagree, say no, or confront someone, you're not in the past anymore. You can remind your young parts that learned to fawn that you're grown up now, and things are different in the present. Now, it's okay to let someone down, challenge someone, or say no, even if the other person isn't happy with your answer.

If someone is demanding an instant answer, say "Maybe" or "I'll let you know later" until you get more clarity. A noncommittal answer buys you time to do Step Two. If someone pressures you, hold your ground. Get backup if needed. Like *No*, *Maybe* is a complete sentence. You don't need to explain yourself. If someone has a tantrum and won't accept your pause, that's information worth having. Any reasonably healthy person who is not trying to control you, exploit you, or sell you something will be patient and give you time to make a decision. If someone refuses to accept your pause, you might need to skip to Step Six, where you create more distance from that person.

What might this look like in real life? Let's explore how Bryce, who struggles with long COVID, took a pause with his partner Eli. Eli called Bryce from work one morning and said, "Hey hon, I invited my boss and his wife to come over for dinner tonight. Do you mind whipping something up?"

Bryce's go-to response would typically be to blend with an accommodating part. He'd agree without even thinking about it or checking in with his parts, and then wind up huffing around or shit-talking Eli in his head, but doing it anyway, resentfully.

This time, because he's learning to slow things down in order to break the reflexive yes, Bryce buys himself some time by saying, "I'm not sure I'm going to be resourced for that. Give me an hour to consider your request."

When you're first getting started with the pause, reminders can be helpful. One client of Lissa's tattooed the word PAUSE on her forearm, to help her remember what to do when she froze, went blank, and was about to say yes without considering the consequences. Another client kept a worry stone in his pocket and stroked it when he was trying not to react without pausing. You could tie a ribbon around your wrist, put a sticky note on your computer, paint your nails red as a reminder to stop, or whatever else will cue you to remember to do things differently. You might even practice the pause with people you feel very safe with. You can let them know what you're up to and ask if they'll be practice partners, so you can try out pausing and notice what gets activated in your body, your emotions, or your thinking, so you can be with those parts compassionately and remind them, "You are safe—with me. You are loved—by me."

WHEN SELF-CARE FEELS SELFISH

If you've been living on emotional breadcrumbs, and especially if you grew up in an emotional desert where little to nothing was invested or nurtured in you, it might feel selfish to pause to think about yourself, like you are trying to create lushness and selfhood out of nothing. This is not uncommon.

Pausing itself can feel like rebellion. To stop, to breathe, to turn your attention inward instead of constantly scanning for others' needs, can awaken old alarms in your nervous system. But that pause is the doorway to Self energy. When you can slow down enough to notice and gently tend both your protective parts and your wounded ones, you begin to practice self-love without selfishness. The pause becomes the moment you shift from doing to being, from performing for love to receiving it from within. That simple act of inward attention can ripple out to transform your physical, emotional, and relational health.

The journey to loving and accepting your own parts is easier if you can find at least one person, and ideally a few people, who are nonjudgmental and accept you as you are, someone you don't have to fawn in order to feel safe. Don't expect them to do for you what ultimately you can only do for yourself, but understand that, paradoxically, you can heal yourself and you can't do it alone. A few safe people can become sanctuaries, holding a field of calm, compassionate presence that helps your nervous system remember what safety feels like. In their company, you may find yourself subtly entrained into Self energy, borrowing their regulated state, until you can more steadily become that sanctuary, that place of refuge, for your own parts.

Ultimately, you will become the one who provides the safety on the inside that you may not have had or do not have on the outside, and when you make that shift, others will show up differently around you. Instead of your nervous system firing threat signals because you rarely feel safe enough; instead of being in a continual fight, flight, freeze, or fawn stress response; instead of always wondering, "Who's got my back?" you can finally relax. Because YOU have your back. You are protecting you, no matter what someone else might do.

PRACTICE

CALL IN SELF ENERGY

During your pause, try practices that can put you in touch with more Self energy and help you unblend from parts.

- Take a few deep breaths or do a few simple yoga poses to get you into your body.
- Listen to music playlists that can calm your parts and open up more space.
- Get on your hands and knees and just move, with or without music, in any ways that feel pleasurable, safe, and embodying.
- Take a quiet walk out in nature while focusing on your breath.

- As long as you're not prone to dissociation, close your eyes and meditate. You might try "The Path" meditation from chapter eight.
- Sit down with a pen and let your Self write to your parts.
- Try an Intentional Creativity practice created by Shiloh Sophia called "metacognitive drawing." With the intention of calling in more Self energy, pick up a pencil or pen and move the writing utensil around the page without picking it up, drawing one long squiggle without concern for how it looks while pondering Self. See what arises in your consciousness as your pen moves.
- Do anything that tends to put you in a flow state. Paint, sing, run, dance, cook, chant mantras, swim, watch a candle flame flicker, do push-ups—whatever works for you!

RESTORING INTEROCEPTION

If you tend to dissociate, interrupting the fawning reflex will likely require more than just knowing what to do. In order to actually break the pattern, you'll need embodiment practices and/or somatic therapies to get back in touch with feelings and sensations in the body that have been numbed; learn to trust your own instincts again; and heal the parts that were not allowed to pause, say no, or protest without severe, often abusive consequences.

Interoception is the awareness of internal bodily sensations (such as heart rate, respiratory rate, hunger, fullness, temperature, and pain) and the way various emotions feel in your body. This includes the ability to determine which nervous system state you're in. When your interoception is working optimally, you should be capable of discerning when you're in a relaxed, socially connected state (ventral vagal parasympathetic), when you're in a hyperaroused fight-or-flight state (sympathetic), and when you're in a hypoaroused freeze-or-fawn shutdown state (dorsal vagal parasympathetic).

Interoception can be interrupted by certain kinds of trauma. If you've been taught to obey or attend to others instead of paying attention to the messages your body and feelings are trying to send you, or if you've suffered under the indoctrination of a religion or way of living that emphasized obedience and conformity over human rights and dignity, then interoception can be challenging. In order for pausing to be a real option, rather than just an idea you forget about in those watershed moments when you need it most, you might need to practice restoring your interoceptive capacities. The following exercises can help. Like any exercise, the more you practice them, the easier they will become.

PRACTICE

DEVELOPING INTEROCEPTIVE INSIGHT

You can begin to increase your capacity for recognizing the state of your nervous system through a few simple exercises.

1. Slow down your breathing.
Focus on the sensation of the breath entering and leaving your body. This helps ground you into your body and enhances your capacity for self-observation.

2. Notice your physical sensations.
Ask yourself, "What is my breathing like?" (for example, shallow, deep, barely noticeable) and "What's my posture?" (for example, open, tense, slumped).

Ventral vagal: You may feel warmth, relaxation, or a gentle flow of pulsing energy. Your breath will be steady and your chest may feel open.

Sympathetic: You may feel tense and jittery, with shallow breathing, a racing heart, and a sense of urgency.
Dorsal vagal: You may feel heaviness, numbness, slowness, or a sense of detachment.

3. Notice what emotions are present.

Ventral vagal: Calm, connection, confidence, curiosity, compassion, gratitude, and a sense of safety.
Sympathetic: Anger, frustration, anxiety, or overwhelm.
Dorsal vagal: Hopelessness, helplessness, powerlessness, terror, shame, disconnection, or apathy.

4. Notice the quality of your thoughts.

Check in with how you feel socially (for example, engaged, loving, irritable, withdrawn). Notice how you feel inside (safe or frightened, secure or insecure, tuned in or checked out). Notice how you feel about your loved ones (connected or disconnected, trusting or paranoid, anxious or relaxed).

Ventral vagal: Clear, organized, safe, trusting, and optimistic.
Sympathetic: Racing, scattered, focused on threats; aggressive or accusatory toward others or feeling an urge to flee.
Dorsal vagal: Foggy, slow, paranoid, disengaged, distracted, disoriented, ashamed, or self-attacking.

5. Journal or reflect on what you observed.

Write down or mentally note your observations, allowing any parts that arise in response to have a voice and take the pen. Over time, patterns will begin to reveal themselves—clues about how your body and your parts work together to create different states, and what tends to trigger certain shifts. For example, a critical email from a boss might send your system into sympathetic overdrive, while a partner's withdrawal might drop you into dorsal shutdown. You might also see how your breathing and thought patterns travel together. Perhaps your breath gets shallow and fast whenever an anxious part takes over, or you get foggy and frozen and stop breathing whenever an exile that feels shame is close to the surface. Some parts rev up the system to keep you safe by taking control, arguing, fixing, or fleeing; others slow you down or shut you off from sensation to avoid overwhelm. The more you can map these links between sensations, emotions, thoughts, and how they relate to your various parts, the more effective you'll be at recognizing what's happening in the moment. Once you can reliably state, "I'm dorsal vagal" or "I'm sympathetic," you'll be on your way to being capable of using Self-led practices to guide your nervous system back toward regulation.

6. Pair this awareness exercise with gentle practices to shift back to ventral vagal.

To upregulate from dorsal vagal hypoarousal:

- *Get active*. Use gentle movement, like stretching or rocking, to wake up your system. Stand on tiptoes or balance on one foot. Do jumping jacks or push-ups. Listen to upbeat music and dance. Hike, run, skip, or engage in other aerobic exercise.
- *Apply cold*. Drink cold water, splash cold water on your face, take a cold shower, open the window and get cold air on your face or body, or chew peppermint gum.
- *Use aromatherapy*. Try a stimulating scent like cinnamon, peppermint, eucalyptus, or a citrus blend.
- *Try the 5-4-3-2-1 exercise:*

  Find 5 things you can see (be specific, noting colors, shapes, or details).

Find 4 things you can physically feel, like the chair under your legs, your feet on the floor, the fabric of your shirt, or the air on your skin.

Find 3 things you can hear, like the birds chirping outside, the hum of the refrigerator, or the sound of your own breathing.

Find 2 things you can smell, like the scent of coffee or the smell of the fire burning in the hearth.

Find 1 thing you can taste, like the toothpaste from brushing your teeth.

To downregulate from sympathetic hyperarousal:

- *Diaphragmatic belly breathing.* Focus on your breath and inhale deeply through your nose for a count of four. Imagine your breath as a wave, gently rising with each inhale and falling with each exhale. Invite tension to leave your body with every exhale. Place a hand over your belly button and let your breath expand your belly, moving your hand outward with each inhale. Exhale slowly through your mouth for a count of six (or longer if it feels natural), as though you're blowing through a straw. Feel your belly deflate as the hand on it moves inward. Repeat for 5–10 minutes, or as long as needed.
- *Body scan and progressive muscle relaxation.* Starting at the top of your head, gently and slowly tense and then release muscle groups in your scalp, then your face, then your neck, then your shoulders, all the way down to your feet.
- *Soothing self-touch.* Place a hand on your heart or hug yourself.

> To move into ventral vagal: The polyvagal ladder shows us that we have to get from dorsal vagal to sympathetic and then get out of sympathetic in order to get to the ventral vagal state. So after doing whatever exercises you might need to facilitate shifting those states, reach out for connection, first connecting your wise, loving Self to your parts, and then asking for safe, coregulating conversation or touch with someone you trust.

STEP TWO: DO THE YOU-TURN

Turn your attention inward and check in with your "parts." Get to know your protectors and unburden your exiles if you can do so yourself, or get help from a therapist. Notice any indoctrinated thought patterns. If need be, get a neutral third party to give you some feedback.

Once you've paused and invited in Self energy, buying yourself a moment to be in choice, rather than automatic reaction, the next step in interrupting fawning patterns is to do the YOU-Turn and hear from all parts involved in the decision, as you learned in chapter eight, so you can determine whether you're blending with a fawning part or whether you're really in consent to give what someone is asking or expecting you to give.

As we saw in part one, fawning parts that override the consent of other parts are often linked to chronic medical conditions. Typically, these parts are trying to ward off what they imagine might happen if you do anything but fawn, feeling terrified that if you say no or do anything other than reflexively comply with what you think someone else wants, you might upset them and get yelled at, beaten, or abandoned. The key is that these parts aren't necessarily rational. Unless you are actively in a risky situation, those parts are often stuck in the past, operating out of unfounded fear.

Fawning parts usually get their protective jobs when we're young—when others were supposed to care for and nurture us, but didn't do so. As a child, part of you knew intuitively that you should have been loved unconditionally, without having to earn it by taking care of others or letting people exploit you. You shouldn't have had to earn this kind of love. It should have been your birthright. But little kids don't understand why some children are well loved, taken care of, and accepted unconditionally, while others either have to earn that love or learn to live on breadcrumbs. And because they rely on their caregivers for survival, they cannot psychologically handle believing that their caregivers are inadequate. It's simply too frightening. Instead, they process neglect, emotional abandonment, and even full-on abuse by deciding they must be the ones who are bad, defective, and flawed.

To compensate for all the overwhelming feelings created through this relational trauma, protective parts come to the rescue. If you didn't believe you were valuable and worthy, just because you exist, then you suppressed what your deeper Self knows. Instead, you learned to believe you're only worth loving if you're being useful, rescuing others, helping out, caregiving, or otherwise giving away all your apples. You learned young how to not only survive without adequate reciprocity in relationships, but how to be needless, wantless, easygoing, and accommodating. This helped you do what you had to do, such as caretaking siblings or managing the emotions of immature, irresponsible, neglectful, or abusive parents. Then, once you grew up, because that was all you'd ever known, you likely attracted romantic partners, friends, bosses, and others who also expected you to be the responsible caregiver and nurturer who expected little care or nurture in return.

This left you with parts that needed you to get physically or mentally ill in order to finally, *finally* get some care for yourself. The firefighters will do anything, even if it actually hurts you or hurts others, to make sure you don't get overwhelmed with emotion and loss. That's your protector parts' biggest fear: that if you actually feel what your young vulnerable exiles were not allowed to feel all those years ago, then you won't survive. They're afraid you'll be so overwhelmed with grief, anger, sadness, or even rage that you won't be able to get out of bed, do your job, care for the kids, and put one foot in front of the other—that you'll just become a nonfunctioning puddle of tears, or be overcome with rage and hurt someone. Since the only way you survived back then was because those parts overfunctioned, they think if they stop functioning, you will literally fail to exist.

Back then, if you hadn't stuffed down your feelings and kept the peace, the consequences to you could have been dire. That's not true anymore. But because your protector parts (managers and firefighters alike) are stuck in the past, they tend to think you're much younger and much less competent than you actually are. Rather than relaxing and trusting that it's safe to do so, they often think they have to work harder, try harder, and get you to neglect your own needs more. And then maybe, finally, someone will love you enough to take care of *you,* for a change.

While you'd never do this on purpose, getting sick can sometimes subconsciously help your parts accomplish that goal. Even if your close loved ones keep neglecting you—because they've learned to expect you to center their needs while ignoring your own—you might at least find a doctor or nurse who sits with you and cares for you, which to some of your parts might feel like a blessed miracle.

Firefighter parts do not understand the damage they can cause. They don't realize being physically or mentally ill can seriously mess with your life or actually kill you. All they care about is making sure the painful emotions and other burdens of your exiles don't overwhelm you. They will do anything to keep those exiles locked up in their inner prisons. They don't realize that the only way to heal is to welcome those little ones out of their cells, learn what they went through and witness their suffering, and help them finally get their needs met.

It's not just fawning parts, caregiving parts, or sick parts that use the body to get your attention or get you a break from caregiving others that we need to become intimate with and find compassion for. Other protectors may have allied with these parts to help you get your core needs met; chronically ill people typically have many protector parts constellated around more than one exile. Healing means systematically attending to all of these related parts. But working with fawning, overfunctioning, and caregiving parts is often a helpful place to start. Doing the YOU-Turn so you can get to know your protectors (and ultimately unburden the exiles they protect) is a key part of interrupting fawning behaviors.

While our main goal in Step Two is to help you stop fawning, the YOU-Turn is also helpful when you're triggered, so you can pause and investigate why. You might find that when you pause and go inside, you feel terror. If you were beaten as a child when you weren't compliant, you might have parts that are frightened someone will hit you if you don't obey, even if you're with someone now who isn't physically violent. You might have parts scared of being abandoned or getting verbally attacked if you fail to fawn. Or they might be afraid that something bad will happen to the other person, like they might die or kill themselves or go bankrupt, if you don't rescue them, caretake them, or give them what they need. You might also be terrified of missing an opportunity, making money, or seeming disloyal to someone who might be testing your fidelity or obedience. Or you might have parts that will call you selfish or blame you, or accuse you of not being kind or spiritual or good enough if you even consider standing up for yourself. No matter what your reaction is, doing the YOU-Turn slows these reactions down, so you can separate from and get to know all involved parts—not just the fawning parts but also those that might not want you to say yes or give away all your apples. When you do the YOU-Turn, you'll realize you probably have a lot of parts with many differing opinions about whether to comply with a request, rebel against it, or negotiate a more equitable arrangement.

Remember, doing a YOU-Turn is not about blaming yourself or accepting responsibility for what others have done wrong. Highly narcissistic individuals will often convince you that you are "at cause" for everything that happens to you—so if someone just mistreated you, it must be your fault. That's how they get away with even the most egregious behaviors. However, we sometimes overreact to something happening right now because of incidents in the past. But we can own that overreaction. When we do the YOU-Turn, we can take responsibility for how our needy, insecure exiles may make us act clingy or desperate. We can make sense of our sometimes-nonsensical behavior and get to know why we do, feel, and say what we do. Instead of just reacting every time someone pushes our buttons, pausing and then doing the YOU-Turn can help us interrupt old, dysfunctional patterns that can keep us stuck in unbalanced or unhealthy relationships. It helps us examine whether any of our parts are getting reactivated because of past traumas, so we can discover what our parts need from us, in Self. That way we can show up for them, and when needed, speak up for them to someone else.

As an example of interrupting old patterns, Lissa once ordered a salad at a fancy restaurant that she was going to split with someone else. She was answering a question, and before she realized it, the other person had eaten the entire salad. Feeling tears burn her eyes, she ran to the bathroom to do the YOU-Turn because she was too embarrassed to have a meltdown in public. When she checked with her parts on the inside, she realized that having her needs overlooked—having the other person fail to consider her own hunger while selfishly indulging their own—was a reenactment of what her father used to do. Understanding the reason she'd reacted so strongly didn't mean not speaking up to the person who ate the whole salad. But when she did go back, after comforting her own parts and finding out what they needed from her and the other person, she was able to speak on her parts' behalf and explain why what might have seemed trivial to the other person activated an eighteen-year history of feeling like her father had selfishly put his own needs ahead of her own.

When you pause and do a YOU-Turn, it gives your chronically dysregulated nervous system a chance to settle down and activate your body's natural self-healing mechanisms. Because bodies can't repair when you feel unsafe, creating more safety for your threatened inner children by protecting them and helping them get their needs met can be serious medicine for your physical body.

PRACTICE

DO THE YOU-TURN

After you've taken a pause to interrupt the reflex to fawn, next do the YOU-Turn to check with any relevant parts, to determine whether you're a yes, no, or maybe.

1. Close your eyes and check inside. Turn your attention to your inner world so you can discern whether your parts are in consent to do what someone has asked of you, or sense what's triggering your parts and tempting you to overgive, for fear of something bad happening if you don't.

2. Focus on your body and emotions, and identify parts using the "Get to Know Your Protectors" protocol described on page 220 in chapter eight. If someone has made a request and you've taken a pause, ask yourself:

- Which parts have an opinion about this request being made?
- Which parts want to do what I'm being asked?
- Which parts don't?
- Which parts aren't sure?

For example, you may have:

- Fawning protectors that fear abandonment or abuse if you don't do as you're told.

- An obedient part that believes a good, kind, or brave person does what others ask them to do.
- Enabling protectors that let others off the hook.
- Parts that spiritually bypass to avoid conflict or confrontation.
- Parts that dissociate the minute someone makes a request.
- FOMO parts that don't want to miss out if they say no.
- Delusionally hopeful, magical-thinking parts that think if you just keep doing what you're asked, you'll get the outcome you want.
- Angry, resentful protectors that are sick and tired of overgiving and feeling unappreciated.
- Parts that defend those who harm you, blaming you instead.
- Protectors that use physical illness to get your attention, distract you from emotional pain, or give you a good reason to stop over-caregiving and take a much-needed break.

Notice, in your body, what it feels like when these parts try to override other parts in order to fawn. See if you can call upon just a bit of Self energy and extend some curiosity or compassion toward your body, emotions, or whatever part emerges for healing. Give yourself a hug if it helps. Let all parts know you're here to listen and comfort them.

WRITING PROMPT: When I ask all my parts, not just the fawning parts, how they feel about what I'm being asked to do, they say . . .

3. Negotiate and seek consensus with your parts. Listen to your parts, honor their points of view, appreciate why they think or act that way, and negotiate with them, from Self, the way a good parent listens to everyone in the family before deciding for the group. See if you can bring your parts to consensus. They won't always agree with each other, just as a large family might never come to a unanimous decision. But even if some parts are not on board for the general agreement, you may be able to help them address their fears and get their needs met. If they still resist the general consensus, use the "Get to Know Your Protectors" protocol. Then you can earn their trust in Self and help them relax, so you, in Self, can take the lead in decision-making. This isn't always easy or straightforward, and you might need professional help if protectors are strongly resisting something the rest of your system overwhelmingly wants you to do (or not do). But with practice, you'll get a clearer sense of what you actually consent to, rather than agree to because you're reflexively fawning.

WRITING PROMPT: Channeling your wise, loving Self, write a love letter to any fawning protector parts, parts that use the body with physical symptoms, or other relevant protector parts. Let them know you've heard their points of view, mirroring, witnessing, validating, and appreciating how hard they've worked to try to keep you safe. Let them know you get it, that it makes sense why you've been fawning for so long, or why parts might be using the body to get your attention, distract you, get core needs met, or avoid unbearable feelings. Notice how those protector parts receive the validation, appreciation, and unconditional compassion and acceptance Self offers.

EXERCISE: Try mapping out any related parts, drawing them on a piece of paper, so you can unblend from them, learn how they relate to each other, and get a visual representation of the complexities of your opinions about any given decisions.

4. Flag any exiles for deeper treatment later. When you do the "Get to Know Your Protectors" protocol, you'll learn what your protectors are afraid will happen if they stop fawning, using your body to get your attention, or whatever else they might be doing to distract you from overwhelming exile feelings. For example, when you took your pause, you might have realized right away which part of you was scared to say no. If you felt panicky even asking for a pause, an exile that's afraid to do anything but automatically people-please (maybe because it got beaten if it failed to instantly obey, or was threatened with abandonment if it didn't do exactly what a caregiver approved of) may have come right to the surface. Or maybe you're not sure which wounded parts your protectors are looking after. If you can't identify an exile on your own, don't worry. You're not doing anything wrong, and you're not alone. It's common for protectors to block us from identifying an exile. You might need the facilitation and coregulation of a skilled IFS therapist.*

If you've been successful in identifying an exile, and if your protectors grant permission, you can make a note to come back later, on your own or with a trained IFS therapist, to follow the "Unburdening Your Exiles" protocol from chapter eight. Unburdening the exiles that are driving protectors helps heal, relax, and interrupt reflexive behaviors like fawning. The more exiles you unburden, the more your protectors will learn to trust your Self-leadership when it comes to decision-making.

* We try to help you do as much self-help IFS practice as is possible, but if this step doesn't come easily to you, for your own safety, don't push it. To find a referral to an IFS therapist, visit https://ifs-institute.com/practitioners.

Once you learn the basics of the YOU-Turn, you can learn more advanced IFS practices, like the Conference Table meditation. The Conference Table is an incredibly helpful tool when it comes to decision-making. It's kind of like a pro-and-con list, only trauma informed and sensitive to all parts. If you need to make a decision, like whether to agree to another person's request, this practice can help you slow down, unblend from your fawning part, attend to all parts, and make a more Self-led decision, rather than letting fawning or enabling parts run the show.

PRACTICE

THE CONFERENCE TABLE MEDITATION

Imagine you're at a conference table with any relevant parts that have an opinion about a decision you're trying to make.

1. Go inside to see if any parts have an opinion about the request that was made. Imagine you're sitting at a conference table with Self at the head.

2. Designate one side of the conference table "Yes" and the other side "No."
Ask any parts that want to weigh in on either side to populate the table (or sides of the bus). One by one, let all parts with a substantial stake in the decision introduce themselves and tell you their opinion about the request you're considering. Let each part know you appreciate their feedback and validate their point of view. Take notes if it helps you keep track of the parts.

3. Let your wise Self mediate among your parts' opinions.
Just as the head of a family, or a good political leader, might listen to all parties involved when making a decision in order to find a fair compromise, Self mediates the discussion to arrive

at a just decision that considers all parts, even if the vote is not unanimous. This takes some practice. Often, parts will take sides. Some will ally with each other. Others will gang up against the other side. Let them hash it out a bit, listening and taking their desires, fears, and concerns seriously. Show your parts you care about all of them, rather than siding with parts you might fear less. If you're considering another person's request, maybe you'll wind up complying with it. Maybe you'll reject it. Or maybe you'll find an answer somewhere in the middle, a compromise negotiated between parts on different sides of the issue.

4. If you can't find consensus among your parts, keep pausing. Mediation is a process, not a quick fix. Clarity will come, but it might take time. Your answer also might not come from critical thinking, but from a gut feeling or an intuitive knowing. It might come to you in a dream, in a flash of insight, or with a wave of emotion that makes the best choice clear.

If someone else is pressuring you to make a decision before you're ready, let them know you're still a maybe, and if they need an answer immediately, they can feel free to interpret your lack of a clear yes as a "no for now." If there's a deadline, the absence of a yes is probably a no. A yes given from pressure and urgency is rarely a Self-led yes; it's a parts-led rush job. Especially if someone is asking you to do something that would be beneficial to them but possibly harmful for you, the lack of a "hell yeah" is probably a "hell no."

5. Thank your parts and celebrate your clarity!
Let your parts know you appreciate that they let you (Self) help out and mediate, rather than letting your fawning part reflexively comply with the request without considering the needs and preferences of the other parts. Check in especially with the fawning part and see how it's doing after the Conference

Table meditation. If it's still stressed and wanting to fawn, see if you can show up in Self and offer comfort, or maybe talk to a trusted friend or therapist to get a second opinion about whether complying with the request seems like a wise choice for you. Those who exploit people who fawn often try to isolate them, so reaching out for advice outside your inner world can often help you get clarity when the Conference Table alone fails to do so.

When you've made a Self-led decision, you will feel relaxation in your body, as well as emotional relief. Even if some parts are scared of the decision you've made, you will feel somatically relaxed overall. Clarity usually softens your system, even if what you're clear on is something you feel afraid to do, like ending a relationship or quitting a job. Even people who don't fawn won't always make perfect, regret-free decisions, but especially when you're new to learning agency and autonomy, be gentle with yourself. Maybe you will regret your decision in the future. But you'll have far fewer regrets than if you say yes from fawning parts alone. That's how we learn new ways of orienting our lives—from a Self-led place, and through trial and error, not perfectionism.

A variation of the Conference Table meditation is the Campfire meditation, which can be especially helpful for decisions that are more complex than a simple yes/no. It allows many parts with nuanced opinions to take a seat around a warm, comforting fire, with Self presiding over a cozy campfire conversation, so they can hash out a decision together. The Campfire meditation is also helpful for gaining insight into the dynamics between your various parts.

You can access recordings of guided meditations of both the Conference Table and the Campfire meditations at Relationsick.com.

Let's look at an example of the YOU-Turn in action. Say your boss asks if you're available to work overtime. You might pause, request a minute, go inside, and check to see who's at your internal conference table, and where they're sitting. Maybe on the "yes" side you've got a fawning part that reflexively wants to agree, a part that doesn't want to let anyone down, a part that likes the idea of earning more money, a part that likes helping the clients, and a part that's gunning for a promotion. On the "no" side, you might have a part that isn't feeling well physically and has a headache, a part that doesn't want to cancel plans with a friend that night, a part that is exhausted and just wants to go home, and a part that is angry at your entitled boss for asking you to work overtime again, when you'd previously tried to set boundaries around overtime work.

Parts-led decisions are often "all or nothing" when it comes to the others' requests or demands—comply or rebel, obey or disobey, defer or defy, be a good girl/boy or a bad girl/boy. But Self-led decisions are compromises that are good enough to suit most of the parts, without exiling or bullying the others. Maybe, after considering the needs of all your parts, you decide to see if your friend can reschedule for a little later that evening, take ibuprofen and have a tea for your headache, and agree to two hours of overtime so you can earn the extra money and be a team player, but say no to the six hours of overtime your boss just assumed you'd take on.

STANDING UP FOR YOUR OWN NEEDS

Checking in with your parts on the inside can help you not only make better decisions, but also build a skill most fawners lack—the ability to know what you need and communicate it to others. Trauma causes fawners to suppress their own needs in order to prioritize the needs of others. To begin relating more reciprocally, you'll need to work on recognizing your own needs (the needs of your parts) so you can speak on their behalf and communicate those needs clearly.

Checking in with your parts using the IFS Daily Parts "Check-In" meditation from chapter eight, and asking them what they need from you or what they might want to request from others, is a beautiful, non-bypassing way to implement a daily IFS practice. Some of those parts will be so young that, when you ask what they need, they might say, in a little baby voice, "Juice"—something Lissa's therapist Nancy Morgan once reported hearing from a client. If it's possible to get them juice, go ahead. Showing up for the needs of your parts in small, simple ways helps you build trust, because it shows your parts that you really do care about them and want to help them get their needs met. Also, when you show up for the needs of your parts, you build the muscle you'll need to stand up to others, on behalf of those parts, even knowing others might reject you or not care about your needs.

PRACTICE

IDENTIFY NEEDS AND PREFERENCES

As you get to know various parts, practice checking in with them once a day to see if they have any needs or requests using the IFS Daily Parts "Check-In" meditation from chapter eight. As you do this, you might also discover, possibly for the first time, what your own preferences are, separate from what other people prefer.

For instance, if you're used to just going along to get along, deferring to the preferences of others, you might not even be aware of whether you prefer vanilla ice cream, chocolate, or something else. What kinds of movies do you like? What are your favorite foods? Do you like your eggs scrambled, fried, over easy, or some other way? What are your values, your morals, the things that fire up your sacred anger and motivate you to protect what you care about? You might be surprised to realize you like the ice cream others like, eat your eggs the way others like, and even take on the values and morals of others.

Without someone else guiding your preferences, you may feel lost and confused, but you'll find your way over time. Try sharing these preferences and distinctions with the people you care about. You might even write up a list of your preferences so you can educate yourself and other people who want to please you.

STEP THREE: NEGOTIATE

In conversation with the person who has made a request or triggered your fawning part, speak on behalf of your parts, making self-advocating requests for what your parts need. Take turns with the other person, listening to what they need and want, sharing power, and negotiating appropriate boundaries and agreements. If helpful, document what you both agree upon.

Let's say someone has made a request, and you've paused, checked in with, and negotiated with your parts. If you're a clear yes or an unequivocal no, you can just say so. But let's say you're prepared to accommodate some of the request, but not all of it. In other words, you're ready to negotiate.

Negotiation is a skill built upon equality and shared power. It helps you avoid both the reflexively accommodating yes and the automatically rebellious no, and allows you to prioritize your own needs while considering someone else's. Negotiation can be challenging for trauma survivors because they must learn to tolerate letting someone down without having a panic attack even imagining doing so. It can be helpful to remind yourself that the way you imagine others responding if you let them down is often much worse than how they *actually* will respond in real life.

In Step Two, you negotiated with parts in your inner world. The next step is to do the same with other people in your outer world. After doing the YOU-Turn and getting clear on what you want to happen, you're now able to negotiate, not just from a fawning part but from a diverse group of parts with different but equally important needs. Negotiation works best when all parties involved know how to pause and do their own YOU-Turn. But even if it's just you, you'll have more success finding a mutually acceptable solution that allows for the consent of both parties when you show up prepared to be a representative of your internal family system.

As you begin the conversation with the person who's made the request, you can explain that you hope to find a satisfying agreement you both feel okay about, but be prepared to hold your ground if they start trying to pressure you to change your stand. The goal is to share power with the other person, rather than overpowering them with bullying demands or blindly submitting to them and getting overpowered. As equals, neither of you one up or one down, and both of you firmly in Terry Real's "center of health," you can negotiate back and forth, listening to each other and showing respectful care for that point of view, without employing undue influence or power moves.

When you speak vulnerably on behalf of scared, hurt, or protective parts, a healthy person will be moved by your vulnerability. While an unhealthy person might weaponize that kind of vulnerability and use it to manipulate you, a person acting from the center of health will care about your needs, requests, safety, and autonomy.

That doesn't mean negotiations will always be easy. You can't assume that you and someone you're in a relationship with are always going to share the same opinions, needs, or values. Sometimes Step Three highlights essential incompatibilities and requires ironing out clashes around world views and preferences. Figuring out how to negotiate equitable agreements can be difficult when one person values earning money over family time, or creative time over housekeeping, or urban living over rural life. But if you take the time to stand up for your needs and preferences, while genuinely caring about those of the other, you can learn a lot about yourself and your relationships. Sometimes we delude ourselves into thinking essential incompatibilities will work themselves out, when they may not. Part of healthy relating is getting to know our magical-thinking parts, so we can face reality head on.

Working out equitable negotiations for everyone's parts in these situations takes effort, but if you're compatible *enough*, this exercise in trust and intimacy can bring you closer together and lead you both to feel safer, enabling a more balanced flow of give and take in the future. The key is for both parties to be willing to make concessions, rather than one person expecting the other to always give up what's important to them or demanding to get their way. In a democracy of two, there's no tie-breaking vote. You have to figure it out creatively, with care for both of your needs as your guide. Sometimes one person will defer to the needs of another, and other times they'll switch. This is the only way to share power equally.

Many trauma survivors have no idea how to share power with others. They don't know how to get consent from their own parts while still caring about whether someone else's parts are consenting. All they know is how to go one up and overpower others (dominate/demand/evade) or go one down and get overpowered (submit/comply/resent). To have "power with" someone requires negotiating relational boundaries, and fair, reciprocal negotiation requires not just getting consent from accommodating parts but also being able to check in with all relevant parts and then communicate on those parts' behalf. It also requires being able to use this information to set and enforce healthy boundaries.

Especially if rigid rules you never consented to were used to control you growing up, if you've been in a cult, or if you've been in a coercively controlling romantic relationship, you might be confused about boundaries. If fawning and conflict avoidance have been your go-to strategies for engaging with others, you might mistakenly think of attempts on your part to set or hold someone else to a boundary as controlling. But boundaries, especially when negotiated between two people, are not controlling. Rather, you're trying to take control of your own life so your body has a chance to recover. Someone who accuses you of being controlling when you're trying to protect yourself is someone who is trying to control *you*.

Speaking up about what's okay and not okay is not controlling. Expecting automatic compliance from someone is. Making requests or saying no on behalf of your parts is not a dominating behavior, although people used to dominating you may perceive it as such. Failing to cooperate with someone else's self-interested agenda for you is not abusive. What's abusive is expecting someone to just go along with their agenda, even if it means you'll wind up a stripped, dead stump.

The antidote to being controlled and overpowered or being controlling and overpowering is mutually consensual boundaries, negotiated together. This can feel scary to conflict-avoidant parts, who often have a lot of indoctrinated beliefs around assertive or confrontational behaviors, because it can require some degree of confrontation. Boundaries can also feel limiting or controlling to lone-wolf parts that prioritize freedom, since boundaries can limit your freedom to act autonomously, without others' consent. People who have been under the influence of coercive control's rigid rules can swing too far the other way, into the boundaryless territory of zero limits, to avoid exercising any control over others or feeling controlled. Understanding the difference between coercive rules and flexible, healthy boundaries therefore can be a learning curve.

YOU'RE WORTHY OF BOUNDARIES THAT PROTECT YOU

Before we talk about the "how" of boundary setting, take a moment to remind yourself that you're entitled (in a good way) to have boundaries that protect you. If you have parts that don't feel worthy of getting your needs met—say, asking someone else to put themselves out, or potentially limiting someone else's freedom to protect you—then participating in boundary setting can be a hard sell. So before you approach any kind of boundary negotiation, remind yourself that you are precious, valuable, and lovable for who you are, not just for how you serve others.

To have your own back and stand up for yourself and your needs, you have to know you're worth advocating for. You're worth saying no for, especially if continuing to say yes keeps you sick or harms you in other ways. You're valuable whether you're resourced and want to give or not.

Trauma survivors often have parts that have come to believe they're valuable because of what they can do for others or for impressive accomplishments. But this kind of self-esteem is fragile, flimsy, and easily lost. Terry Real teaches that there are three forms of false self-esteem: performative self-esteem (*I'm worthy because of what I achieve or produce*), attribute-based self-esteem (*I'm valuable because I have a Ferrari, muscles, a trophy spouse*), or other-based self-esteem (*I have worth because others think I do*). Healthy relational self-esteem requires the ability to hold both your goodness and your imperfections at once, without inflation or deflation. It's grounded not in superiority, performance, or attachment, but in truth, humility, accountability, and love both for self and others.

Think of babies—they don't have to do anything in order to be loved and lovable. We never look at a baby and think, *This baby will have value if it goes to Harvard or grows up to look like a supermodel.* We know every baby is precious and has inherent worth and value. To participate in healthy, fair, balanced negotiations, we have to get back in touch with the value that is our birthright.

PRACTICE

PRACTICES TO CULTIVATE AUTHENTIC, RELATIONAL SELF-ESTEEM

The following practices can help you remember your inherent value—not because of what you do, how you look, or what others think, but because you exist. They invite your parts to feel loved and worthy, not through the strategies they've used to earn belonging, but through inherent self-esteem.

1. Explore the Roots of False Self-Esteem.

Before you can build authentic esteem, it helps to know which parts have learned to equate worth with performance, specific attributes, or others' approval.

Close your eyes, breathe, and invite forward the part of you that tries to "earn" worth. Ask with curiosity:

- "What are you afraid would happen if you didn't prove your value?"
- "Where did you first learn that love had to be earned?"
- "What are you trying to protect me from?"

Thank the part for how hard it has worked to keep you safe and loved. Let it know you're not trying to get rid of it—you just want it to rest in the truth that its worth is not conditional. Visualize the Self—calm, compassionate, present—holding that part with tenderness. Let it begin to absorb the message: You are good and valuable, just as you are.

2. Use the FAST Acronym.

This tool from dialectical behavior therapy can be part of a daily life practice for building healthy self-esteem. Post this reminder of what FAST stands for on the bathroom mirror, your fridge, or your computer.

F—Fair: Balance fairness toward self and others. Fairness includes allowing others to disappoint you without collapsing into unworthiness.

A—Apologies: Notice if your "sorry" is a bid for safety or approval. If so, pause and offer internal reassurance instead.

S—Stick to values: Identify which of your values are intrinsic (truth, love, compassion) versus performative (being seen as nice, competent, spiritual). Stay anchored in the intrinsic ones.

T—Truthful: Include inner truth. Notice if you minimize your pain to seem "good." Radical honesty with yourself restores integrity and real esteem.

3. The Baby Mirror Practice.

Find a photograph of yourself as a baby or small child. Look into that child's eyes for one full minute. Say (silently or aloud): "You don't have to do anything to earn love."

Notice any parts that resist or want to argue. Let Self reassure them: You're safe to rest now.

HOW TO PRACTICE GENEROUS LISTENING

Once we can pull ourselves up by our bootstraps into the center of health, with real self-esteem and without going too far into grandiosity, we're ready to have hard conversations with shared power. One way to negotiate respectfully and democratically, that makes sure both parties get a voice, is to use a talking stick. The talking stick is an ancient Aboriginal tool that allows two or more individuals to share power by creating a container that allows all parties to have their say in negotiations, disputes, or conflict resolution and repair. By passing a stick or other object between them, each person has a turn to speak and be heard, without interruption, making democratic decision-making possible.

Beyond decision-making, another reason you might need to pick up the talking stick and negotiate is if someone else is doing something that's not okay with you. Maybe everyone in your family leaves all their dirty clothes on the floor, and you're up to your eyeballs in resentment every time you walk around the house, picking up all the smelly socks and feeling like the family servant. This is when you might need to pause, do the YOU-Turn, then call a family conference and pick up the talking stick, passing it around to hear others' perspectives after you've shared what you need to say.

PRACTICE

TALKING STICK EXERCISE

If you're new to communicating clearly on behalf of your parts, you can use the talking stick exercise to remind your parts that you have a right to speak up, be heard, negotiate, protest if necessary, and hold your boundaries with someone else.

Here's how it works:

1. Find an actual stick or a token that can represent the talking stick. Or you can use a metaphorical talking stick by just saying, "I have the talking stick now."
2. Establish talking stick boundaries, especially if the other person isn't familiar with the concept of the talking stick and how it works. For example:
   - Only the person holding the talking stick can speak.
   - If speaking up is scary for some of your parts, set any boundaries you need for safety. For example, make it clear you won't tolerate any attempts to manipulate you into changing your mind. You can set other boundaries as well, like no yelling, gaslighting, name-calling, sarcasm, unsolicited advice, psychoanalyzing, defensiveness, blame-shifting, or other interruptions until it's the other person's turn for the talking stick.
   - While the person with the talking stick speaks, it's the other person's job to listen attentively, without interruption. It's important that the listener hold this space with kindness, understanding that the person with the talking stick is trying to get out what is turbulent within them, so that the issue can be resolved in the most effective way. If the listener feels triggered or tempted to interrupt when the speaker has the talking

stick, the listener pauses, breathes, and continues to hold space until it's their turn.

- After the person with the talking stick is finished, the listener should repeat what they've heard so the speaker knows they were listening and to validate what is true about the speaker's experiences, even if it's just their feelings.

3. Once the speaker feels empathically heard, seen, and validated for at least their feelings and as much of their experience as the other person can honestly validate, they hand the talking stick to the listener and hear their reaction to what the speaker shared. It's then the first speaker's job to practice generous listening, extend empathy, validate what's happening for the other person, and contain any temptation to be defensive.
4. This process is repeated as necessary until everyone feels adequately heard and the issue has been thoroughly addressed.
5. If you're negotiating an agreement together, you can do so by passing the talking stick back and forth until you arrive at a mutually satisfying outcome. For example, you might make a first offer, hear the other person's counteroffer, then keep going back and forth until you can both agree upon a compromise.
6. If you find it hard to make sure all parties get equal time being heard, consider setting a timer.
7. If you're in a larger group, such as a family, pass the talking stick between each person until everyone has had a chance to speak, including the quieter ones or those who are less likely to make their voices heard. In the interest of streamlining the group-share process, listeners can skip the mirroring and witnessing process.

For an example, let's reimagine the story of *The Giving Tree*. The boy comes to the tree and asks for apples, and the tree considers his request. After pausing (Step One), she offers him twenty of her apples and saves the rest for some of her other favorite children. When the boy says he wants a house, the tree pauses yet again. The only way she can help the boy get his housing needs met is to offer her branches. She does the YOU-Turn (Step Two), and realizes that while she has parts that want to please the boy, she also has health-conscious parts that don't feel like it's wise to just hand all her branches and photosynthesizing leaves over to the boy. Her justice-seeking parts don't feel like it's a fair or reciprocal trade. And she has parts that want to encourage the boy to grow up into a mature, responsible man, rather than enabling his unhealthy entitlement. She realizes his housing needs are not ultimately her responsibility. Most of all, she doesn't want to jeopardize her ability to survive.

So, the tree approaches Step Three, prepared to negotiate. She asks for the talking stick and lets the boy know she's not going to harm her health by letting him cut down all her branches. But since she's gotten kind of bushy, it might be a win-win if he could prune her down to a more svelte shape and keep the pruned branches. He'd just need to find other trees willing to be pruned, and he could use the wood he collects to build himself a house. Then she passes the talking stick to the boy to give him a chance to respond.

Unlike the giving tree, the boy doesn't know how to do the YOU-Turn. He just blends with one part after another. He feels a wave of entitled rage over not getting his way—but he loves the tree and realizes she has a good point. His rageful parts settle down, and disappointed parts rise to the surface. His bartering parts try to pressure the tree to change her mind, but she remains firm with her generous offer and her self-protective boundary. He tries countering her offer, asking if he can also collect more than twenty apples this time, so he can buy more wood. She raises her offer to thirty apples, saving a hundred more to be shared with others.

The boy huffs and puffs and has a little tantrum, but agrees to her offer. He trims her into a nice shape, taking some of her wayward branches, and harvests thirty apples, reluctantly leaving the rest. He is grateful for the tree for what she has given him, even though it is not what he originally wanted. He feels a wave of respect and love for the tree, and tells her so.

And the tree is happy.

A SIMPLE WAY TO MAKE A NEEDS-BASED REQUEST

Typically, giving tree–type people like us keep our needs silent or don't even know what we need. We suppress our feelings and abdicate our right to make requests. We don't stand up for justice, accountability, or fairness. All of this makes negotiation difficult if not impossible.

Especially if you're learning how to communicate about needs for the first time, there's a simple framework you can use to make this process easier, adapted from both Marshall Rosenberg's Nonviolent Communication (NVC) and Terry Real's Feedback Wheel.

NVC is based on the idea that when we simply state the facts of what triggers us (while resisting the temptation to interpret someone else's behavior), when we're willing to be vulnerable about our emotions, and when we're clear on our needs and express them, we can make a request or set a boundary in a way that doesn't cause emotional violence. "Emotional violence" refers to using words, tone, or behavior in ways that shame, blame, judge, manipulate, or diminish another person's sense of worth or safety. Its forms include criticism, contempt, guilt-tripping, threats, or withdrawal meant to control or punish. Through the lens of NVC, emotional violence happens whenever we disconnect from our own or another's humanity, speaking from judgment rather than from feelings and needs, which creates separation instead of understanding.

Anger is not inherently emotionally violent. When Jeff discusses healthy anger with psychiatry patients, he explains that anger is like the furnace in a home—when it's contained, it warms the home so life and love can occur. But when that fire isn't contained, it can be destructive, burning the house down. Anger can be a healthy emotion that helps us protect our boundaries and stand up for others whose boundaries are getting violated. When it is integrated, it doesn't seek to harm or dominate; it seeks to negotiate, mediate differences, repair ruptures, and restore balance. It says, "Something's not okay here. Please stop" or "I deserve better than this."

But giving-tree types tend to suppress or dissociate from their own anger, driving it underground. We may not even feel our anger when someone is abusing us or overriding our rights. But anger is like a volcano that builds until it blows. If we're not in touch with our healthy anger—if we're not pausing when our parts get triggered, doing the YOU-Turn to figure out which parts are upset and why, speaking up for what we need and making requests or setting boundaries—our understandable anger tends to blow out sideways as passive-aggressive resentment or punishing behaviors like withdrawing affection, giving the silent treatment, threatening to leave the relationship, or quietly sabotaging the connection in other ways. These are unhealthy forms of covert protest—ways our parts try to express anger when we don't feel safe expressing it directly. But these strategies don't protect us; they just gradually corrode intimacy and self-respect.

We have to take responsibility for knowing our rights, speaking up when something upsets us, and asking for what we need, rather than punishing others who might not even know they've upset us. Healthy anger is what helps us do this.

In the Accountability Feedback Practice, we've married NVC with the steps in Terry Real's Feedback Wheel, which gives us a way to own our natural storytelling and meaning-making tendencies when we're triggered, something NVC doesn't leave room for. This non-bypassing approach to feedback allows space for honest meaning-making without blame or tone policing. Naming the stories we make up about what someone else says or does helps us own our stories and unblend from the storytelling parts, so we can get a little space from the story and speak for those parts, rather than blending.

PRACTICE

THE ACCOUNTABILITY FEEDBACK PRACTICE

1. Share your observations. Describe the triggering event, what you saw or heard, with a "just the facts, ma'am" objectivity. It's much harder to dispute facts than judgments we make about those facts. We simply share what we noticed, without making evaluations, interpretations, or accusations about the event. For example, "You came home two hours late without calling and dinner got cold" rather than "You selfish asshole! You never think about me one bit, do you? I'm at home waiting for hours while you're doing Lord knows what with Lord knows who at work."

2. Own your storytelling. Terry Real suggests starting with "What I made up about that is . . ." Share the story or meaning your mind attached to the triggering behavior—what you assumed or interpreted it to mean. For example, "I told myself you didn't respect my time or the labor I put into making your dinner, and that you think your needs are more important than mine or the kids'." Some people who criticize NVC feel that it tone-polices people who are protesting certain behaviors. "What I made up about that is . . ." leaves room for more honesty and less tone policing.

3. Express your feelings. When an event triggers us, emotions arise. Name the emotions that arose for you in response to that story or interpretation. For example, "I felt hurt, devalued, angry, and dismissed."

4. Speak up for what you need. We can't expect others to be mind readers when we stuff down our feelings and suppress our legitimate needs, and it's not fair to punish others when we're not taking responsibility for speaking up. Directly communicating our needs sets the other person up for success. Once we have gone inside and gotten to know our younger parts and their needs, it's our job to speak clearly on their behalf, as their spokesperson, from Self. For example, "I have a respect-seeking part that needs to feel like I matter and am a priority to you. This part needs to know that, even if you're busy at work, you care enough about the effort I put into getting dinner on the table on time to let me know ahead of time that you're running late."

5. Make a request. Sometimes our loved ones want to please us, but they have no idea how. Making a clear request that can easily be carried out gives others a way to make repairs and show that they care when we're upset. Your loved one does not have to fulfill this request, because it may violate their own needs, but it's a starting place for negotiation. "My request is that you give me a head's up as soon as you realize you're going to be home late. Ideally, you'd give me enough advance notice that I could either eat without you or delay dinner so it doesn't get cold."

The basic outline of the Accountability Feedback Practice:

When ____________,
the story I told myself was ____________.
I felt ____________,
because my need for ____________ was not met.
Would you be willing to ________________?

The Accountability Feedback Practice requires giving-tree types to stretch way beyond our likely comfort zone. If we've been fawning and saying yes when we're not really a yes, it may take courage and exercising of new muscles to start paying attention to the feelings in our bodies, speaking up about what triggers us, owning the stories we make up, expressing our needs, and making clear requests to get them met. We may feel frightened of holding others accountable for behaviors that upset us or of putting others out. We might feel guilty about prioritizing our own needs, especially when our personal sacrifice might have helped someone else. We might feel terrified of risking our vulnerable requests being rejected. But if we want to heal relationsickness, then learning to hold others accountable and stand up for our own needs, rather than putting others' needs first, is crucial medicine.

We know implementing this practice may seem like a utopian fantasy. You may learn this intellectually and memorize the steps, but then fail to implement them when it matters most. You might dissociate the minute someone makes a request, and next thing you know, your fawning part and accountability-bypassing part have joined forces, and you're doling out hall passes right and left. That's normal. You might need to print the steps out and post them all over your house. You'll need to practice, practice, practice. But change is possible. We know it works, with the right support, because we've made that shift from fawning to freedom ourselves. We believe in you.

The Accountability Feedback Practice will not always work. Someone high on the narcissism spectrum might cut you off and gaslight you right out of the gate when you state your version of objective reality. If they dispute your facts before you've even finished offering your feedback, you're likely to get even more triggered, and then things can escalate into conflict and emotional violence. Understandably so, because it's maddeningly frustrating to have your factual reality disputed. If that's the case, remember: You're getting discernment information about how narcissistic someone is, how unwilling they are to be held accountable, and whether they're safe to have in your life when you're in recovery from relationsickness.

Sometimes the request you'll make as the final step of the Accountability Feedback Practice will be the first step in a boundary negotiation, such as, "My request is that you hold to our time boundaries. If we've previously agreed that dinner is at six, unless there's an unexpected emergency, please honor our agreement and make an effort to be home at six, even if it means letting someone down at work." To shift the balance of unbalanced relationships, boundary setting is the next essential relational skill to master.

A NOTE ON BOUNDARIES

Now that you're working on speaking up more and fawning less, it's time for a brief lesson in boundaries. A boundary is a conscious, ethical request we make to protect our safety, honor the needs of our parts, or preserve our well-being. Put simply, a boundary is how we communicate what's okay with us and what's not. Think of it as a gate that lets blessings in while keeping toxicity out. Boundaries are not walls. Walls are indiscriminate; they block everything, both love and harm. When walls come down, everything floods in at once—the nourishing and the toxic alike. Gates can be filters, admitting what is nourishing and barring what is not good for you, being opened more for people who have proven to be trustworthy and staying closed for those who have betrayed our trust without good repair.

A healthy boundary never seeks to control another person; it respects their freedom to choose. They can choose to honor your boundary, or not. If they don't, you have the right to protect yourself by enacting consequences—not as punishment or revenge, though it may be perceived that way, but as an act of self-care and self-respect. While some conflict-avoidant types fail to make those consequences clear from the start, it's fair to spell out what will happen if the boundaries are crossed, so everyone knows ahead of time what honoring or violating the boundary will mean, and people clearly see that you're serious and not just issuing an empty threat.

Boundary setting is the healthy alternative to passive-aggressive punishment. Rather than lashing out, withdrawing, or justifying betraying someone because you don't like how they're treating you, boundaries restore us to greater integrity and give others the chance to act with integrity as well. Whether or not someone is willing to negotiate good boundaries with us, and then honor them, is part of our discernment process. When you're relationsick, the process of negotiating boundaries is part of the decision tree that helps us determine whether our various relationships can change in health-inducing ways or not.

The goal of boundary setting is healing, solving a problem, or preventing future harm. By setting limits—after you do the YOU-Turn to figure out what's upsetting your parts—you can avoid giving too much and then getting resentful. To negotiate boundaries fairly, you'll need to practice taking responsibility for your own limits. The other person is not responsible for determining your limits. You are. It's your job to say, "This is okay with me. That is not." Only you and your parts know what you can and want to give, and only you can be responsible for drawing that line.

When you don't draw that line, you can end up seething inside, but that's not the other person's fault. That's on you. The person you are chronically upset with may have no idea that what they're doing irritates the crap out of you. So it's important to be proactive about communicating your needs, rather than using passive-aggressive punishment. Acting out passive-aggressively is not setting a boundary; it's unhealthy manipulation.

So, how do you set a clear, healthy boundary?

PRACTICE

HOW TO NEGOTIATE BOUNDARIES

1. Get clear with your own parts on what's okay and not okay. The Conference Table or Campfire meditation can be helpful here to get a clear sense of what your various parts need and what boundary you need to assert.

WRITING PROMPT: Let all parts that are upset about the issue at hand express how they feel, what they're scared of, what they need, and whether they have any requests.

2. Speak on behalf of your parts. Do your best to give voice to your parts in a way the other person can hear. Blaming, shaming, attacking, and condescending language doesn't help. Instead, provide detailed examples of the behaviors you don't like. For example, "When you make plans that impact me but don't run them by me to make sure I'm okay with them, I have a part that feels angry, disrespected, and unappreciated."

3. Gently but clearly request a different behavior. Make it abundantly clear what you are requesting! Some people might freeze or dissociate when you approach them with a new boundary request. Especially if the person you're talking to has a neurodivergent nervous system and might need more processing time, try to go slow, speak calmly, and resist the temptation to monologue. Write it down if necessary. A request that is straightforward, clear, and simple—delivered with as much neutrality as you can muster—will get the best result.

For example, "If you're thinking about committing to something that impacts me, my request is that you consult me first. Give me the choice to consent, and if I say no, I'd prefer if you respect my no without arguing with me or pressuring me to change my mind."

4. Let the other person respond, but hold your ground. Once you've clearly stated your boundary request, give the other person a chance to respond or speak on behalf of their own parts. But don't get knocked off your center by their response. Whatever feelings the other person expresses, it's important to stay centered in Self, rather than enmeshing with the other person. Remember, their feelings are their feelings. Your feelings are your feelings. As long as the other person is not physically violent, allow them to feel angry or disappointed, while tending to the parts in you that might react to their feelings. If need be, go back to Step Two and do the YOU-Turn, checking inside with your own parts again.

You might worry that other people will perceive your holding your ground as a separate person, entitled to your own needs and feelings, as selfish or lacking in closeness. But remember, this separateness is not an absence of love. It actually complements love, providing enough space to stay connected even as you are setting and enforcing clear boundaries.

If the other person's reaction does knock you off your center, do the YOU-Turn again. Take a few deep breaths. Reassure your parts that you've got them. Reorient them to present time, in case they get whooshed into a flashback. The other person is allowed to be upset about your boundary; that doesn't mean you're not entitled to it. You also don't want to reward extreme reactions by giving in, the same way you don't want to reward children who melt down at the grocery store when they don't get what they want. Giving in is enabling behavior, which is a pattern you'll need to break if you hope to optimize your health outcome.

EXERCISE: To hold onto your center when someone else has an extreme reaction to your boundary request, before saying anything, try counting backward: 5-4-3-2-1. This helps interrupt the reflexive fawning pattern and gives you a chance to bring in a little Self energy before you reply.

5. Warn the other person in advance what will happen if the boundary is violated. You've set the other person up for success by letting them know clearly what will help resolve the situation. Next, make sure they understand what will happen if the boundary isn't respected. For example, if you're requesting that someone who is always late to appointments show up on time, let them know that if this problem doesn't get solved, you'll no longer make appointments with them. They will have lost the right to a spot on your calendar.

Assuming the issue you're setting a boundary around is a small one, you might want to give people a few chances to get it right. Reasonably healthy people might violate a boundary once or twice simply because they didn't understand it, or because they forgot. But if they break the boundary a third time, you're most likely dealing with someone who doesn't intend to respect that boundary.

Some requests are not small, though. If the boundary you're setting is "No violence" or "No cheating," one strike might be all you need to skip to Step 6 and create space.

6. Make sure you allow the other person to retain their right to consent to your boundary or not. It's not okay to use force or coercion to get someone to respect your boundary. If you become threatening, coercive, manipulative, shaming, or otherwise abusive in your attempt to set or enforce your boundary, you're no longer having a fair, shared power negotiation. Instead, you've just gone one up. You don't have the right to control someone else's decisions. Let them make a free-will choice about whether to respect your request.

7. Be open to negotiation. Sometimes you'll set a clear boundary and someone else will have a valid reaction to it, speaking on behalf of their own parts and expressing something you might not have considered when requesting the boundary. The best, most relational boundaries are negotiated between all parties involved. You can pass the talking stick back and forth until you settle on a mutually agreed-upon boundary that works for everyone.

Let's say you make a boundary request around walking the dog. You're feeling resentful that there are four people in the family and yet you're the only one doing the dog-walking. You say you're willing to walk the dog three days per week, and someone else will need to walk the dog the other four days. Maybe everyone else gets defensive and starts pushing back against your boundary, but you stay firm. Three days, that's it. Then your daughter says she can do Sundays. Your son says he can do Saturdays. Finally, your husband, who has been silent while considering his own needs, suggests, "What if I pay a dog walker to do the other two days?" You'd still only be walking the dog three days per week, even though he's not directly taking responsibility for helping out more. His solution respects your boundary, while also honoring his own needs.

8. Get it in writing. Write down the boundary you've set. You might also discuss what will happen if the boundary is breached. What are the consequences of breaking the agreement? Don't threaten a consequence you're not willing to carry out. A boundary is only useful if you're willing to hold the other person accountable should they violate it. If the other person (or people) involved agrees to the terms of the boundary, you can both sign it. If they don't, you're still negotiating—and may need to pay a counselor or mediator to help you resolve your impasse. Getting boundary agreements in writing helps prevent confusion. If the other person later acts like you never made the request or they never agreed to it, at least you can pull out the contract and head off any dispute about the facts.

9. If the boundary is breached, be sure to follow through on consequences. Sometimes people forget an agreement, especially at first, and need a gentle reminder. If Sally was supposed to walk the dog on Saturdays, and forgets, you might need to provide a nudge that helps her remember her commitment. But if Sally is willfully defying the boundary, or refuses to set alarms for herself so she doesn't forget, you have to be strong enough to hold your line. If the other person breaks the boundary and you fail to enforce the consequence, it will be harder for them to take your boundaries seriously in the future. You've also now violated your own boundaries and risk losing trust between you and your parts.

10. Be liberal with praise. If the other person does respect your boundary and you notice them going out of their way to do so, verbalize your appreciation! Remember, sugar goes down easier than vinegar.

DEAD-STOP CONTRACTS

Sometimes negotiations and boundary conversations go south. Instead of seeking to negotiate a boundary fairly, one person loses their shit, while the other freezes. Or both start trying to one-up each other in an escalating one-up ladder, and two people who otherwise care about each other start seriously hurting each other.

If the person you're talking to is refusing to respect talking stick boundaries or listen to your healthy protests or boundary requests with curiosity, respect, and humility, or if things escalate into verbal attacks instead of healthy, fair conflict, you can employ the "dead-stop contract": an instant time out that you've both agreed you'll respect, no matter what. Taught by Terry Real, this tool is an advance agreement that says when either party recognizes that they're falling into old, unhealthy patterns, blending with parts that go one up or one down or mutually escalating, they can call a dead stop—and the other will immediately halt the interaction until their partner is calm enough to have a repair conversation. (Or, a safe third-party mediator, like a couples therapist, can facilitate the conversation to help protect both parties.) A dead-stop contract helps interrupt hurtful repetitive patterns by giving both people's nervous systems a chance to deescalate, so they can unblend with activated parts and allow more Self energy to return.

If, during a negotiation, one or both of you have spiraled into what couples therapists John and Julie Gottman (marriage researchers at the Love Lab in Seattle) call the "Four Horsemen of the Apocalypse"—defensiveness, criticism, contempt, and stonewalling—things are only going to get worse if you try to continue. But a dead-stop contract doesn't mean the negotiation is abandoned. The key is to return to the issue when your nervous systems have calmed down. There's no shame in getting activated, but it's important to know when to stop, before things get out of hand.

Last, remember: If you are trying to set a boundary and the other person is reflexively pulling out narcissistic defenses like DARVO (Deny, Attach, Reverse Victim and Offender), you have a right to set a firmer boundary. If the dead-stop contract doesn't work, and if all of your best talking stick negotiations and boundary-setting skills fail to get you the safety, empathy, behavior change, and accountability you deserve, you might need to skip straight to Step Six and create space.

STEP FOUR: TROUBLESHOOTING

If you've been successful in coming to a negotiated boundary agreement, the next step is to troubleshoot whether both of you are able to follow through on what you've agreed upon.

Hopefully, both parties will keep to the agreement you've made. If this is the case, you can proceed to Step Five if any repair of hurt feelings is needed from the trigger that originally initiated the pause. And if all you need is a celebration, you can go straight to Step Six!

Unfortunately, it's not always quite that simple. For whatever reason, we can struggle to keep the agreements we make. Maybe the other person struggles to respect the boundary. Maybe you struggle to enforce it. Maybe you're the one breaking your own negotiated agreement. We're human; we inevitably make mistakes, especially if we're new to boundary work.

If the other person breaks the agreed-upon plan, knows they've done so, and owns it, you can move to Step Five for repair, reinstate the boundary, and (ideally) move on. However, if they don't catch their mistake or own up to the breached boundary, you will have to initiate a conversation about it and figure out why. If you're the one who has broken the agreement, you'll have to do a postmortem on yourself, so you can troubleshoot what went wrong. Either way, this process requires personal accountability and sometimes holding someone to account.

When you first start negotiating boundaries, misunderstandings abound. If someone else isn't respecting your boundary, the first step of troubleshooting is double-checking with yourself that you weren't fuzzy in the way you communicated your boundary.

You might think you've set a boundary or made a request, but realize in retrospect that your conflict-avoidant parts caused you to hedge. When Jeff was new to setting boundaries, he'd set the boundary and then immediately invalidate it, often in the same sentence. When discussing dinner once with someone who always wanted to eat at 5 PM, before Jeff was done with his workday, he said, "I'd prefer we eat dinner at seven at least half the time we get together." But then he quickly followed it with, "But if you'd rather eat at five, that works too."

He called it "softening," which was intended to minimize upset feelings in the other person—but it often just resulted in their missing the memo. For example, let's say you want to end a dual relationship with a friend you're also doing business with. Instead of just saying, "My therapist is advising me to untangle my dual relationships. I'd like to stay friends but stop doing business together," you add, "But maybe it'll be fine if we do business at some future time." That's not clear; that's confusing.

If you communicated the boundary clearly, but the other person has broken the agreement, the problem might be that they said yes when they weren't really a yes, fawning you and then getting pushback from their parts afterward. Sometimes someone will agree to something during a negotiation, but then discover from triggered, resentful, or passive-aggressive parts afterward that they weren't really in consent with all parts. People also can feel coerced into agreeing to something they're really not okay with, because of the circumstances of the request. This is why it's so important during negotiations that both people stay in choice and speak up on behalf of all relevant parts. Otherwise, rebellious parts might push back against fawning parts, or there might be backlash from other parts that weren't represented during the negotiation.

Important negotiations can't be rushed. Even the law thinks so. For example, the day before baseball player Barry Bonds married bartender Sun Branco, he and his lawyers asked her to sign a prenuptial agreement. She signed, but when they got divorced six years later, she challenged the agreement, saying that because the wedding was the next day, she felt coerced into compliance because it was too late to negotiate a fair prenup. The case went all the way to the Supreme Court, and the laws around California prenuptial agreements changed as a result, making all prenups signed after 2002 invalid unless there was enough time to pause and consider the request before the wedding, with both parties having access to fair legal counsel. If the goal is a truly democratic, consensual, shared power negotiation, be ready to slow things down.

Especially when someone is under the undue influence of coercive control (Level 3 relationship) or in a domestic violence situation (Level 4), they may not feel safe enough to say no during a negotiation. Even when someone *is* safe to say no, past traumas from former times when it wasn't safe can cause reflexive compliance. This can look and sound like consent, but consent really isn't present.

It's because this can get so complicated that Step Four is such a necessary troubleshooting period. If an agreement isn't kept, figure out what went wrong and, if needed, renegotiate the terms of the agreement. Unless you're dealing with someone malignantly high on the narcissism spectrum, the two people negotiating a boundary usually do care about each other. It's worth investing in figuring out why an agreement wasn't kept and what can be done to shore it up.

That said, there are many coercive controllers who willfully make agreements they have no intention of keeping. The feigned agreements are manipulations intended to trick someone into behaving the way the controller wants. They may outright maliciously lie because they are trying to harm, exploit, or criminally violate their victim. It can be difficult to discern the difference between an honest mistake born of generally benevolent intentions and a deliberate boundary crossing intended to intimidate, confuse, or disempower. If you aren't sure which it is, you might need a third party to help, whether it's a therapist, a lawyer, or law enforcement. Assuming that you're dealing with a garden-variety boundary violator who's more clumsy oaf than criminal predator, Step Four can help you both find the right solution for shoring up and reinstating your negotiated agreements.

THE IMPORTANCE OF HEALTHY PROTEST

Let's say two of you agreed to terms for a boundary, agreement, or plan of action, but then the other person crosses the boundary or fails to follow through with the plan. Now it's your job to do the opposite of what most of us have done our whole lives. Instead of avoiding conflict, telling yourself things will never get better, and ignoring your need for justice, you need to protest.

Why? Because protest is a necessary first step toward troubleshooting what's gone wrong. If you don't protest, others might not realize how serious you are about the boundaries and agreements you've made—or how upset you are. If you don't speak up, you also won't have a chance to understand the other person's perspective, so you can figure out how to fix the problem and get justice for you both.

If you're not motivated by the pure quest for justice, maybe you'll be motivated by the health implications of failing to protest. Remember the learned helplessness study with the rats from chapter one? The rats who learned to press the lever to escape the shocks not only fought off the cancer they were injected with more often than the rats who learned helplessness; they even had a survival advantage over the rats who were never shocked at all!

If you're being mistreated or your boundaries are being violated, you have to press the lever. If you want to improve your chances of healing, you can't just roll over, listless and helpless, when someone is crossing your boundaries. You're going to have to protest. Doing so could be legitimate medicine for your body.

Just as when people take to the streets when the government does something they don't like, protesting is a way of exercising your rights and fighting for equality. It's also a form of fighting for the relationship. Sure, it doesn't always feel good when someone else tells us we're doing something they don't like. But it sure beats being abandoned by someone who tolerates, tolerates, tolerates . . . then leaves.

A therapist once told me I should date horses, not camels. Horses, he said, can take you across a desert, and when they start getting thirsty or tired, you can tell. They slow down and lose the spring in their step. They give you warning signs that you need to find a nice oasis soon, so they can take a drink and a nap. Camels, on the other hand, keep on going, giving zero warning signs, until they drop dead. Then you're stranded in a desert without a backup plan.

Humans who protest when you cross their boundaries are like horses. They give you warning signs that something's not right and that you need to shape up if you want to avoid being abandoned. Camel types, on the other hand, keep their mouth shut, build up resentment, and then abandon you with no warning. Learning how to register a healthy protest can transform you from a camel into a horse and makes you a more trustworthy person to relate with.

When you tell someone that what they're doing is hurting you, you're being loving rather than enabling. You're trusting that the other person cares about you and wants to correct the imbalance in the relationship, rather than acting out with punishing, passive-aggressive behaviors because you're afraid they don't.

PRACTICE

PRACTICE YOUR PROTEST

If you're used to avoiding conflict, learning how to protest ethically is no small feat. People with fawning tendencies often fail to voice our protests, choosing to tolerate injustice rather than fight it. If bad things happened when you protested in the past, the natural inclination to protest when you're being mistreated may get exiled, causing you to suffer in silence—sometimes not even admitting to yourself that you're suffering—until you get relationsick. When you abdicate your right to pick up the talking stick when someone else crosses an agreed-upon boundary, breaks a plan, or otherwise triggers you, you're failing to get justice for your parts.

Because it can be scary for some of our young parts to hold someone else to account when a boundary has been crossed or an agreement has been broken, it can help to write down what you want to say and practice by reading it out loud to someone safe. If you have no one, try reading it out loud to yourself instead. That way, you can notice what happens in your body, do the YOU-Turn if fears or other emotions arise, and start to rewire those neural pathways, showing your parts before you do the real thing that confronting someone can be safe.

Here's a sample protest, using the Accountability Feedback Practice we learned in Step Three: "We had an agreement that we would both put our clothes away before bedtime, but although my clothes are put away, there are now three days' worth of your clothes on the floor. The story I made up about this is that you don't respect our agreements or care that a neat house matters to me, and that you think I should have to pick up your dirty clothes because you think I'm less than you, like I'm your servant and will just pick up after you. This makes me feel angry and exploited. We agreed that if you broke this agreement, you'd do both of our laundry this week. Will you please take care of this by Friday?"

When practicing crafting a protest, it helps to remember that the goal isn't to attack or control the other person. It's to advocate for your parts with dignity and clarity. A protest is most likely to be heard when it's specific, nonshaming, and emotionally honest without being emotionally violent. That means describing observable behavior rather than making global judgments ("You left your clothes on the floor," not "You're lazy and selfish"), naming the meaning your parts created about it, expressing how that story makes you feel, and making a clear, time-bound request for repair.

Tone of voice is also important. If your tone is contemptuous or superior, the other person will likely feel attacked and defend instead of listening. Using first-person perspective ("I felt sad when . . .", "I felt hurt when . . ."), a steady tone, and Self-led energy helps your protest land as an invitation to accountability rather than an accusation or indictment of their character.

ACCOUNTABILITY

Everyone messes up sometimes when making agreements with other people. If we're in the habit of doing something on autopilot (like throwing our clothes on the floor), and now we've agreed to make a change, it may take time to break the habit. We might forget we've made an agreement and need to be reminded. Or we might misunderstand the agreement from the get-go. Or maybe we said yes when we meant maybe or no, because we forgot to pause and do the YOU-Turn.

Regardless of why we broke an agreement, accountability is key. The person who broke the agreement needs to own up to the mistake, express regret and remorse, and be willing to participate in a repair process. If they fail to take ownership, the other person needs to protest—as kindly but firmly as possible—to hold the other person to account.

Holding yourself or someone you care about accountable takes courage, which is one of the qualities of Self. Holding yourself accountable means that when someone approaches you with their upset feelings, you need to examine whether even 1 percent of what they're saying is true. If so, own it, validate them as best you can, and express remorse—but don't own what you haven't done. You don't have to take responsibility for what's not true, if the other person is blame-shifting and falsely accusing you. It's okay to hold your ground and reset your boundaries if someone is trying to blame you when you're innocent, a common tactic that people high on the narcissism spectrum use to deflect accountability.

Holding someone else accountable means getting to know your conflict-avoidant parts so that, when a boundary or agreement has been broken, you can confront the person in a healthy way, and follow through with consequences. Accountability should involve kindness and some flexibility, but ultimately the boundary needs to be enforced. Otherwise, it's meaningless to set a boundary in the first place, and the people you're setting boundaries with will not take your boundaries seriously.

WHEN THE OTHER PERSON VIOLATES THE BOUNDARY

If the other person breaks a boundary but immediately owns it, apologizes, and shows willingness to repair, it's often safe to assume they made an honest mistake and move on to Step Five for repair. But when someone struggles to take responsibility, it's important to slow things down, hold your ground, and refuse to let them off the hook. Some people are remarkably slippery when it comes to owning their mistakes, often because it wasn't safe to do so when they were young. But that's no excuse for shirking responsibility when they screw up in the present.

It helps to approach someone who is struggling with accountability with both discernment and fierce compassion. Many people who resist accountability aren't consciously trying to gaslight or manipulate you. They may be flooded with shame or fear of rejection, or be stuck in old trauma patterns that make it feel unbearable to admit they messed up. Defensiveness, minimization, and denial can be a form of self-protection, not malice, even though it may feel cruel, confusing, and disorienting when you're the receiving party. Compassion doesn't mean tolerating repeat violations or pretending harm didn't occur. Your job is to stay grounded in reality, name what happened clearly, and hold the boundary with kindness and firmness. This permits people who are very sensitive or frightened when they make a mistake and struggle to own their mistake in the moment to repair the relationship once their nervous system settles.

That's different from when someone chronically distorts reality or refuses all accountability, despite receiving both calm, clear communication and time to let the nervous system settle. When someone keeps shirking accountability and can't come back to a discussion about the conflict later without blowing up or avoiding the issue, that may signal a deeper issue, especially if they sit high on the narcissism spectrum and uses gaslighting or DARVO to maintain control.

Such a person might deny you ever set the boundary or that they ever agreed to abide by it, which is why writing down your agreements can be helpful. They might invalidate your reality, claiming they put the clothes away even when there's factual evidence they did not, because the clothes are all over the floor. They'll accuse you of not putting away your own clothes, even when none of the clothes on the floor are yours. They'll minimize your distress, accuse you of exaggerating, claim that you're misunderstanding, and mock you for making a mountain out of a molehill—anything to shirk accountability and prevent you from pinning them to account.

If that doesn't silence your protest, they may start tone policing you, accusing you of being shrill, nagging, or aggressive, or otherwise using a tone they judge as imperfect, even if you've used your Accountability Feedback Practice perfectly. If you continue to hold your ground and refuse to back down, they're likely to start hurling false accusations. When this happens, you'll often be on the receiving end of projection (being accused of something they're actually guilty of doing to you) or displacement (being accused of something someone else did to them in the past).

If none of this works to dissuade you from holding your ground, and you resist collapsing in the face of their one-up bullying, you'll most likely get insulted, with attacks on your character. You'll get accused of having "two sets of rules," being controlling, or otherwise abusing your power. And then you'll feel so confused and head-spinningly disoriented that you might not even remember what you were protesting. That's what narcissistic defenses are intended to do—disable your legitimate protest, make you doubt yourself, and avoid accountability for the boundary violator.

If your legitimate protest is met with narcissistic defenses, call a dead stop and hold your ground. Some people who initially resist accountability can come around in the postmortem. Once the initial trigger has passed and the other person is not in the midst of a nervous system hijack, you might be able to revisit a boundary breach. It's easier to be reflective when our brains aren't on fire. You can try revisiting the protest twenty-four to forty-eight hours later, during a redo conversation about what happened. Maybe the other person will then be able to cop to the mistake. Or you may need to outsource the boundary conversation and conflict resolution to a couples therapist.* Or, if they continue to shirk accountability and won't see a couples therapist, you may need to skip to Step Six and create space.

---

* If they will agree to see a couples therapist, we highly recommend finding one trained in Relational Life Therapy (RLT). Unlike most couples therapists, who take a neutral stance and can easily get manipulated by someone highly narcissistic, RLT therapists take sides and will back up the party who is one down and help hold the one-up person accountable, with compassion and a trauma-informed understanding of why it's so hard for some people to be held to account.

If the other person will not accept accountability no matter how hard you try, remember that you can still advocate for yourself and stand up for your parts even if the other person won't acknowledge wrongdoing. You can't force someone to be accountable when they mess up—you can't control that. But you *can* make changes in the nature of your relationship. Create more distance, if it's possible to do so. If that still doesn't work, remember, you are allowed to leave the relationship. You are never obligated to stay and suffer, whether those ongoing stressors might be exacerbating relationsickness or not.

Last, you'll need to grieve, whether you need to actually leave the relationship or just create more emotional distance. Grieve that you've chosen someone, or been born to someone or took a job with someone, who doesn't believe in accountability.

WHEN YOU'RE THE ONE WHO VIOLATES THE BOUNDARY

Let's say you participated in a mutually negotiated boundary agreement. You agreed to put your clothes away at the end of the day. But then you dropped the ball, and the other person is protesting. The ethical response is to admit your mistake, apologize for the boundary breach, and hold yourself to account, without resistance, when your partner protests that your clothes are all over the floor.

But don't stop there. Get curious about what might be happening with your parts. If you agreed to put your clothes away, and then didn't, why? Maybe strewing your clothes all over the bedroom is a habit, and you just forgot because the boundary is new. In which case, saying you made a mistake is an acceptable response.

However, it's possible that it's not quite so simple. This is when you might need to do some inner investigating, going back to Step Two and doing the YOU-Turn again. When people who fawn are first trying to break the fawning pattern, it's common to agree to something without consent from all of your parts. To the other person, it might look like you're 100 percent on board. But then you procrastinate, find yourself getting pissy and feeling resentful, second-guess yourself, or just passive-aggressively rebel against the plan you agreed to. You might not even remember agreeing to it if you were dissociating or otherwise checked out. If you then say "I never agreed to that plan!" to the other person, this can feel like gaslighting and be very confusing.

Perhaps you agreed to put your clothes away, but when it came time to do so, another part of you came in and started making a case for why your partner should put away both your clothes and theirs. You did the shopping, cooked the meals, did the dishes, watched the kids, and worked all day in your full-time job, while your partner has done nothing but go to work and come home and watch the game. Your overfunctioning parts are pissed, and what you actually want is for your partner to put away all the clothes before bedtime and do all the laundry, to help even the score. But maybe you didn't know how unfair you'd feel it was until it came time to put those clothes away.

If you find yourself having second thoughts about whether what you originally said was okay, you may need to return to Step Two and do another YOU-Turn. Go back to the conference table and find out which parts got left out the first time. If there's strong resistance to what you said yes to after the fact, you might need to renegotiate the boundary or agreement. This also applies if you realize you failed to speak on behalf of all parts in Step Three, but that's never a justification for breaking the initial agreement. You'll still need to repair the rupture.

After hearing the other person's protest, you can ask for the talking stick and own up to not putting your clothes away for the past three days when your partner kept to the agreement. Validate your partner's right to be upset about the boundary violation. Then express why you're feeling resentful about the agreement you previously said was okay. Ask if you can open up negotiation again, since you experienced backlash from your parts when the time came to do more household chores after spending all day doing more than your fair share of household tasks.

You can ask if your partner will share cooking and cleaning duty. Maybe you need more breaks from childcare and permission to veg out in front of the TV after work some of the time too. Maybe then you'd feel okay with both of you putting your own clothes away. Or maybe you're fine doing those other tasks, and all you want, just before bed, is for your partner to put away both of your clothes.

It's okay to reopen the negotiation and let your partner respond. But you still have to own up to breaking the agreement and validate your partner's right to feel upset if they kept it. You might have to go to Step Five to repair the rupture before you negotiate a new deal.

WHEN FAWNING CAUSES US TO HURT OTHERS

Often, people who fawn become the victims of others who take advantage of their generous nature. But as they say in twelve-step programs, part of healing is taking a moral inventory of how your compulsions, in this case the compulsion to fawn, may have harmed others. While we all deserve repair from the people who hurt us, we are also morally obligated to show up for repair with the people we've harmed.

How might we have inadvertently hurt people because of our fawning? Those who fawn can struggle because trauma has oriented our moral compass not toward keeping our word and staying true to our core values, but toward accommodating anyone we see as one up, even if they're asking us to do something that requires us to compromise our values or betray people we love. One client of Lissa's wound up coerced into giving all her money away to a spiritual guru because her fawning parts kicked in the minute she felt pressured by the pushy, fraudulent "holy man." This meant being disloyal to her family, giving away money that belonged to all of them without anyone else's consent.

A patient of Jeff's wound up cheating on his beloved wife with his boss at work, whom he wasn't attracted to, when his boss showed up in his office wearing only a bathrobe that she dropped before coming on to him. He was so afraid of humiliating her or her attacking or firing him if he rejected her that he reflexively complied, only to realize after the fawning fog wore off that he had just destroyed his marriage. His wife divorced him when he confessed to her what he'd done that same day.

It's inevitable that people who fawn will sometimes betray others, because we can't please everyone, and sometimes we have to choose between two people with competing interests. For example, if you're a divorced mom and you get involved with someone who feels entitled to make you choose between them and your child, you obviously can't both please your new partner and remain true to your responsibilities as a parent. If a mother rejects her child in favor of fawning a new partner she fears upsetting, that mother is breaking the contract for care and betraying her child.

Fawning is not our fault, but any harmful consequences that our fawning may lead to, for ourselves or others, are our responsibility to sort out. If we have strong fawning parts, we are likely to be the one who is the most victimized by them, because those parts can interfere with the parts of us that would otherwise protect us. But when we silence the justice-seeking parts of us that would otherwise hold others accountable, we may also fail to protect the ones we love. Even as we let other people stomp all over our own boundaries, we may also end up stomping all over other people's.

If you've been responsible for hurting other people because of your fawning, take the lead in your relational recovery by engaging in healthy repair with those you have hurt or betrayed due to your inability to say no to those who didn't have the best interests of the people you love at heart. You can start with simply saying "I messed up" or any other expression of remorse you can muster. If you caused significant harm, you'll want to participate in the full repair process described in Step Five.

WHEN ADMITTING YOU MESSED UP DOESN'T FEEL SAFE

If you're new to setting, enforcing, or being held accountable to boundaries, you're sure to screw up a few times. As we mentioned, that's normal. You're imperfect and human. So is the other person. Nobody with a history of trauma is going to get an instant gold star in boundaries.

While it's okay to make mistakes, it's not okay to cover up those mistakes, lie, deny someone else's reality, or shirk accountability, just because you might not have meant to hurt anyone. Some people who were not allowed to make mistakes without sustaining severe abuse in childhood learn to gaslight themselves when they've done something wrong. If you were forbidden from making mistakes, expected to be perfect, or beaten even if you did everything perfectly, the terror of being wrong or making an error can be so strong that you develop a part that convinces you that you haven't done anything wrong, even when you have.

If this happens, getting to know that protector part that tries to cover up mistakes instead of taking responsibility for them with the 6 F's on page 220 can help relax that part and allow for more honest admissions of guilt when you do inevitably make mistakes. Remember, it's okay to mess up, as long as you own it and then do your best to make changes, make repairs, and make amends.

STEP FIVE: REPAIR THE RUPTURE

If trust has been breached, work together to heal the breach and agree on a change in behavior for the future.

Lissa was attending an IFS workshop led by its founder, Dick Schwartz. Everyone had been diving deep into trauma healing all week, and the air in the retreat center felt tender and charged, as if everyone was walking around with freshly opened hearts. Wanting to help the group lighten up and have some fun, Lissa and two of her girlfriends decided to host a spontaneous dance party that evening, a way to shake off the intensity and move some energy through. Her friends had offered to help her set it up, DJ, and get people on the dance floor, and Lissa felt grateful not to be doing it alone.

At first, everything was going beautifully. The lights were low, the music was pulsing, people were laughing, and the room felt alive. But about fifteen minutes into it, Lissa looked around and realized her two friends were gone. A part of her tried to stay upbeat, leading the dancing and keeping the vibe fun. Everyone else seemed to be having a great time, and she didn't want to bring it down. But underneath, a younger part of her was quietly aching. Where did they go? Why didn't they tell her they were leaving?

When the dance wound down and people started to head out, Lissa went looking for her friends. She found them a little later at the retreat center, sitting around a fire pit. They looked sheepish when they saw her. "Where did you go?" Lissa asked, tears welling in her eyes. "You promised to help me, and I felt abandoned and lonely without you. I wouldn't have offered to host this if I'd known the two of you weren't going to be there to dance with me."

Her friends instantly softened. They didn't get defensive. They validated her feelings, admitted they'd messed up, and confessed that when the men's group, who'd been sequestered from the women all week, was released right as the dance started, they'd both gotten a little boy-crazy and temporarily lost track of their prior commitment.

They apologized sincerely; acknowledged how much that must have hurt; validated Lissa's upset feelings; and expressed regret and sadness over their impulsive, insensitive choice. One of them opened her arms. Lissa stepped into the hug, and the other friend joined, wrapping around them both. Then her friends offered to take her out for ice cream—their treat. It wasn't about the ice cream, of course. It was about accountability, care, and coming back into connection after rupture. The whole repair lasted about five minutes, which is what can happen when there's no defensiveness, justification, minimization of someone's upset, blame-shifting, or shirking of accountability. And isn't that what we all crave when we're brave enough to confront someone who's hurt us?

Many trauma survivors have zero lived experience of this kind of relational repair. When Lissa inquired about the subject at a month-long healing retreat she was teaching for frontline COVID-19 doctors and nurses after the pandemic, asking how many people in the group came from families of origin where relational repair was taught and modeled, she was shocked to be the only person raising her hand. The truth is, most people, trauma survivors or not, grew up in cultures and family systems that prized performance, obedience, or self-sufficiency over emotional repair. In many homes, conflict is avoided, minimized, or punished rather than resolved through accountability and reconnection. As a result, even securely attached, high-functioning adults may find themselves ill equipped to recognize and name harm, stay present in rupture, or move through repair.

Some people are quickly remorseful when they mess up and may apologize right away. Some who are more conflict avoidant might apologize even if they don't believe they've done anything wrong, just to keep the peace. Others go silent, stonewalling any attempt at repair, either because they have no idea how to do it or because they simply freeze. Some people instantaneously become defensive, even if they know they're guilty of doing something hurtful. Still others go on the attack, denying they've done anything wrong and blaming others for the very thing they themselves did. It's difficult to see, accept, and admit what we've done wrong when we hurt someone. But we must learn the art of repair if we want to have sustainable, healthy relationships that don't make us sick.

The talking stick works great to facilitate repair conversations. Whoever initiates the repair conversation gets the talking stick first. If you've hurt someone and are initiating repair by owning up to what you did that was hurtful, lead off with a humble confession, being specific about what you've done and admitting guilt. If it's the hurt party who is initiating the repair conversation, the one who did the hurting needs to pause and breathe through any inclination toward defensiveness, to give the hurt party a chance to express their feelings and have them validated. Often, when there's a rupture in a relationship, both parties are guilty of hurtful behavior, in which case whoever initiates the repair conversation goes first, and the talking stick is passed back and forth until there's understanding, compassion, ownership, and a plan to prevent future harm.

PRACTICE

HOW TO REPAIR A RELATIONSHIP RUPTURE

1. Be mindful of timing. When there's a rupture in a relationship, whether because an agreement has been violated or a boundary has been broken, both parties are usually upset, but the damage isn't always equal. It's rare that repair is initiated by the person who caused the rupture, so if you're the hurt one, you might need to protest first and then ask for the repair proactively. When doing so, be mindful of timing. Early in the morning when the other person is racing out the door for work, or late at night when they are tired or one or both of you have been drinking, are not great times to initiate a repair conversation. If you want a good outcome, ask for consent around the timing of what may be a difficult conversation.

2. Decide who takes the talking stick first. Ideally, the person who violated the boundary will know what they've done, go first, and lead off by clearly confessing the boundary breach and expressing empathy, followed by apologizing sincerely.

> *"I know I agreed to put my clothes away before bed, and I failed to do so three nights in a row. Then I got passive-aggressive about it because of the part of me that felt overextended. But that wasn't your fault. I shouldn't have agreed to something I wasn't actually prepared to do. I'm sorry I broke our agreement and then got huffy about it when you were trying to hold me to account."*

If the boundary violator isn't prepared to initiate, then the hurt party bears the burden of initiating repair. You might have to repeat your protest. Be direct, firm, and clear about what you're upset about. Don't be cruel, but also don't mince words. You can revisit your Accountability Feedback Practice communication tools from page 286 if it helps.

> *"When you said yes to working on the weekend, without consulting me, after we agreed you'd stay home with the family on weekends, I felt betrayed, sad, and angry. I need for you not to override my consent again by agreeing to work overtime without even discussing it with me."*

3. The listener holds space, listening for what's true, then mirrors back what they've heard so the speaking party knows the listener has understood. If the one going first is the hurt party, the hurting party validates why the hurt party has a right to be upset. If both parties have engaged in hurtful behavior, they take turns owning what they can about whatever happened. When someone has been hurt, if there's any chance at repair, they need to feel witnessed and validated, not only by their own Self in Step Two, but also by the person who hurt them, if at all possible. Assuming a valid protest has been registered, the listener needs to contain any defensiveness and focus on the person who has been hurt, summarizing what was said to show the hurt party that they were accurately understood.

It's possible that the listener will disagree completely with what the hurt party claims. They may remember the incident differently, and may not feel that they can validate anything the protesting party is saying. But even if they can only validate the hurt party's feelings, it can still help facilitate repair. In other words, if they can validate any facts at all about the other person's reality, they should do so. As Terry Real teaches, even if you can only validate 1 percent of what the other person says is true, try that.

For example, Lissa has a friend who veers into paranoia sometimes when she's triggered. She'll start accusing Lissa of outlandish things that aren't even close to reality, like how Lissa is going to steal her bitcoin or turn her into her slave. Lissa can't validate what she's being accused of, but because Lissa knows her—and her trauma history—really well, Lissa can say, "You're really scared right now, aren't you?" This still lets her friend feel seen and heard, which allows her nervous system to start to relax, allowing repair to happen even without Lissa validating her friend's exact story.

It helps to remind the person you're repairing with that you care, and that you're fighting for the relationship because the relationship matters to you. In their book *Fight Right*, Love Lab researchers and couples therapists John and Julie Gottman recommend adding positivity to moments of conflict with smiles, nods, and reassuring physical touch, emphasizing what you and the other person have in common, pointing out what the other person does right, and saying things like "Good point" or "Fair enough." You get bonus points if you're practicing IFS with someone else and can remember the other person's parts and why they might get triggered by certain behaviors.

> *"I hear that you feel betrayed, sad, and angry because I said I wouldn't work weekends and then I did. You want assurances that it's not going to happen again. It makes sense to me that you'd feel that way, after I promised I would start being less of a workaholic. Of course you feel betrayed, and scared that I'm just going to keep doing it and never change. I also get that this might be needling the parts of you that got neglected by your father when he didn't prioritize you or the family."*

4. The listener takes ownership for hurtful behaviors and extends a sincere apology. Assuming the hurt party spoke first, the next step is for whoever did the hurting to honestly confess what they've done, whether it's a boundary-violating trust breach, pulling out all the narcissistic defenses when they got caught, or otherwise messing up.

As V, formerly Eve Ensler, says in her book, *The Apology*, and her TED Talk, "The Profound Power of an Authentic Apology," this confession cannot be vague. It's not enough to say,

"I'm sorry you feel angry." The ownership needs to include a retelling of the hurtful thing that is as accurate as possible.

People who grew up not feeling safe to mess up frequently will avoid admitting wrongdoing, even if they're with someone with whom it would be safe to do so now. They may fear that they'll be the one getting stuck with all the blame and the other person won't own any part of the conflict. Or they might be afraid of someone else's verbally or physically violent response. Or they may be afraid of getting rejected and losing the connection altogether. Asking, "What are you afraid would happen if you admitted what you did?" can sometimes point to an exile that got hurt when confessing wrongdoing in the past.

If someone cannot acknowledge that what they've done is hurtful and that the other person has a right to be upset, you might need a couples or family therapist. If that isn't an option, you may choose to skip to Step Six and create space.

> *"It's true that I worked all weekend after promising you I would say no the next time my boss asked me to work overtime. I know I promised to at least take Monday and Tuesday off if I absolutely couldn't find a way to get the job done without working on the weekend, and I failed to follow through on our compromise. Then, when you confronted me about it, I blamed you and accused you of being controlling and not being supportive of my work, which is not true. You have every right to be upset, and I'm really sorry."*

5. The protesting party responds. If the person who did the hurting has done a decent job taking ownership for what they've done, this usually opens the heart of the protesting party and makes it easier for them to forgive. The person who was hurt might still be upset, and the listener might need to let them vent a bit before moving on. But the more the hurt party can reward real ownership, the better the repair will go. A lot of people who were punished as children for making mistakes or being vulnerable may be terrified of what will happen when they confess rather than avoid accountability. If the hurt party can extend bids for connection to begin to soften the tension, this can help reward healing behavior and encourage an easier repair next time.

> *"Thank you for not being defensive. I know you're trying hard to be more available to me and the kids, and I know it's hard when your boss gets pushy and you get scared of pushing back. I appreciate you owning up to the boundary breach, and I know you're working really hard on doing better."*

6. The listener can now offer explanations. Timing is important here. If the listener disagrees with some of what the hurt party said, if there's been a misunderstanding or if the hurting party wants to explain why they did what they did, this is the time—*after* the hurt party has been validated and feels at least a little less upset.

Maybe the boundary wasn't clear or the listener misunderstood. Maybe they felt so much pressure to break the boundary (in order to fawn someone else) that they felt justified in the moment. Maybe they felt inappropriately entitled to break the boundary because they have issues with power and control and are struggling with the idea of a more equal relationship. The "why" often plagues victims, so giving the person who did the hurting a chance to explain can be helpful toward the hurt party letting go and moving on, as long as the explanation is used to provide context and understanding, and not to minimize personal responsibility.

"When my boss came bursting into my office in a panic and threatened to overlook me for a promotion—again—if I didn't demonstrate my loyalty to the company now that it's crunch time, I just froze. I blended with my obedient part and honestly wasn't even thinking about you and the kids until I got in the car and realized I'd just done it again and there would probably be hell to pay."

7. The listener can also protest if they need to. It's rare that one party is 100 percent guilty and the other is 100 percent innocent. Once the person who broke the boundary has owned up to the boundary breach and the hurt party feels better, the original offender can air any feelings or protests they have around the way things played out. After they get their chance at the talking stick, the original protester needs to offer the same empathy, mirroring, validation, and, if need be, apologies. Keep in mind that this doesn't mean that the blame is shared equally or that ownership has to be equally shared.

"I know I screwed up, but you don't have to yell or call me names when I make a mistake. When I mess up, you sound like my mother, and my young protectors just want to get away from you, even though I know I need to stay relational and own up to what I've done. It would help if you could be less verbally abusive and superior when you catch me making a mistake."

"I hear that I remind you of your mother when I get verbally abusive after you've broken an agreement. It's wrong of me to call you names and get sarcastic. I lose it because it's happened so many times, and I'm just so frustrated, but that doesn't excuse me from weaponizing my words. I'm sorry for the way I reacted."

8. Reestablish boundaries and make amends. The boundary-violating party asks what the hurt party needs in order to feel repaired, restored, and able to move forward. If both parties are hurt, both people can address what amends might be needed.

"How can I make it up to you?"

"Mostly, I just need assurances that you won't do it again."

"I know I need to work on the part of me that just freezes and fawns my boss, without thinking about how it impacts you and the kids. I'm willing to pay for us to see a therapist together, so you can see I'm really committed to changing that pattern. I'm also going to work on setting firmer boundaries with my boss. Nowhere in my contract does it obligate me to work overtime, and if that's what is expected for a promotion, I might just have to let go of that hope. Honestly, if I had to choose between the promotion and our family, I'd choose you and the kids. No amount of money, power, or status is worth losing you all. Is there anything I can do to make it up to the kids?"

"Maybe we can all go out for pizza tonight? And yes, let's go talk to a therapist about all this, because I don't yet trust that you won't just do this again next month. If this keeps happening, I'm scared our marriage might fail."

"I'd hate that. Yes, let's go see a therapist together. I feel ashamed that I let you all down. I think I need help getting my priorities straight."

REBUILDING TRUST AFTER RUPTURE

Sometimes a full repair isn't possible at the time of a rupture. We may need to take some space to calm our nervous systems, fully understand what happened, own our part, hold ourselves and/or the other person accountable for our/their part, and find our way back to compassion for ourselves and each other. What sometimes helps is inviting the other person into a "redo."

In the IFS unburdening process, part of healing our wounded parts is asking them what they wish had happened differently and letting them experience that imagined alternative reality. When we experience relational ruptures with other people, we can sometimes do the same thing in real time.

For example, let's say Marta and her friend Elsie, both fluent in IFS and capable of pausing and doing the YOU-Turn, negotiated an agreement together, which they signed and documented, in which Marta, a professional editor, would help Elsie with her grad school essay, and Elsie, a personal trainer, would in exchange provide Marta with some training sessions.

Elsie's essays were on a tight deadline, so Marta put aside some of her own urgent business to prioritize helping Elsie meet her deadline. And then months went by without Marta receiving the agreed-upon training sessions. Marta has a hard time standing up for herself, and was waiting for Elsie to initiate making good on her end of the bargain. Rather than speak up and ask when it would be convenient for Elsie to schedule the training sessions, Marta got increasingly annoyed, resentful, and hurt. But Elsie was so caught up in grad school prep that not only did she forget to reach out about the sessions, she didn't even notice that Marta had stopped responding to her texts or making bids for connection.

Six months later, when Elsie invited Marta to meet her out at the local pub for a drink, Marta blew up and started attacking Elsie for breaching their contract and taking advantage of her with the essay help.

Elsie felt blindsided. So much time had elapsed that she'd forgotten what she'd promised altogether and didn't understand why Marta was coming unhinged.

After the initial shock, Elsie vaguely remembered that they'd agreed to a trade and felt a rush of shame when she realized she'd failed to keep up her end of the deal. But she also felt angry at Marta for waiting so long to remind her and for attacking her over something she fully intended to do when she agreed to the bargain and had simply forgotten about.

After composing herself and calming her defensiveness, Elsie invited Marta into a repair conversation. She started by going through the repair steps until Marta felt restored, including putting not only the original training sessions on the calendar, but also a few extra.

But in order to protect their friendship, Elsie asked for one more step—a redo. She asked Marta if she'd be willing to go back in time and talk about how the two of them could have negotiated the whole thing in a healthier, more respectful fashion.

Elsie started the redo by admitting that she should have put training sessions on the calendar with Marta right out of the gate. She knew she was swamped with grad school prep and should have known herself well enough to realize she might just space on what she'd agreed to do. With that acknowledgment, Elsie added that she wished Marta would have just reached out to remind her, rather than staying silent, making assumptions about Elsie's motivations, and then lashing out six months later.

Feeling validated by Elsie's acknowledgment that Elsie had screwed up by not being more proactive, Marta owned up to her part in the confusion around their agreement. She acknowledged and took responsibility for her conflict-avoidant, passive-aggressive behavior, and apologized for the immature way she handled feeling blown off. They both agreed that, next time they made an agreement, they'd include a plan for its implementation. If they'd just scheduled Marta's training sessions at the same time they scheduled Elsie's essay help—even if they'd scheduled the sessions further out, when Elsie wasn't so busy—they'd have prevented damage to their relationship and avoided a lot of hurt feelings.

Every time we complete a successful repair and then go through the redo process, we learn how to relate more sensitively to someone we love and teach them what our parts need in order to develop trust, safety, and healthy closeness. Once they went through the redo, Marta and Elsie knew each other a little better, and also gained valuable insight into how to more fairly follow through with future agreements.

PRACTICE

HOW TO HAVE A REDO CONVERSATION

1. Either party suggests a redo and requests a better way to handle things next time. If the one initiating the redo can own any part of the conflict, this is a good way to start. Even if one party is the primary agreement-breaker, the one who feels betrayed can, if they choose, begin by owning their conflict-avoidant parts that didn't speak up or their passive-aggressive parts that acted out. This requires getting to know the parts that might have contributed to the dynamic, and speaking on behalf of those parts.

> *"Marta, I'm sorry I forgot to reach out and initiate scheduling your training sessions. I know I have scattered, disorganized ADHD parts that can make me forgetful or insensitive, and I could have been more proactive about getting those sessions on the calendar as soon as you started helping me with my essays."*

2. The other party owns their part and makes requests for how they wish things had gone down differently.

> *"I get it, Elsie. I could have been much more proactive about reminding you what we'd agreed upon, rather than waiting for you to initiate. I knew you were*

> *swamped and stressed about grad school applications, and I could have been more sensitive to that and given you the benefit of the doubt, rather than letting my catastrophizing parts assume the worst about your intentions."*
>
> **3. Both parties discuss what they need in the future in order to communicate better; troubleshoot issues if they arise again; and improve trust, intimacy, and connection going forward.**
>
> *"Let's go one step further in the future and plan our follow-through as part of negotiating the agreement. That way we can get ahead of any possible misunderstandings."*

STEP SIX: REWARD OR CREATE SPACE

Depending on whether or not repair was successful, reinforce positive behavior or be proactive about creating more distance in the relationship.

If you've been successful in repairing the rupture, celebrate and appreciate! A little cherishing can go a long way when you're trying to reinforce positive behavior change. Especially if you're trying to repair with someone who is used to being met with shame and humiliation instead of compassion when they admit wrongdoing, this is your chance to help them lay down new neural pathways. By showing them they can mess up and be held accountable without anything horrible happening, you improve their ability to own up to mistakes.

We cannot stress it enough: If you got through these first five steps successfully, you and the other person deserve a gold star! For anyone with a long history of nervous system dysregulation and relational trauma, these relational skills can be monumentally challenging. If you struggled along the way, things didn't go as you hoped, or you're worried you somehow got it wrong, please go easy on yourself. These are the kinds of skills people often need years of therapy to master. Even with a Level 2 relationship, it may take months or even years of therapy to make it all the way through all six steps. If you're in a Level 3 or 4 relationship, you might not have even made it past Step One before discovering you need to skip straight here to create space.

If you're with someone really controlling, you might have been pressured to instantaneously comply or face hell to pay. You might have been trying to negotiate with someone who has no interest in sharing power with you, compromising, or helping you get your needs met. You might be with someone who says they're going to respect your boundaries but then refuses to do so. Or you might have discovered that you're with someone who has a real accountability problem and gets defensive rather than taking ownership when they mess up. Regardless of the path you took to get to Step Six, you can always celebrate the strength and courage of your own brave internal family system, even if you realize you need to create space with someone else.

If you do need to create space, we can help support you in figuring out how to do so with care for both yourself and the other person, in a relational way that leaves you feeling like you took the high road, even if your self-protective actions cause discomfort in others. Working through the Six Steps, you might have collected useful but disappointing discernment data about some of the people you've been trying to relate with, evidence that suggests you'll need more space from this person if you want to optimize your health outcome. In extreme cases, you might have even discovered a need to go "no contact" and cut them out of your life altogether.

Hang onto this mantra: *Unconditional love, conditional access.*

Some people assume that loving someone means tolerating all their behaviors, no matter what. But that's the kind of mindset that causes people to get relationsick. Loving someone doesn't mean infinite hall passes. You can love someone and still end the relationship. You can love someone from the other side of prison bars. No matter how much you care about someone, no matter how attached you are to them or how much affection you feel, even if you've promised to never leave them, you can't protect your health without healthy boundaries.

Intimacy is not all or nothing. It's also ever-changing. Depending on what happens between two people in real time, trust and feelings of safety (or the lack thereof) go up and down. The closeness in a relationship will, and should, fluctuate depending on how much trust is present.

HOW MANY MARBLES ARE IN YOUR RELATIONAL JAR?

Brené Brown says that trust in relationships is like a jar of marbles. Every trustworthy action adds a marble or two to the jar, while one big betrayal can empty the whole darn thing. Some people enter relationships by giving new people an empty jar, requiring that they earn every single marble. Others give total strangers a completely full jar of marbles, without waiting to see if they deserve such a gift. We believe it's fair to give new people half a jar of good faith marbles, letting them earn the rest or lose them.

Take a moment and check how many marbles are in the jars of the people you're in close relationships with. How much trust do you have, and was that trust earned or blindly gifted? Did you bother to take marbles out of the jar if someone did something untrustworthy? Trust is something that builds over time, not something we should just give people who haven't earned it or who have repetitively betrayed our trust.

How will you know whether someone deserves more marbles or less? You'll have to pay attention. We can learn a lot about whether someone is worth keeping in our inner circle by doing the healing work in this chapter. Seeing how people respond to your efforts to get relationally healthier is part of how you can tell who can be trusted—and who really shouldn't be.

UNCONDITIONAL LOVE, CONDITIONAL ACCESS

People with a tendency to fawn also tend to see intimacy as binary: You're either "all in" or "all out." But if negotiations, boundaries, accountability, and repair attempts have failed, it's not safe to be all in, and you may need to adjust intimacy to a level that *is* safe. We're not just talking about sexual intimacy, although that's sometimes included. Intimacy can mean how emotionally exposed you allow yourself to be, how much access someone has to your time, energy, or home, or whether or not you commingle finances. It's the degree to which you let someone see and affect you. Adjusting intimacy isn't punishment; it's an act of self-protection and discernment. Healthy intimacy requires mutual trust and safety, and when that isn't present, protecting your heart by limiting contact or depth of sharing is an act of love—for yourself and even for the other person, who may not yet have the capacity to meet you in that deeper space.

The reasons you might wind up needing to adjust your intimacy level can vary. Maybe someone blew up the minute you asked for a pause. Or maybe they dug their heels in and refused to negotiate, insisting, "It's my way or the highway." Or maybe they agreed to respect a boundary but then refused to do so. Or maybe you tried to repair but couldn't get past their narcissistic defenses, and even revisiting the conversation after your nervous systems had calmed down failed to lead to repair. But in each of these circumstances, there needs to be consequences—not as a punishment, but as a way to protect yourself and create the nervous system conditions necessary for your nervous system to relax and your health to improve. That's where creating space comes in.

Sometimes, it's enough to just create temporary physical distance between you and someone else. If you choose this route, it helps to warn the other person how long you'll be gone. Especially if they have an anxious or disorganized attachment style, you don't want to activate their fear of abandonment and trigger unnecessary panic. Also, if you say you need an hour, and then it turns out you need twelve or twenty-four, be sure to communicate that clearly.

Sometimes taking temporary space isn't enough. If someone you're close with has proved untrustworthy, you may need to escalate the consequences by withholding certain privileges that come with intimacy. Rather than all or nothing, healthy people with good boundaries see intimacy on more of a dial, making the respect, care, trustworthiness, and willingness to cooperate mutually during the Six Steps a precondition of certain degrees of closeness.

To employ the intimacy dial, imagine in your mind's eye a dial from 0 to 10, with 0 meaning zero contact, in person or digitally, and 10 meaning the other person lives in your house, shares your finances, has access to your social network, and/or sleeps in your bed. Certain privileges should only be shared with safe people. While you do not have the right to control another person, you do have the right to grant these privileges or take them away, depending on how someone is behaving and whether they're proving to be trustworthy. Losing privileges is a natural consequence when enough attempts at setting boundaries or engaging in repair fail.

The way the intimacy dial works is that, moment by moment, you can choose to turn it up or down, based on whether or not the other person is respecting your expressed needs and boundaries. If things are going well, you might dial them up. You might spend more time together, have sex together, join your households, enjoy emotionally deep conversations, and spend a lot of time investing in the intimacy between you. If things are going badly, you might dial them down. This might mean sleeping in another bedroom, converting a romance into a friendship, divvying up your finances, or spending less time with them one on one. This is not a manipulation or a way to punish someone; it's a way to break the enabling pattern, to enact consequences when you're being mistreated, to keep yourself and your parts safe from further harm. We teach people how to treat us by communicating through our actions what we're willing to tolerate and ignore and showing that we respect ourselves enough to protect ourselves.

The intimacy dial mostly applies to adults with adults. Children have a right to survival needs no matter what: things like food, a roof over their head, and your loving attention. It would be cruel and abusive to withhold them because a child doesn't act the way we wish they would or doesn't yet have the skills and maturity for accountability and repair. But when we're talking about adult-to-adult relationships, nobody is automatically entitled to receive these things from you. Within the limits of marital and domestic partnership law, privileges can be granted or taken away depending on whether someone demonstrates the ability to respect the limits you set.

Whether someone else chooses to respect those limits is not something you can control, but you can control what happens if they don't. If someone isn't treating you and your boundaries with respect, you have the right to restrict access. Once again: *Unconditional love, conditional access.* It isn't selfish to care for ourselves in this way; it is loving and self-compassionate. And it just might make the difference between disease recovery and staying relationsick.

PRACTICE

USING THE INTIMACY DIAL

1. Consider the privileges you offer your core relationships. What privileges do you currently offer in various relationships that could be withheld (where ethical and legal) as a way to take your power back and establish consequences for someone who won't respect your boundaries? For example:

- Access to your vulnerable emotions, secrets, traumas, and tender heart.
- Coming over to your house, sleeping over in your home, or living with you.
- Privileged access to time alone with you, your energy, and your help when things get rough.
- Texts, phone calls, or visits with you.
- Physical touch and/or sex.
- Eating meals you shop for, pay for, and prepare.
- Access to your social network of friends and family.
- Invitations to your parties and social events.
- Traveling with you.
- Use of your property, such as driving your car.

2. Consider which, if any, privileges you might choose to take away. Notice what feelings arise as you think about how this might impact you, the other person, or anyone else who might be affected, like kids.

WRITING PROMPT: When you think about withholding privileges as a consequence of someone else's refusal to respect your boundaries, negotiate agreements, or participate in repair, what feelings come up? Go around the conference table and check in with your parts. Give the pen to any parts that hold fear, anxiety, guilt, or any other feelings or reactions.

3. Troubleshoot your plan. Before withdrawing your chosen privileges, think about the details of what might need to happen in order to do so. Talking to a therapist about strategies to make sure you're not blending with punishing or vengeful parts or being overly severe can be helpful.

When we have unconditional love for ourselves—when we use our boundaries to protect our vulnerability—abusive relationships naturally begin to fall away. Likewise, when we show compassion to each other, as well as our parts inside, respectful, balanced relationships built upon kindness and genuine intimacy become possible. If you keep finding yourself in relationships with people who disrespect you, you can be sure that, somewhere underneath, you're disrespecting yourself by enabling others to get away with treating you poorly. Teaching others how you deserve to be treated, by modeling for yourself the kind of nurturing care you have a right to expect from those in your inner circle, isn't some kind of entitled, demanding way of being. It's simply an invitation, one others can choose to accept, reject, or negotiate with.

You don't have to be Hindu to take a lesson from the goddesses of yoga, which can be grouped into the fierce goddesses (like the goddess of death and destruction, Kali) and the gentle goddesses (like the goddess of abundance, Lakshmi, or the goddess of marriage, fertility, and beauty, Parvati). If you disrespect the fierce goddesses, they'll cut off your head. But if you disrespect the gentle goddesses, they simply turn away, taking their boons and gifts elsewhere, leaving you wondering where all the blessings and beauty went. You don't have to cut off anyone's head to demonstrate what works for you and what doesn't. Instead, you can just choose to bestow upon the people you respect (and who respect you) the gifts and blessings that come with being close to you.

If you've been granting someone privileged access to your boons and blessings without expecting them to treat you with respect, kindness, and fairness, suddenly withdrawing those boons and blessings might create conflict, if they have come to feel entitled to them. But remember, enabling someone else's bad behavior is not doing that person any real favors.

Behaviors that violate boundaries are *supposed* to result in painful outcomes for the violator. When others violate your boundaries, they're supposed to feel bad. Their empathy for your sadness, anger, disappointment, or frustration is supposed to motivate better behavior going forward. But if someone has had their empathy traumatized out of them, witnessing your distress is usually not enough.

Losing a privilege or boon they cherish, on the other hand, can be more motivating. You can't make someone do this work, and you don't have a right to apply undue pressure on them to do so. But you *can* take responsibility for your own intimacy dial and decide who you let close and how close you let them. It might affect the other person in ways complaining alone might not, and could help you get through to them in ways your distress alone could not. Most importantly, it helps you protect yourself and your parts. This allows you to build self-trust, which is especially important when you're dealing with people whose trustworthiness might be questionable.

FINDING YOUR SWEET SPOT

It might take some trial and error with the intimacy dial to find your relationship's "sweet spot," the place where you don't trigger each other constantly, where you're close enough that you feel connected but maintain enough separateness that your attachment styles don't ping off each other and create unnecessary drama.

Finding your sweet spot may take trial and error. For example, you might try dialing a romantic partner down to a 7/10, only to realize you're still activating each other or getting physical symptoms. In that case, you might need to dial down to 3/10. If your symptoms get better and the relationship stabilizes, great! You might then try dialing up to 4/10 or 5/10 to see what happens. If you're dealing with someone reasonably healthy, the relationship will usually rebalance into a new normal, even if that means changing a romance into a more boundaried friendship or becoming friends-only with someone you used to work with.

Over time, if trust builds, you can try dialing back up. Sometimes this happens when couples separate, go to therapy, and then move back in together; the trial separation creates space for the couple to interrupt long-embedded patterns. Other times, you might find that you have to keep dialing down and down and down . . . until you go "no contact." But often, setting good boundaries—and being willing to respect the other person's—can help you find your sweet spot.

You'll know you've found your sweet spot when extreme triggers dissipate and there's more harmony. Especially if you're trying to be close to someone with avoidant or disorganized attachment, or who suffered from too much enmeshment and intrusion growing up—and *especially* if they are not getting help in therapy—creating more space can actually be good for the relationship, even if it's sad that you have to sacrifice an element of closeness.

ETHICAL WAYS TO CREATE SPACE OR END A RELATIONSHIP

When you begin using the Six Steps, you may not be clear what level your relationship is. You might think you're in a Level 2 relationship only to discover it's worse than you thought. Or you might have thought you were in a Level 3 relationship, only to find that the other person is very responsive to your clear boundaries and willing to change the dynamics of your relationship. We created the Six Steps to help you figure that out, as safely as possible: to find out whether healing relationsickness while staying in your relationships is possible, and whether your unbalanced relationships can be successfully rebalanced.

Sometimes, all efforts at salvaging a relationship fail, and you simply have no choice but to turn the intimacy dial down to zero and go no contact. This can mean divorce from a partner, estrangement from a parent, leaving a job, cutting off a friendship completely, or firing your coach. When dealing with a Level 3 or 4 relationship, this may be your best option. Going no contact means clearly stating that you don't wish to have any further contact and making that an immovable boundary. Delete them from your phone. Block them from your email. Do not let them in your house. Get a restraining order if they stalk you after you've asked them to leave you alone.

It won't always be possible to go no contact—for example, if you're coparenting a young child or otherwise unable to get away completely. In that case, experts in narcissism recommend going "gray rock" or "yellow rock." Gray-rocking means deliberately disengaging, making yourself so bland and nonreactive that you become as uninteresting to the narcissist as a gray rock, in order to protect yourself from further abuse. Narcissists thrive off attention, even negative attention. By minimizing the narcissist's ability to manipulate or provoke you, you deprive them of the emotional reaction or attention they seek. In doing so, you essentially disappear from the narcissist's radar, making it more likely they'll get their attention-seeking needs met elsewhere and torment you less.

To gray rock, give minimal responses, avoid personal details, and maintain a neutral demeanor, no matter how much they try to provoke or engage you. You do not need to let them know you're gray-rocking them. That can be used against you. Just limit your interactions to the bare minimum. Just the facts.

"Yellow-rocking" is a slightly sunnier version of gray-rocking. It's gray-rocking with a few pleasantries, which can be useful if you're coparenting, for example, since seeing their parents engaging in mildly pleasant behavior can be easier on children.

Be aware that if you go no contact, gray rock, or yellow rock with a narcissist, this withdrawal might result in "hoovering" behavior, wherein the narcissist tries to vacuum you back into their life with new manipulations, like fresh bouts of love bombing or "future faking"—promises of grand things to come that never materialize. Even if you've been the one getting abused, the psychological fragility of narcissism can cause the narcissist to start flattering and manipulating *you* the minute they think they might get abandoned.

If you notice yourself getting hoovered back in, you may need to remind yourself why you decided to create space in the first place; recalling what someone has put you through can help motivate you to stay firm with your boundaries. It's tempting to just gloss over hurtful and abusive behaviors if you're on the conflict-avoidant side. Keep in mind what's at stake: your nervous system, your health, and potentially your life.

One way to remind yourself why you're removing someone from your life, especially if they start a love-bombing campaign when you try to create space, is writing a victim impact statement. Traditionally used in courts of law to aid in sentencing, victim impact statements typically include all the potential ways you've been harmed by someone else's abuse. They include emotional effects (fear, trauma, PTSD, pain and suffering, other mental health issues), physical injuries or illnesses (relationsickness), financial losses (medical bills, lost wages, property damage), career damage or opportunity cost, and impact on children or other relationships.

Although it can be healing and validating to write a victim impact statement just for yourself as part of your healing, victim impact statements also can be a tool for healing your relationship. Consider sending your victim impact statement to the person you're going no contact with, or even to someone you've already cut out of your life, if you have any interest in giving that person a final chance to reclaim space back in your life. While you may get no response, in rare instances a victim impact statement may break through a perpetrator's denial and open a window for reconciliation and repair.

A client of Jeff's who is estranged from his children received victim impact statements from all four of his kids after behaving in ways that ended his marriage to their mother and caused his children unspeakable suffering. He was in a twelve-step program at the time, trying to take a moral inventory of his life and make amends for harm he caused. As he told Jeff, he never would have had a chance at amends had his children not been brave enough to send those victim impact statements. He wouldn't have been able to craft a specific-enough apology without the details they provided, some of which he couldn't remember. While he is still estranged from one of his children because he can't yet bear to read another victim impact statement, he's back in touch with three of his kids and working hard to complete the repair and amends process so he can have them all back in his life.

It's impossible to know whether someone who has hurt you will be moved by a victim impact statement. While many people who perpetrate abusive behavior will shirk accountability indefinitely, some self-aware individuals will break out of the trance of denial and do right by the people they've hurt. You never know if the person who's hurt you will be one of those people unless you try.

Be prepared to be ignored, however. Make sure you work with your own parts before deciding whether to send the statement, ensuring that your parts are in consent and that you're not just blended with one justice-seeking part. If being ignored would worsen your distress, you might reconsider whether it's worth the vulnerability of opening yourself up to even more rejection and pain. Especially if confronting your abuser may lead to further abuse, including gaslighting, stalking, or physical violence, your attempt at getting justice and healing could backfire. For your own safety, be careful and consult appropriate authorities for guidance if there's any question whether it's safe to share your victim impact statement.

You can write your victim statement either in third person, as you would to a judge or, if you wish, in second person, as if directly addressed to your perpetrator.

PRACTICE

WRITE A VICTIM IMPACT STATEMENT

1. Summarize the relationship.

For over eleven years, I was in a relationship with someone highly narcissistic who presented themselves as caring, charismatic, and trustworthy but who gradually isolated, manipulated, controlled, exploited, and gaslit me.

2. Describe the abuse. You don't need to recount every incident. Focus on recurring tactics and how they made you feel, highlighting key patterns (gaslighting, blame-shifting, silent treatment, love bombing, devaluation, exploitation, etc.).

He repeatedly manipulated me in order to get me to cooperate with his self-absorbed and exploitative plans, coercing me, without my consent, into giving him money for so-called emergencies that turned out to be scams. When I tried to stand up for myself, he told me that my memories were inaccurate, disputed facts I could readily prove, accused me of being selfish for standing up for what I needed, and blamed me for the very things he was doing. He told me that my friends, who protected and supported me, were untrustworthy; that I was cheating when I wasn't; that I was exploiting him when it was actually me getting exploited; and that my emotional reactions were signs of psychological instability. He drove a wedge between me and my daughter, and I was too frightened of him to stand up for the responsibilities of mothering her.

3. Itemize the impact on your mental and physical health. Be explicit about the toll the abuse took on you: chronic pain, autoimmune conditions, insomnia, eating disorders, headaches, anxiety, depression, C-PTSD, and the like. Mention any diagnoses, medications, hospitalizations, and/or therapy you've required as a result.

> *The chronic stress led to adrenal collapse, panic attacks, fibromyalgia, and eventually a diagnosis of complex PTSD. I now live with chronic migraines and multiple inflammatory medical conditions that my doctors directly link to prolonged emotional trauma.*

4. List the impact on your daily functioning. How has your ability to work, maintain relationships, parent, and/or care for yourself been affected? Mention financial repercussions if applicable.

> *There were months when I couldn't work due to medical problems, chronic fatigue, and panic attacks triggered by authority figures or raised voices. I lost income, missed job opportunities, drained my savings on medical and therapeutic care, and lost touch with most of my supportive friends because I was intentionally isolated and coerced into turning my back on people who actually loved me.*

5. Be honest about emotional consequences. Describe how your sense of self, trust in others, relationship with children or family, and/or hope for the future has been altered. Avoid exaggeration, but don't minimize.

> *I no longer trust my own instincts. I second-guess every decision and have had to rebuild my identity from the*

ground up. I lost custody of my daughter and regret terribly that my abuser caused me to lose my most precious of identities—mother. Now, the world seems like a scary place and I feel hopeless about my future.

6. Be specific about what you need and any amends you want. What could your abuser do to even begin to make it up to you? What do you need in order to feel safe again? In legal or restitution settings, state clearly what you hope will result: acknowledgment, accountability, protection orders, and/or reparations. Outside of legal situations, make it clear what would help you recover: money for therapy, admitting the truth about what was done to you to others who have been affected, cooperation with any legal proceedings without defensiveness, and/or any boundaries you're setting.

I am asking that he not be allowed to contact me for at least a year. If he would like to participate in my healing, I would appreciate it if he would be required to pay for my $300/week therapy, my daughter's therapy, and the balance of my unpaid medical bills.

7. Offer a closing statement. Conclude with a powerful, truthful message about your resilience, recovery, or ongoing needs.

Though I've been deeply wounded, I'm committed to my healing and recovery, whether he chooses to participate in my healing or not. I write this not because I actually believe he'll read it or respond, but because I owe it to my own hurt parts to speak the truth, whether he listens to me and validates what I'm saying or not. I speak out not only for myself, but for others who suffer in silence under the grip of coercive control.

LETTING GO WHEN NOTHING ELSE HAS WORKED

You might be wondering: Where does forgiveness fit into all this? Teachings around forgiveness can be some of the most confusing for people in abusive relationships. It's true that holding grudges and carrying seething rage indefinitely is not good for anyone. It's also true that abusers often try to pressure victims to forgive them as a way of letting them off the hook and carrying on in the relationship as if nothing bad has happened, putting the burden of responsibility for forgiveness on the victim, not the perpetrator.

Real forgiveness happens most authentically when someone who has hurt us makes sincere efforts at repair and amends. In *The Apology* and *The Profound Power of an Authentic Apology*, V says that if perpetrators of abuse want to offer those they've hurt a real apology, they need to engage in four steps:

1. Engage in humble self-interrogation, in which abusers get curious about the perpetrator parts that made them capable of doing whatever they did, and what in our culture might have caused them to justify this behavior.
2. Create a detailed accounting of exactly what they've done, and making a full confession.
3. Put themselves in the shoes of the person they hurt and feeling their pain, so their own heart can break. This step requires empathy and perspective taking. They have to be willing to acknowledge the long-term damage they might have caused and really let themselves feel that deep but healthy shame that can motivate repair.
4. Practice radical ownership, taking responsibility for what they've done, and making amends and reparations where possible. The victim must fully understand that the perpetrator is profoundly changed and that they will never repeat the offense, not ever.

It's easier to forgive if you're received a real apology. But sometimes that's impossible. Maybe your abuser is a malignant narcissist or a sociopath and you're just never going to get a real repair. Or maybe they're dead and you still feel burdened by what's happened. IFS can help. So can V.

For those who will never get this kind of apology but want to heal, you can do this for your own parts, as part of the "redo" step of unburdening your exiles, giving yourself the apology your parts need to hear, but from you in Self. You can also try doing what V did. In her book *The Apology*, V shares a letter she wrote to herself on behalf of her deceased, sexually abusive father. It includes a detailed, graphic accounting of exactly what happened, and features him taking complete ownership of his actions and validating how her parts were hurt.

You can't force a perpetrator to participate in repair or give you a real apology. But you can go no contact with your perpetrator and give your own parts the apology you'll only get in the inner world, the way V did. Sometimes this will help you let go, grieve, and move on, releasing the perpetrator's grip on you, even when nothing else has helped. It may sound silly, but having participated in this process ourselves, we can both attest to its profound healing power.

PRACTICE

GIVE YOUR PARTS THE APOLOGY THEY'LL ONLY GET FROM YOU

Channeling your perpetrator and taking notes from your victim impact statement, follow the four steps to give your parts what they need to hear but are not going to get from the one who hurt you.

Start by writing the apology down, so you can get it out of your body and onto the page. But don't stop there. Although it might sound weird, it's very healing to record yourself reading the apology letter and then play it out loud. When your hurt parts hear your own voice reading those words, those parts—and the parts that protect them—have the potential to feel profound relief and finally let the hurt go. Even though the apology is not being given by the one who hurt you, it can be deeply healing for your parts to hear that YOU believe them, that YOU are sorry, that YOU want to be with them as they heal. You might even ask a trusted friend to read you the letter so your parts can fully absorb what's being said.

While this might sound like gaslighting your parts, from your parts' perspective, getting this healing from you in Self is absolutely real. As neuroscience has shown, this is how neuroplasticity happens. When we revisit those traumatic memories, we open up the trauma-related neural pathways, making them capable of change. When our parts hear the apology, when we register it in our nervous systems, we can rewrite those neural superhighways, replacing the pathways of trauma with the new neural circuitry of repair, thereby calming our dysregulated nervous system and letting our body's natural self-healing mechanisms get to work.

For a sample four-step apology letter, visit Relationsick.com.

REBUILDING TRUST AND LETTING GRIEF FLOW

When we're kids and we're abused, we do not need to forgive ourselves. We were kids. We were innocent. It was not in any way our fault. But when we've been abused in adulthood, and especially if an adult relationship was a reenactment of a childhood trauma, we often *do* have to forgive ourselves, especially if we've stayed in the relationship beyond when it might have been wiser and kinder to ourselves to leave. While fawning may have been a powerful survival strategy in childhood, when we blend with fawning parts or others that interfere with our protection in the present day, the trust between Self and our hurt parts can be lost. Also, some parts may not trust other parts. Because our safety/danger compass may have been upside down due to early trauma, our hurt parts might distrust the parts that choose our close attachments over self-protection. We might have parts that hate our gullible trusting parts and others that are hell bent on distrusting everyone going forward.

In order to heal the rift between Self and our parts, rebuilding trust so Self can lead, we might have to forgive ourselves and make repairs on the inside, between our parts and between parts and Self. We can make those repairs by writing a four-step apology letter from Self to the parts that were hurt because we didn't adequately protect them. If you're privileged enough to have an IFS-informed therapist, your therapist can help you repair those inner bonds.

Because of all that distrust inside our internal family system, we might also project that distrust onto other people in our lives, even when they're trustworthy. Part of relational recovery work is doing outer repairs with those we have unfairly distrusted, including apologizing for any hurtful behaviors stemming from that distrust.

Once you've forgiven yourself, and once you've reestablished connection between your parts and your Self, you'll need to hold space for your parts to grieve. If all attempts at repair have failed, grieve that the person or people you allowed to get close to you were not capable of respecting your no, tolerating your boundaries, taking ownership for how they violated them, or participating in repair. Grieve that you picked someone who mistreated you for years and you didn't yet know how to protect yourself. Grieve that you've been loving someone incapable of giving you what you deserve—justice, fairness, kindness, empathy, reciprocity, real love.

If you've had to withdraw privileges because someone was not willing to or capable of cooperating with the Six Steps, you've probably lost some of the intimacy you previously enjoyed, and will miss it, even though you know it was necessary to take it away. And if you've had to go no contact, you're probably looking at a massive loss. As empathy researcher and author of *The Language of Emotions* Karla McLaren says, "Grief arises when something has been lost irretrievably or when someone has died." When we go no contact with someone, this can be more painful than an actual death, because the loss is ambiguous. There's no funeral to give closure. But that doesn't mean grieving that loss isn't just as important.

As tempting as it might be to skip this step or just get stuck in outrage, we have to really feel the loss and sadness to be capable of moving on and letting go. Let the tears come up. Don't blink them back. Put on music and let your emotions move through you. Grief is like childbirth, in a way. The heart is a muscle, and grief clenches your heart just like a uterus contracts. Just like a woman in labor, you breathe . . . and push. Grief comes in waves, and in between the contractions, you get a break. Over time, the contractions space out, and one day, you might find that you've actually healed. You don't forget, but you no longer feel the charge of grief so intensely.

PRACTICE

A RITUAL FOR GRIEVING YOUR LOSSES

It's terribly sad when we have to withdraw or create more space in a relationship that matters to us. Ritualizing your grief can help you create a sense of closure, so you can move on, prioritize the relationships that made it through the Six Steps, and attract healthier relationships in the future. Try the following grief ritual:

1. Let your hurt, grieving parts write down how they feel and what they'll miss. Allow any feelings that arise to flow through you. Tears are welcome and respected as a natural cleansing.

2. Make an altar to honor your grieving. Light a candle; collect stones, flowers, shells, or pine cones; and choose a few objects that remind you of the person or relationship you're grieving. Allow yourself to visit the altar periodically when you need to grieve.

3. Safely discharge your anger. Part of the grieving process includes feeling the anger at how you've been mistreated. You might also have parts that feel angry at you for tolerating so much before setting limits. Let it be okay to feel that anger and discharge it in safe ways—punching a pillow, screaming out loud somewhere that it's safe to do so, kickboxing, or ranting to someone you trust to hold your anger with you, like a close friend or therapist.

4. Practice ritually letting go. Maybe you'll burn letters from the person or some of the objects from your altar—or the apology letter you had to write to yourself—in a fire ceremony. Maybe you'll bury someone's photo in the ground, or set your wedding ring afloat on a shell into a body of water. Maybe you'll get rid of everything they ever gave you. Maybe you'll pick up stones on the beach, imbue each one of them with a memory you need to release, then throw them into the water.

5. Dance it off. Make sure your body is involved when you're letting go. Make yourself a letting-go playlist and put on some music that helps you move the anger, sadness, and grief energy through your body so you can get it out.

FROM FAWNING TO FREEDOM

If you've made it to the end, take a breath. These six steps aren't just concepts—they're courageous acts of reorientation. You're learning to stop betraying yourself to preserve connection, and that's no small thing. Interrupting the fawning patterns that once kept you safe can feel like walking barefoot over the shards of old loyalty—especially when people you've long cared for fall away because they can't tolerate your newfound boundaries.

It's natural to grieve. You may ache for the harmony you once worked so hard to maintain, or fear that setting limits makes you "cold," "selfish," or "unspiritual." But what if true spiritual maturity isn't self-erasure, but self-respect? What if compassion that excludes yourself isn't actually compassion at all? As you grow, you may realize that what once felt noble—enduring mistreatment, overfunctioning, keeping the peace at any cost—wasn't sainthood, but self-abandonment dressed in virtue. And yet, there's no shame in that. You were doing your best with the tools you had.

Now, freedom invites you to a different kind of love—one that includes you. One where your empathy isn't weaponized against you, your boundaries aren't punishable offenses, and your worth doesn't hinge on your usefulness to others. There will be grief. But there will also be peace. There will be space for genuine reciprocity. And as you learn to show up for your own tender parts—the ones who once thought love required disappearing—you'll discover a deeper kind of belonging, one rooted not in fawning, but in freedom.

CONCLUSION
The Cracked Pot

We began this book with a parable and we're going to end with one as well: the story of the cracked pot.

Every day, a water bearer in India walked to the stream with a large pot hanging from each end of a pole, which he carried over his shoulders. One pot was perfectly intact and delivered a full portion of water after the long walk from the stream to the house where the water got used. The other pot had a crack in it and leaked water all the way home, so that it always arrived holding only half the water.

For two years, the water bearer delivered only one and a half pots of water to the house. The perfect pot was very proud of its accomplishments, thinking itself superior to the pot with the crack, while the cracked pot was ashamed of its imperfection. It felt miserable that it was able to accomplish only half of what it had been created to do.

One day by the stream, the cracked pot spoke to the water bearer. "I feel ashamed of myself and I want to apologize to you."

"Why?" the water bearer asked. "You've done nothing wrong."

"But I have. I am only able to deliver half of the water to the house because this crack in my side causes the water to leak. Because of my flaw, you do all this work and don't get the full value of your effort."

The water bearer softened and said, "Ah, sweet pot. I hear that you feel inferior because your crack makes you leak, and I'm sorry for the pain you feel because of your crack. As we return to the house, you might feel better if you pay attention to the beautiful flowers blooming along the path."

As they climbed up the hill toward the house, the cracked pot did feel slightly cheered up by the warm sun beaming on the beautiful wild flowers beside the path. But when they arrived at the house, the pot still felt bad about itself because it had leaked out half its load.

Once again, it apologized for being such a failure.

"Dear pot," the water bearer said, smiling, "did you happen to notice that there were wildflowers only on your side of the path? That's because I have always known about your flaw, and I thought it would be lovely to make good use of it. So I planted flower seeds on your side of the path two years ago, and every day, when we walk from the stream to the house, you've watered those flowers. Haven't you noticed the flower bouquets on the dining room table? Without you being just exactly the way you are, we would not have these radiant flowers to grace our home."

The cracked pot grew quiet, and for the first time, it saw itself not as broken, but as belonging.

THE BROKEN HEART AT THE CORE OF RELATIONAL TRAUMA

We are all cracked pots with unique flaws that can make us feel bad about ourselves, but can also bless us with particular gifts. Many blossom because of the care and nurturing we offer others. We are nurses and therapists, social workers and mothers, caregivers for the disabled and healers in our respective fields. Those of us who fawn are often experienced by others as the most loving, compassionate, generous, accommodating, and good-natured people on the planet. Our cracks make us extremely lovable, even if those cracks also put us at risk of exploitation, unbalanced relationships, narcissistic abuse, and chronic or even terminal illness. Our fawning is a generous gift we give to others, and our fawning can also make us sick. Both are simultaneously true.

More than anything, we need to hold ourselves gently as we recover from the broken heart at the core of all relational trauma. The tragedy of relational trauma is its fragmenting of the wholeness of the soul. It unravels us more deeply than mere betrayal and cuts into us as a primal wound, one that leaves us feeling far less than the wholeness that is our natural state, our birthright. To dare to move beyond this kind of wound, to reach out to the injured, heartbroken child within ourselves and say, "Come, sit, stay for a while, let us rest here together," to trust enough to heal that broken heart and really start to live again, requires profound courage and knee-trembling risk.

The feeling that one is existentially alone—the chronic unmet longing to be seen, heard, understood, validated, and, most of all, loved and accepted for all of who we are—lies at the heart of all trauma. To offer up even a moment of unconditional positive regard to the inner child inside, to hold our own vulnerability safe, to remind ourselves that we are not and never have been broken, to offer up admiration for our parts and for the ways we have managed to survive in a world that has not always been kind, to dare to love intimately instead of selling ourselves out—this is brave stuff.

We cannot heal in isolation. Trauma that happens in relationship must be healed *in relationship.* The primary relationship to heal is the one within. This healing starts within our own hearts, where we celebrate a long-overdue reunion between the soul that cannot be broken and the brokenhearted little child who didn't get loved enough. When the bereft little child sees that we are here to rescue them, when they can finally experience a redo of what went wrong.

Then we have to learn discernment and risk, trusting other trustworthy beings. After allowing ourselves to receive solace inside our own hearts, we must risk reaching out, to seek that same solace in the arms of another, to dare to open our hearts without collapsing our right to have wants, needs, fears, and boundaries that keep us separate. This is the promise of healthy, reciprocal relationships, where we open the door to the intimacy without erecting walls or engaging in "power over" or "power under" dynamics that foreclose intimacy.

It is the paucity of intimacy, the starvation of real, nourishing connection, that makes trauma survivors so lonely. In the absence of the intimacy we crave, we settle for transacting, and if we're the giving tree, we get the raw end of the transactional deal. Because transactional relationships will never fill the void we yearn to fill with real love and intimacy, this way of selling ourselves short makes us even more lonely.

We wall up to protect our broken hearts, but then we're encouraged to open up, to be vulnerable, to spill our guts and bare our souls, to divulge our secrets, to unguard our hearts. Yet not all who wish us to be open wish us well, and without good boundaries, openness can be masochistic. We may splay ourselves open, but at what cost? We need not let ourselves come to harm in order to be worthy of being loved.

Souls are more robust than hearts. They can't be broken and are never damaged. But as Stanford chaplain and physician Bruce Feldstein, MD, warns, when we experience too much heartbreak, the soul can become sore. This "soul soreness" needs the kind of medicine no drug can provide. Only safe, intimate relationships—with ourselves and our inner children, with other safe-enough, trustworthy people, with nature and the Earth, and with whatever we might call "God"—can nurture and heal the broken heart at the core of soul soreness. This is what we wish for you, dear reader: a balm for the soul soreness and brokenheartedness, and hopefully, medicine for your healing heart and body.

If you've ever felt like that cracked pot, ashamed of the leak that makes you different, I hope you'll remember this: Our cracks are where our humanity shines through. You were never meant to be a perfect pot—you were meant to be a healer, a lighthouse, a warrior of tenderness forged in the fire of your own pain. Our cracks are not liabilities; they are invitations to grow flowers, to offer beauty in ways perfection never could. Your tenderness is not a weakness—it's a sacred strength. We are not broken. We are breaking open. And from that opening, intimacy, connection, sovereignty, and self-love can take root.

So gather up your courage, unfurl your boundaries like wings, and refuse to pour your life force into those who do not cherish your water. Let this be the season we stop bleeding for those who won't tend our wounds—and start blooming for those who will water our wildest becoming.

To all the givers who've poured yourselves dry trying to be loved: You are not here to prove your worth by how much you endure. You are here to remember that you were always worthy, just as you are. Healing is not about becoming perfect; it's about returning to wholeness, to the untouchable soul-self that never stopped deserving love. So dare to rest. Dare to receive. Dare to hold boundaries like holy scripture. And above all, dare to love yourself with the same devotion you once gave away for crumbs. That love—fierce, wild, and true—is the medicine that will make you whole again.

May you reclaim your sacred "no," your holy boundaries, and your birthright to be cherished, not used. May you rise, not in spite of your wounds, but because you dared to honor them. The roots remember, dear one—but so does the soul. And the soul is calling you home.

RESOURCES

Note: Some of these resources may be activating. Please engage at your own pace and prioritize nervous system safety. Healing relational sickness is not a solo endeavor. These resources are offered as companions—not prescriptions—on the path back to Self-led connection, sovereignty, and repair.

HEALING RESOURCES WITH DR. LISSA RANKIN

LissaRankin.com

Heal at Last, https://healatlast.org/

Love School (IFS community of relational recovery practice), https://courses.lissarankin.com/love-school

One-on-One IFS-informed Transformational Mentoring support, https://courses.lissarankin.com/mentor

Selected online programs at LissaRankin.com:

1. Becoming Unf*ckwithable
2. Dating from Self
3. Heal Your Wounded Boundaries
4. Healing Attachment Wounds in Relationship
5. Healing the Trauma That Surrounds Medical Symptoms
6. IFS as Medical Treatment

7. Mothering as Medicine
8. Preparing the Heart to Love Again
9. The Six Steps to Radical Self-Healing

HEALING RESOURCES WITH DR. JEFFREY REDIGER

DrJeffreyRediger.com

The Mysteries of Spontaneous Healing with Lissa Rankin, https://courses.lissarankin.com/mysteries-of-spontaneous-healing

One-on-One Cured Consults (on Zoom anywhere in the world), https://drjeffreyrediger.com/services/

One-on-One Trauma-Informed Integrative Psychiatry (in California and Massachusetts), https://drjeffreyrediger.com/services/

BOOKS AND AUDIO PROGRAMS

Mind–Body Medicine and Healing

The Anatomy of a Calling, Lissa Rankin

Cured, Jeffrey Rediger

The Daily Flame, Lissa Rankin

Mind over Medicine, Lissa Rankin

Sacred Medicine, Lissa Rankin

Attachment and Trauma

The Art of Receiving and Giving, Betty Martin

The Body Keeps the Score, Bessel van der Kolk

Fawning, Ingrid Clayton

Healing Developmental Trauma, Laurence Heller and Aline Lapierre

How Can I Get Through to You?, Terry Real

I Don't Want to Talk About It, Terry Real

In an Unspoken Voice, Peter Levine

The Modern Trauma Toolkit, Christy Gibson, MD

No Bad Parts, Dick Schwartz

Not the Price of Admission, Laura Brown

Nurturing Resilience, Kathy Kain and Stephen Terrell

The Polyvagal Theory in Therapy, Deb Dana

The Power of Attachment, Diane Poole Heller

Trauma and Dissociation Informed Internal Family Systems, Joanne Twombly

Waking the Tiger, Peter Levine

What Happened to You?, Bruce Perry and Oprah Winfrey

What My Bones Know: A Memoir of Healing from Complex Trauma, Stephanie Foo

You Are the One You've Been Waiting For, Dick Schwartz

Narcissism, Abuse, and Power

Combating Cult Mind Control, Steven Hassan

Rethinking Narcissism, Craig Malkin

Take Back Your Life, Janja Lalich

Traumatic Narcissism and Recovery, Daniel Shaw

Why Does He Do That?, Lundy Bancroft

The Wizard of Oz and Other Narcissists, Eleanor Payson

Boundaries and Differentiation

Boundaries, Henry Cloud and John Townsend

Set Boundaries, Find Peace, Nedra Glover Tawwab

When I Say No, I Feel Guilty, Manuel J. Smith

Where to Draw the Line, Anne Katherine

Codependency and Relational Addiction

Adult Children of Emotionally Immature Parents, Lindsay Gibson

Codependent No More, Melody Beattie

Facing Codependence, Pia Mellody

Facing Love Addiction, Pia Mellody

The Intimacy Factor, Pia Mellody

Repair, Accountability, and Relational Maturity

The Apology, V (Eve Ensler)

Fierce Intimacy, Terry Real

Spiritual Bypassing, Robert Augustus Masters

Us, Terry Real

WEBSITES

The Attachment Project, https://www.attachmentproject.com/

Mark Ettersohn, https://www.healnpd.org/

Internal Family Systems Institute, https://ifs-institute.com/

International Cultic Studies Association, http://www.internationalculticstudies.org/

International Society for the Study of Trauma and Dissociation, https://www.isst-d.org

National Domestic Violence Hotline, https://www.thehotline.org

RAINN (sexual trauma support), https://www.rainn.org

Dr. Ramani's YouTube channel, https://www.youtube.com/doctorramani

Relational Life Therapy, https://relationallife.com/

Somatic Experiencing International, https://traumahealing.org

Trauma Research Foundation, https://traumaresearchfoundation.org

PODCASTS

Heal NPD with Mark Ettensohn

Hot Buttered Epiphanies with Lissa Rankin, MD and Axel Monsoor

Indoctrination with Rachel Bernstein

A Little Bit Culty with Sarah Edmondson and Anthony "Nippy" Ames

Navigating Narcissism with Dr. Ramani

Relationsick with Lissa Rankin

Therapy Chat with Laura Reagan

The Trauma Therapist Podcast with Guy MacPherson

Where Should We Begin? with Esther Perel

TED/TEDX TALKS

"Is There Scientific Proof We Can Heal Ourselves?," Lissa Rankin, https://www.youtube.com/watch?v=LWQfe__fNbs

"A Medicine of Hope and Possibility," Jeffrey Rediger, https://www.youtube.com/watch?v=8mjVHIB0FhI

"The #1 Public Health Issue Doctors Aren't Talking About," Lissa Rankin, https://www.youtube.com/watch?v=s2hLhWSlOl0

"The Profound Power of an Authentic Apology," V (Eve Ensler), https://www.youtube.com/watch?v=gQ-0oR3C1UM

"The Shocking Truth About Your Health," Lissa Rankin, https://www.youtube.com/watch?v=7tu9nJmr4Xs

ACKNOWLEDGMENTS

From Lissa and Jeff

Our deepest thank-yous to the countless patients who dared to share their secrets about how their relationships were making them sick, and especially to the ones who allowed us to tell their stories in this book so we could help others heal. We are infinitely grateful to our literary agent Michele Martin, who always tells it to us straight and cheerleads us until we find our way to something we hope comes close to universal truth. Huge appreciation to Leah Wilson, our editor at BenBella Books, who took a far-too-wordy manuscript and cobbled it down to something not only readable, but far more piercing than we could have crafted without her. Thank you to Glenn Yeffeth, the founder of BenBella Books, for giving us the opportunity to bring our shared message to you, dear reader.

To Dick Schwartz, Frank Anderson, Nancy Morgan, Laura Schmidt, Tracy Juliao, and other Internal Family Systems colleagues who inspired so much of this book, thank you for spreading the IFS medicine to those who need it and for supporting us every step of our own healing journeys from fawning to freedom.

To Terry Real, Erika Boissiere, and others in the Relational Life Therapy family, we so appreciate your inspiration, therapeutic support, and compassionate framework for one-up/one-down relationships.

From Lissa

I'm so grateful to my inspiring coauthor and brave, badass partner in relational recovery, Jeffrey Rediger. We met at a trauma conference near Santa Fe in 2019, where we sat outside on Native American reservation land near the Rio Grande, downloading everything we'd learned from studying radical remission survivors and concluding from day one that nonreciprocal relationships might be the single greatest unacknowledged health risk we'd come across. Thank you for what you have brought to the world with *Cured*—and for helping me bring the vision of this book to life. I will always be grateful to you for being my sanity during the insane pandemic years, for teaching me how to love a trauma survivor, and especially for your courage in being vulnerable with your own personal stories of abuse, indoctrination, and healing in this book. You really have proven to be that injured Olympic high jumper who nobody could keep from the gold medal. Here's to continuing to climb Mount Everest together and teaching others what we've learned along the way.

I'm so grateful to my daughter, Mira Klein, for giving me a reason to want to educate young people, so they know early on whether a relationship has the potential to be medicine or poison. Thank you for allowing me to enter your therapy rooms so we can heal your Mommy wounds together, before your body has to take any hits. You've always supported my writing, Mira, and I so appreciate how you understand my need to create and have come to find your own creative voice. I love you to the moon and back.

So much appreciation to Téa Elizabeth Blake, who has been the billowing wind beneath my wings through child-rearing, Hen House maintenance, book writing, sappy Netflix binges, *Driving Miss Daisy* days, surviving dinner parties, and the daily joys of spending fifteen years living together. You will always be my family.

To Jonathan McCloud, thank you for all of the frank feedback and cogent insight you've given me throughout the writing of this book, as you were also busy writing *Thrive* and *Chaos Is the New Black*. I'm so relieved you survived your cancer, so you could bring the double gifts of that ordeal to those you now serve. Thank you for always having my back. Please know I always have yours.

To Emma Harper, my daily peer-to-peer IFS parts-processing partner—*whoa, sister.* What our parts have been through! Bless you for holding space for all my parts, no matter how things are shaking down. And to Agnis Peña-Toro and Emily Liu, thank you for all of your empathy for my parts when Emma was busy or when shit hit the fan in US time zones!

To Nicolay Kreidler, Caitlin Nelson, and Karoline Monkvik, the team that makes all of my creative work beyond my book writing possible, so many thank-yous for putting up with me, helping me handle my overwhelm, and supporting me in bringing my visions to fruition. I couldn't do it without you all.

To Diane Hunter, Maja Rode, Nicki Clark, Shannon Rose, Katsy Johnson, Chris Horton, Rachel Gilgoff, Emma Jarrett, Lindy Bragg, Cari Hernandez, Christy Gibson, Chris Rutgers, Rachel and Doug Carlton Abrams, Jim Griffeth, Nancy and Joel Aronie, Kira Siebert, Mariana Caplan, Debbie Rosas, and all the rest of you who were sounding boards for me during the process of visioning and writing this book, thank you for being such thoughtful, patient, honest, and insightful listeners, storytellers, and visionaries.

To Chris, Keli, Trudy, Larry, Jana, Kim, Malen, Nick, and other Rankins whom I love, and to Mom and Dad on the other side, thank you for helping me always know I am a Rankin, and I am never alone in the world. I'll never forget what you always told me, Mom: "I have to live with myself, and so I have to be fit for myself to know." In stormy times, it's such a comfort to know we're all on the ethical, human rights–supporting side of our country's many conflicts. As Paul Farmer said, "The idea that some lives matter less is the root of all that is wrong with the world." I feel so lucky to have my roots in a family that all believes this.

Last but not least, I want to express my heartfelt gratitude to my patients from my integrative medicine practice in Mill Valley, who opened my eyes to how privileged Marin County patients could have the best conventional medical care, top-of-the-line nutrition, excellent alternative medicine support, yoga and meditation teachers, cutting-edge personal trainers, and all the supplements, pharmaceuticals, and good health habits in the world, yet it still wasn't enough to protect their bodies from the power-hungry narcissists in their lives who were making them relationsick. Had I not learned what I did from all of you, both *Relationsick* and *Mind over Medicine* would not have been written.

From Jeff

There is no way that I could have participated in whatever new knowledge and, hopefully, wisdom is distilled in these pages without the exceptional resilience and staying power of my brave partner, Lissa Rankin. Many details, insights, and points of clarity were worked out during endless hours of discussions, occurring during our morning café times and a nearly infinite number of days-long discussions, sometimes intense, sometimes intensely intellectual, sometimes intensely personal. This book would not be what it is without her unparalleled capacity to go deep and stay there until we could, together, begin hammering out real understanding and tangible solutions.

I also feel a debt of profound gratitude to all the people who have so graciously opened their hearts, lives, and medical records to me over the past twenty-plus years and helped me begin understanding the kind of insight and courage it takes to create a life where deep healing genuinely occurs and can be medically substantiated. You all are the true Olympians of health and well-being, the flagship of a new era in medicine and psychology, where we actually study how people heal and what it takes. *Relationsick* is the next step beyond *Cured*, where we go even deeper into the healing of identity, and I could not have done that without the many hours of interviews that you so graciously granted.

I also owe a deep debt of gratitude to all the patients and staff at McLean Hospital and Boston Medical Center–South, who also have been such profound teachers for me about both what does work and does not work when it comes to the deepest healing. It's nuts that we create such a false divide between medicine, psychology, and spirituality in Western culture, including the segregation of medical and psychiatric campuses to separate buildings and addresses as if they are completely different worlds. You all have helped me overcome the conditioning of my medical training and begin understanding how much mental there is in the physical and how much physical in the mental. You've also revealed to me how deeply spirit penetrates and suffuses all aspects of our being, animating both mental and physical—ever present, ready to be activated, and incapable of being either eliminated or destroyed.

This book also would not be what it is without the never-ending compassion, kindness, and profoundly trauma-informed work of the staff at the Santa Rosa Behavioral Health Partial Hospital Program. You have graciously allowed me to become part of your well-established, well-crafted team in beautiful Sonoma County and taught me what it means to truly change lives on a regular basis. Thank you for allowing me to become a part of the beautiful work that you do.

I also feel unendingly grateful to my new friends in California who have accepted me, warts and all, and helped me in my long quest to integrate what I've been learning from my long study into a personal, real life, one that is more balanced and human than what I've known in the past. You know who you are: Jonathan McCloud, Ed Savay, Maja Rode, Emma Harper, Diane Hunter, Rachel Vinkey . . . I love you all. Thank you for supporting me and for also supporting Lissa in our journey together. It truly takes a village to figure out what genuine intimacy requires, to deconstruct all the conditioning that gets in the way of that, especially for men, and to find a path to sharing deep love and thriving.

And then there's my dear Boston friends. Chris and Monna Katavolos, you have been with me through thick and thin, and have been unendingly wise, patient, and loving with me through all the byways and travails of my experiences and decisions. Anne Cuvelier, you have been like a mother to me, with endless patience and acceptance of me as I only slowly learn what it means to be a better friend and less of a workaholic. Thank you, thank you, thank you, to all of you. Thank you, each of you, for being exactly you.

Now, Duncan MacCourt, who left all of us suddenly and far too soon. The world is not the same without you, and neither is McLean. I will never forget our long walks and conversations, or going to the gym every day at noon. I will never forget all that we talked about—your sensitivity and compassion for those we were seeking to serve, and how you always sought to bring your great intellect to bear on what would best serve those who are most invisible and most unseen. Thank you for teaching me all you did.

To my daily IFS parts-processing partner, Jim Griffeth, I am so grateful that we can go on this journey together, this effort to bare our inner lives and struggles and give words to what we can share with no one else, or at least nearly no one else. To find a path together, with equal measures of support and accountability, as we walk this fetid and beautiful earth together.

Finally, to my children, Landon, Bryn, and Simeon. Thank you for being exactly who you are. Behind all this research is the undying hope that I can contribute in some small way to halting the cycle of secrets, violence, and trauma that have been visited with such ferocity on the lives and genes of our intergenerational family system. Each of you is such an unrepeatable light in the world, and I am so proud of you, not only of who you are but also who you are becoming. Thank you for being as patient with me as you have been.

NOTES

1. Alastair Cunningham et al., "A Prospective, Longitudinal Study of the Relationship of Psychological Work to Duration of Survival in Patients with Metastatic Cancer," *Psycho-Oncology* 9, no. 4 (2000): 323–39, https://doi.org/10.1002/1099-1611(200007/08)9:4%3C323::aid-pon465%3E3.0.co;2-b.
2. Alastair Cunningham et al., "Fighting for Life: A Qualitative Analysis of the Process of Psychotherapy-Assisted Self-Help in Patients with Metastatic Cancer," *Integrative Cancer Therapies* 1, no. 2 (2002): 146–61, https://doi.org/10.1177/1534735402001002006.
3. Madelon A. Visintainer et al., "Tumor Rejection in Rats After Inescapable or Escapable Shock," *Science* 216, no. 4544 (1982): 437–39, https://doi.org/10.1126/science.7200261.
4. Compiled from Jeff's research for *Cured,* Lissa's research for *Mind over Medicine* and *Sacred Medicine,* and Alistair Cunningham's research.
5. David Spiegel et al., "Effect of Psychosocial Treatment on Survival of Patients with Metastatic Breast Cancer," *The Lancet* 334, no. 8668 (1989): 888–91, https://doi.org/10.1016/s0140-6736(89)91551-1.
6. Helané Wahbeh, "Spontaneous Remission Bibliography Project," Institute of Noetic Sciences, accessed December 28, 2025, https://noetic.org/research/spontaneous-remission-bibliography-project/.
7. Barbara L. Fredrickson, *Love 2.0: How Our Supreme Emotion Affects Everything We Feel, Think, Do, and Become* (New York: Hudson Street Press, 2013).

8. "Spontaneous Synchronization," posted January 22, 2013, by uclaphysicsvideo, YouTube, 1:09, https://www.youtube.com/watch?v=T58l GKREubo.
9. Wendy Xin and Jonah R. Chan, "Myelin Plasticity: Sculpting Circuits in Learning and Memory," *Nature Reviews Neuroscience* 21, no. 12 (2020): 682–94, https://doi.org/10.1038/s41583-020-00379-8.
10. Jonathan Shaw, "Inflammation Causes Many Common Diseases of Aging," *Harvard Magazine*, April 5, 2019, https://www.harvard magazine.com/2019/04/inflammation-disease-diet.
11. Vincent Felitti et al., "Relationship of Childhood Abuse and Household Dysfunction to Many of the Leading Causes of Death in Adults: The Adverse Childhood Experiences (ACE) Study," *American Journal of Preventive Medicine* 14, no. 4 (1998): 245–58, https://doi.org/10 .1016/s0749-3797(98)00017-8; David Brown et al., "Adverse Childhood Experiences and the Risk of Premature Mortality," *American Journal of Preventative Medicine* 37, no. 5 (2009): 389–96, https://doi .org/10.1016/j.amepre.2009.06.021.
12. David Baumeister et al., "Childhood Trauma and Adulthood Inflammation: A Meta-Analysis of Peripheral C-Reactive Protein, Interleukin-6 and Tumour Necrosis Factor-α," *Molecular Psychiatry* 21, no. 5 (2016): 642–49. https://doi.org/10.1038/mp.2015.67.
13. Pete Walker, *Complex PTSD: From Surviving to Thriving: A Guide and Map for Recovering from Childhood Trauma* (Boulder, CO: Sounds True, 2013).
14. Laura S. Brown, *Not the Price of Admission: Healthy Relationships After Childhood Trauma* (New York: W. W. Norton & Company, 2018).
15. Ibid.
16. "Still Face Experiment Dr Edward Tronick," YouTube video, 2:49, posted March 5, 2016, by Mindyour class, https://www.youtube.com /watch?v=YTTSXc6sARg.
17. Linda G. Russek and Gary E. Schwartz, "Perceptions of Parental Caring Predict Health Status in Midlife: A 35-Year Follow-Up of the Harvard Mastery of Stress Study," *Psychosomatic Medicine* 59, no. 2 (1997): 144–49, https://doi.org/10.1097/00006842-199703000-00005.

18. John Bowlby, *Attachment and Loss, Volume 1: Attachment* (Basic Books, 1969); John Bowlby, "Attachment Theory and Its Therapeutic Implications," *Adolescent Psychiatry* 6 (1978): 5–33.
19. Nadine Burke Harris, "How Childhood Trauma Affects Health Across a Lifetime," TEDMED, September 2014, https://www.ted.com/talks/nadine_burke_harris_how_childhood_trauma_affects_health_across_a_lifetime.
20. Adapted from ACEsAware.org.
21. James House et al., "Social Relationships and Health," *Science* 241, no. 4865 (1988): 540–45, https://doi.org/10.1126/science.3399889.
22. Monica M. Williams-Farrelly et al., "Loneliness in Older Primary Care Patients and Its Relationship to Physical and Mental Health-Related Quality of Life," *Journal of the American Geriatrics Society* 72, no. 3 (2024): 811–21, https://doi.org/10.1111/jgs.18762; Julianne Holt-Lunstad et al., "Advancing Social Connection as a Public Health Priority in the United States," *American Psychologist* 72, no. 6 (2017): 517–30, https://doi.org/10.1037/amp0000103; Tiffany Petitte et al., "A Systematic Review of Loneliness and Common Chronic Physical Conditions in Adults," *Open Psychology Journal* 8 (Suppl. 2) (2015): 113–32, https://doi.org/10.2174/1874350101508010113.
23. Julianne Holt-Lunstad et al., "Loneliness and Social Isolation as Risk Factors for Mortality: A Meta-Analytic Review," *Perspectives on Psychological Science* 10, no. 2 (2015): 227–37, https://doi.org/10.1177/1745691614568352.
24. Lisa F. Berkman and S. Leonard Syme, "Social Networks, Host Resistance, and Mortality: A Nine-Year Follow-Up Study of Alameda County Residents," *American Journal of Epidemiology* 109, no. 2 (1979): 186–204, https://doi.org/10.1093/oxfordjournals.aje.a112674.
25. Julianne Holt-Lunstad et al., "Social Relationships and Mortality Risk: A Meta-Analytic Review," *PLoS Medicine* 7, no. 7 (2010): e1000316, https://doi.org/10.1371/journal.pmed.1000316.
26. Christian Albus, "Psychological and Social Factors in Coronary Heart Disease," *Annals of Medicine* 42, no. 7 (2010): 487–94, https://doi.org/10.3109/07853890.2010.515605; Nia Xia and Huige Li, "Loneliness,

Social Isolation, and Cardiovascular Health," *Antioxidants & Redox Signaling* 28, no. 9 (2018): 837–51, https://doi.org/10.1089/ars.2017.7312; Bert Uchino et al., "Size, Strength of Social Networks, Influence Heart Disease Risk," *UF Health News*, February 16, 2005, https://ufhealth.org/news/2005/size-strength-social-networks-influence-heart-disease-risk; Li Liu et al., "Social Support Mediates Loneliness and Depression in Elderly People," *Journal of Health Psychology* 21, no. 5 (2016): 750–58, https://doi.org/10.1177/1359105314536941; Bryan James et al., "Late-Life Social Activity and Cognitive Decline in Old Age," *Journal of the International Neuropsychological Society* 17, no. 6 (2011): 998–1005, https://doi.org/10.1017/S1355617711000531; André Hajek et al., "Social Support and Functional Decline in the Oldest Old," *Gerontology* 68, no. 2 (2022): 200–208, https://doi.org/10.1159/000516077.

27. Ayal A. Aizer et al., "Marital Status and Survival in Patients with Cancer," *Journal of Clinical Oncology* 31, no. 31 (2013): 3869–3876, https://doi/10.1200/JCO.2013.49.6489.
28. Chiara Acquati et al., "Social Wellbeing in Cancer Survivorship: A Cross-Sectional Analysis of Self-Reported Relationship Closeness and Ambivalence from a Community Sample," *Current Oncology* 30, no. 2 (2023): 1720–32, https://doi.org/10.3390/curroncol30020133.
29. Hae-Chung Yang and Tammy A. Schuler, "Marital Quality and Survivorship: Slowed Recovery for Breast Cancer Patients in Distressed Relationships," *Cancer* 115, no. 1 (2009): 217–28, https://doi.org/10.1002/cncr.23964.
30. He backs up this claim by citing, among other research, a 2024 study in which eight patients diagnosed with NPD underwent psychotherapy over two and a half to five years. At follow-up, all eight no longer met diagnostic criteria on the Diagnostic Interview for Narcissism assessment (DIN) and in the fifth edition of the *Diagnostic and Statistical Manual of Mental Disorders* (*DSM-5*). While this small retrospective study does not in any way prove that everyone with NPD will get better with treatment, it does refute the popular notion that NPD and other variations of narcissism are untreatable and irredeemable. See:

Elsa Ronningstam and Igor Weinberg, "Narcissistic Personality Disorder: Patterns, Processes, and Indicators of Change in Long-Term Psychotherapy," *Journal of Personality Disorders* 37, no. 3 (2023): 337–57, https://doi.org/10.1521/pedi.2023.37.3.337; Anthony D. Mancini et al., "Pathological Narcissism and Grief: A Longitudinal Study of Interpersonal Loss," *Personality Disorders: Theory, Research, and Treatment* 11, no. 3 (2020): 200–209, https://doi.org/10.1037/per0000372; Igor Weinberg et al., "Can Patients with Narcissistic Personality Disorder Change? A Clinical Study," *Journal of Nervous and Mental Disease* 212, no. 7 (2024): 392–97, https://doi.org/10.1097/NMD.0000000000001777.

31. Ramani Durvasula, "Are You an Enabler? Ask Dr. Ramani," *Navigating Narcissism with Dr. Ramani*, podcast, August 24, 2023, https://podcasts.apple.com/us/podcast/are-you-an-enabler-ask-dr-ramani/id1629909313?i=1000625519150.
32. Dacher Keltner et al., "Power, Approach, and Inhibition," *Psychological Review* 110, no. 2 (2003): 265–84, https://doi.org/10.1037/0033-295X.110.2.265.
33. Jeremy Hogeveen et al., "Power Changes How the Brain Responds to Others," *Journal of Experimental Psychology: General* 143, no. 2 (2014): 755–62, https://doi.org/10.1037/a0033477.
34. Janko Međedović and Boban Petrović, "The Dark Tetrad: Structural Properties and Location in the Personality Space," *Journal of Individual Differences* 36, no. 4 (2015): 228–36, https://doi.org/10.1027/1614-0001/a000179.
35. A large body of research has established that a significant gap exists between what people believe they would do in a situation where someone is being treated badly and what they actually do. For a great summary of bystander research, please see Catherine Sanderson, *Why We Act: Turning Bystanders into Moral Rebels* (Belknap Press of Harvard University Press, 2020).
36. Richard Schwartz, *No Bad Parts: Healing Trauma and Restoring Wholeness with the Internal Family Systems Model* (Sounds True, 2021).
37. Robert Scaer, *The Body Bears the Burden: Trauma, Dissociation, and Disease*, 3rd ed. (New York: Routledge, 2014).

INDEX

S

ABOUT THE AUTHORS

Lissa Rankin, MD, *New York Times* bestselling author of *Mind over Medicine* and seven other books, is a former OB/GYN physician, founder of the Whole Health Medicine Institute training program for doctors and therapists, radical remission researcher, and founder of the health-equity, trauma healing–based nonprofit Heal At Last. After leaving her job in conventional medicine in 2007, Lissa began experimenting in her integrative medicine practice with what really helps resolve symptoms in people with chronic illness who have failed to improve with either conventional or alternative medicine. All roads led to the same conclusion: People who are not responding to other treatments often have untreated, unhealed relational trauma, and treating that trauma can sometimes lead to seemingly miraculous radical remissions.

Upon realizing this, Lissa became a passionate ambassador for raising awareness about the importance of diagnosing and treating relational trauma as both preventive medicine and medical treatment for hard-to-treat mental and physical illnesses. Because old-school psychoanalysis (talk therapy) and therapies like cognitive behavioral therapy do not effectively treat trauma on their own, and because medication, surgeries, and even most alternative medicine and spiritual healing techniques (e.g., acupuncture, meditation, or energy healing) only treat the symptoms of trauma, Lissa became a devoted student of many forms of trauma therapy, including Dick Schwartz's Internal Family Systems, Peter Levine's Somatic Experiencing, Lawrence Heller's NeuroAffective Relational Model, and Asha Clinton, PhD's Advanced Integrative Therapy. She also teaches about spiritual bypassing recovery for those who have used spirituality as a way to avoid healing their trauma.

Along with her public health advocacy and healthcare reform activism, Lissa leads workshops about relational healing and medicine online at US retreat centers like Esalen, 1440, Omega, and Kripalu, and internationally. During the pandemic, Lissa played a public role in debunking the COVID-19 denialism, antivaccination propaganda, and conspiracy theories promoted by many wellness, yoga, mind–body medicine, alternative medicine, and spirituality influencers who got "red-pilled" during 2020. This shakeout anchored her as a physician influencer to trust who is grounded in science, open to the mystical, spiritually aware, relationally focused, and trauma informed.

Lissa lives in West Sonoma County with her partner, now that her daughter has gone off to New York for art school. She thrives on daily hikes in nature, making art, dancing, singing, writing, gardening, upcycling clothing, DJing music whenever she can, and healthy gourmet cooking.

Jeffrey Rediger, MD, MDiv, is a bestselling author and a licensed physician and psychiatrist on the faculty of Harvard Medical School. He is also the medical director of Providence Santa Rosa Memorial Hospital Behavioral Health Services in Sonoma County, California. He was the medical director of McLean SE and Community Affairs at McLean Hospital in Boston for twenty-two years, and concurrently for many years also the Chief of Behavioral Medicine at Good Samaritan Medical Center. In addition to his medical and psychiatric training, he has a Master of Divinity in theology and philosophy of science from Princeton Theological Seminary. His investigations into remarkable recoveries from incurable or fatal illnesses have been featured on *The Oprah Winfrey Show*, *The Dr. Oz Show*, and *Anderson Cooper 360°*, among others. He has been nominated for the National Bravewell Leadership Award and has received many awards for leadership and patient care. His bestselling book, *Cured: Strengthen Your Immune System and Heal Your Life* (a.k.a. *Cured: The New Science of Spontaneous Healing*), has been published in thirty-two languages so far and is available at both local bookstores and online.

Jeff grew up on a farm in the rural Midwest with a father who heralded from the Amish tradition and a mother from the ranches in Montana. It was a home he would come to understand was defined by fear and violence and it didn't take long for Jeff to sense the difference between what was said to be true and what was actually emotionally true. After experiencing years of dissociation and a few spiritual experiences, during which he forced himself to submit and obey as a way to survive, Jeff escaped to college, where education served as both flight and a way out. Although seminary was the most important part of his preparation for becoming a physician, it also became a way to pound in the indoctrination of his youth even deeper, this time by himself, and therefore later became the next thing to deconstruct.

Shortly after accepting his faculty position at Harvard and the medical directorship of McLean SE at McLean Hospital in 2002, he began gathering medical evidence from the Olympians of health and well-being. This was a kind of empirical theology in its quest, an intense need to move beyond conflicting opinions into the hard evidence and patterns associated with recovery when all else appeared grim. He was able to document that it's not doctors or medications that get people better, nor was it nutrition, stress reduction, or any of the other commonly touted external or material treatments; the deepest healings are also about the healing of identity and false beliefs, both conscious and unconscious. Along the way, he experienced a rebuilding of his own mind, body, and nervous system, and eventually was able to begin understanding that healing at the deepest levels requires both understanding and experiencing one's value as a human being and the value of all others, none of whom are one up or one down from anyone else.

He now considers himself an antipsychiatrist, one who loves psychiatry and believes in medical science and all that it can offer but who is also aware of the authoritarian, oppressive, and economic structures of medicine and psychiatry that often prevent people from obtaining the level of healing, well-being, and freedom from control that they need and deserve. He is deeply committed to a type of psychiatry that is built on what is right and good about every human being and does not pathologize or overly medicalize human problems of living. He cares about the democratization of medicine and psychiatry and helping people become the CEOs of their own health and well-being rather than passive patients who are far too often taught to be compliant, passive recipients of treatments that reduce symptoms but ignore the deeper causes.

Although he will always love Boston and New England, Jeff now lives with his partner and golden retriever in rural West Sonoma County, California, in a renovated barn where on a daily basis he is captivated by the natural beauty of the outdoors and the abundance of artists, writers, and creative types, as well as the cornucopia of local produce, wine, music, and high-quality food that characterizes all of West Sonoma County and the Pacific coast.